# HOUSE OF CARDS
# AND PHILOSOPHY

**The Blackwell Philosophy and Pop Culture Series**
*Series editor William Irwin*

A spoonful of sugar helps the medicine go down, and a healthy helping of popular culture clears the cobwebs from Kant. Philosophy has had a public relations problem for a few centuries now. This series aims to change that, showing that philosophy is relevant to your life—and not just for answering the big questions like "To be or not to be?" but for answering the little questions: "To watch or not to watch *South Park*?" Thinking deeply about TV, movies, and music doesn't make you a "complete idiot." In fact it might make you a philosopher, someone who believes the unexamined life is not worth living and the unexamined cartoon is not worth watching.

Already published in the series:

# HOUSE OF CARDS AND PHILOSOPHY
## UNDERWOOD'S REPUBLIC

**Edited by J. Edward Hackett**

**WILEY** Blackwell

This edition first published 2016
© 2016 John Wiley & Sons Ltd

*Registered Office*
John Wiley & Sons Ltd, The Atrium, Southern Gate, Chichester, West Sussex, PO19 8SQ, UK

*Editorial Offices*
350 Main Street, Malden, MA 02148-5020, USA
9600 Garsington Road, Oxford, OX4 2DQ, UK
The Atrium, Southern Gate, Chichester, West Sussex, PO19 8SQ, UK

For details of our global editorial offices, for customer services, and for information about how to apply for permission to reuse the copyright material in this book please see our website at www.wiley.com/wiley-blackwell.

The right of J. Edward Hackett to be identified as the author of the editorial material in this work has been asserted in accordance with the UK Copyright, Designs and Patents Act 1988.

*Library of Congress Cataloging-in-Publication Data*

House of Cards and philosophy : Underwood's republic / edited by J. Edward Hackett.
    pages cm – (Blackwell philosophy and pop culture series)
  Includes index.
  ISBN 978-1-119-09277-3 (pbk.)
 1. House of cards (Television program : U.S.)  2. Television programs–Philosophy.
I. Hackett, J. Edward, 1979– editor.   II. Series: Blackwell philosophy and popculture series.
  PN1992.77.H634H68 2015
  791.45'72–dc23

                                                                            2015021568

A catalogue record for this book is available from the British Library.

Cover image: Aleksandar Nakic/Getty

Set in 10.5/13pt SabonLTStd by Aptara Inc., New Delhi, India
Printed and bound in Malaysia by Vivar Printing Sdn Bhd

1   2016

# Contents

# Introduction
## Contemplating a House of Cards

When we first see Frank Underwood, a dog whimpers while he prepares to put it out of its misery. The senator's visage takes on a sinister, villainous look when he tells us directly that he has "no patience for useless things." From that moment, the visceral darkness of *House of Cards* sucks us in.

The first time Frank sits down at Freddy's BBQ he licks his lips, ready to devour a rack of ribs. The message is clear: Underwood is a lion and other politicians are the lambs on which he feeds. The Machiavellian senator disposes of his enemies left and right, and his only superhuman power is his inhuman ability to predict the movements of his prey.

*House of Cards* plays off the anxieties of our current realities, portraying a political world that is captivating and wounding at the same time, provoking our worst fears that politics cannot deliver on the promise of justice. People should reap what they sow, but that doesn't seem to apply to Frank Underwood, who transgresses our deep commitment to morality and violates everything sacred with impunity. Transfixed, we watch as he maneuvers his way to the vice presidency— "One heartbeat away from the presidency and not a single vote cast in my name. Democracy is *so overrated*"—and then to the presidency.

Our Shakespearian antihero and his Lady Macbeth (played to perfection by Robin Wright) constantly undermine the narrative that

*House of Cards and Philosophy: Underwood's Republic*,
First Edition. Edited by J. Edward Hackett.
© 2016 John Wiley & Sons, Ltd. Published 2016 by John Wiley & Sons, Ltd.

truth, justice, and the American way prevail. *House of Cards* makes us worry, as it should. We should worry that we are not doing better economically than previous generations. We should worry that the promise of postracial America has never been delivered in full. We should worry that corporations have more influence in politics than individual voters. We should worry about the rising inequality that divides opportunity and privilege. We should worry that lesser Franks lurk in corners of the real world. We should worry about many things, and that's the point of the title's imagery: The house of cards may come tumbling down.

To confront the nearly certain risk and danger of politics—even the fictional representation of *House of Cards*—requires courage. To act politically means risking the very fabric of the human world, yet political action risks the world every day, especially in the postnuclear age. With one mistake, the world can be undone.

In truth, *House of Cards* offers us a half-truth about our own undoing. Our worries may outstrip concrete realities. Philosophers, though, are very good at worrying, or what they like to call "contemplating," and this can put them at odds with the concrete practical ends of life depicted in *House of Cards*. In the contemplative life, you withdraw from the political world to think deeply before returning to the world of action. Indeed, that is the purpose of this book. In these pages, we reflect on Frank and the other political insiders and ask: Will the cards ever fall? And if they do fall, what then? The anxiety is productive, returning us to ourselves, putting us in the state of wonder that Plato and Aristotle say is the beginning of philosophy. Wonder begets courage. So, let us begin.

# Part I

# SOCRATES, PLATO, AND FRANK

# Of Sheep, Shepherds, and a Wolf in Sheep's Clothing

## The Cynical View of Politics in *House of Cards* and Plato's *Republic*

*James Ketchen and Michael Yeo*

*The road to power is paved with hypocrisy.*
*—Frank Underwood*

The reviews all seem to agree: "The Empty Cynicism of *House of Cards*," reads one. "The Most Cynical Show on TV," reads another. And "The Very American Cynicism of *House of Cards*," reads yet another.

The reviews are still coming in on Plato's (428–348 BCE) *Republic*,[1] which ends more optimistically than *House of Cards* probably will. Frank Underwood and *House of Cards* in general are modern manifestations of a deeply cynical view of politics, and as such they reflect the challenge of the Sophists presented by Plato in Books 1 and 2 of the *Republic*. In Plato's day, professional teachers called Sophists taught the youth of Athens the political skills purported to be necessary for success in public life. Key to their teaching was a cynicism about the political world in which the strong get the better of the weak, and where exploitation, manipulation, and, yes, hypocrisy "paved the road to power."

*House of Cards and Philosophy: Underwood's Republic*,
First Edition. Edited by J. Edward Hackett.
© 2016 John Wiley & Sons, Ltd. Published 2016 by John Wiley & Sons, Ltd.

## Justice and Power

The *Republic* is very much a philosophical set piece, each part carefully designed to further the arguments and ideas under consideration. Early on in Book 1, the character Socrates turns the discussion to the nature of justice.[2] In the ensuing discussion, Socrates' interlocutors give several definitions like "justice is telling the truth and paying one's debts,"[3] or "justice is helping one's friends and hurting one's enemies."[4] None of these definitions stands up to scrutiny as Socrates exposes weaknesses in them.

A decisive transition in the dialogue occurs when the character Thrasymachus—a Sophist—forcefully intervenes like a "wild beast,"[5] saying that the discussion of justice to that point has been stupid and naïve. Thrasymachus offers his own definition: Justice "is nothing but the advantage of the stronger."[6] This account is not so much about how we ought to live as it is about the de facto status of what norms guide us. The rules benefit the powerful. That's just how it goes.

Thrasymachus' view of politics, like Frank's, is deeply cynical. Politics is about power, and nothing more. The powerful will see to it that the rules serve their interest. From the standpoint of those who don't have power, the rules will not be to their advantage but to someone else's advantage. In the course of his defense, Thrasymachus slides from a descriptive statement to an evaluative one: Those who are just (who follow the rules) are dupes or suckers. One would be better off not following the rules, if one had the power and ability, and so living the life of injustice is supremely preferable to the life of justice. It is, in short, better to be ruthless and unjust than it is to be just and taken advantage of.

## Underwood's Cynical Use of "His People"

Frank often asserts a kind of ownership over people. Certainly, this "ownership" is not in the form of chattel slavery, but in important respects his relations with other characters go beyond just manipulation.

One of Frank's central strategies is to place people in thrall to him. At one point he refers to his Gaffney, South Carolina, constituents as "my people," and this means more than just "those like me" or "the people from which I come." There is a sense of proprietorship in his attitude, as though Gaffney were a kind of fiefdom or, perhaps, apropos of the *Republic* and Thrasymachus, a flock of sheep. Evocative of this latter image is Frank's admiration for Tusk, who, he tells us, "Measures wealth not in jets but in purchased souls."

Arguably the most tragic of Frank's "sheep" is Peter Russo, who upon coming to the end of the line with Frank, bleats forlornly, "Whenever has your help helped me?" Frank even gets Russo to sacrifice and slaughter some of his own sheep with the closing of the naval base in Russo's district. Countless lives were ruined, and the social upheaval was immeasurable.

Stamper, Meechum, Sharp, Seth, his Gaffney constituents—all are, for Frank, merely sheep to be used as the shepherd sees fit: groomed and perhaps pampered one moment, fleeced and even sacrificed the next. Admittedly, some of his sheep are more wolf-like than others (Stamper, Seth, and Jackie, for example). In keeping with a metaphor from the *Republic*, we might think of them rather as "sheepdogs" than "sheep." Nonetheless, all are at his mercy, all serve at his pleasure, and he makes it clear that he can and will do with them as he pleases. Notably, the most significant early falling out between Frank and Claire, which foreshadows the decisive falling out at the end of Season 3, occurs when she accuses him of using her "like you use everyone else." Claire is a fellow shepherd, not merely Frank's "head sheep" or, as Jackie Sharp refers to herself, his "pit bull." She is quick to remind Frank of that status. All of this cynical manipulation was long anticipated in the *Republic*.

Socrates deploys the shepherd–sheep analogy in attempting to refute Thrasymachus' view that justice is the advantage of the stronger. As this analogy would have it, the relationship between ruler and ruled is like that between shepherd and flock. As a shepherd's charge is to look after and care for the sheep, so too a proper ruler should act only to secure the advantage of the ruled. Thrasymachus will have none of this argument. He turns the analogy around on Socrates: It may be true that the shepherd cares for the wellbeing of his flock, but only insofar as it is ultimately to his advantage to do so. Thrasymachus scoffs smugly (as Frank often does),

> [Y]ou do not even recognize sheep or shepherd.... You suppose shepherds or cowherds consider the good of the sheep or the cows and fatten

them and take care of them looking to something other than their masters' good and their own; and so you also believe that the rulers in the cities, those who truly rule, think about the ruled differently from the way a man would regard sheep, and that night and day they consider anything else than how they will benefit themselves.[7]

Much in this exchange comes to life and is reflected in how Frank uses people. The exchange contrasts two views. On one view, politicians ought to strive not for their own interests but rather for those who they are said to represent. On the second view, as a matter of fact politicians ultimately serve their own interests; they serve the interests of the people only to the extent that this advances their own interests. The reason the latter, "realist" view is thought to be cynical is precisely because it grates against the former, "idealist" view. Thus, if the view of politics presented by Thrasymachus and *House of Cards* is cynical, it is so because it grates against some idealist view we hold about what politics should be.

It's clear enough that Frank has a cynical, or realist, view of politics. Even when it appears that he is acting on behalf of his constituents, like the parents of the girl who drove off the road distracted by the giant peach, he is really acting to advance his own interests (avoiding lawsuits and bad publicity). Everything that Frank does is calculated to advance his immediate and ultimate interests and to augment his power. That is precisely as Thrasymachus would have it. And, if we are honest with ourselves, we will admit that we too often find the realist view attractive. Frank both repels and attracts us after all. As we shall see, it is precisely this tension, between our idealist and realist selves, that makes the Sophist's (not to mention Frank's) challenge so powerful.

## It's Good to Be Bad

As if to appeal to the realist in all of us, Thrasymachus shifts the focus of the debate. Not only does he insist that "justice is the interest of the stronger," but he adds that the unjust life is better and to be preferred to the just life.

To be just, or to act justly, is a "high-minded innocence" or naivety in one's view of the world that sets one up to be used and manipulated.

To practice injustice is the best sort of life because it allows the unjust to get the better of the just and to attain what they desire. Justice is either for fools (like Blythe) who don't understand that the stronger have pulled the wool over their eyes, or for those who are too weak (like Zoe's colleague Janine) to challenge the strong.

Early in the series we actually see Frank suffer what, on this realist view, would surely be an "injustice." Frank is "cheated" out of his appointment as secretary of state. It is a tough blow after all of his hard, loyal work. Frank didn't see it coming because he underestimated his opponents. In this situation, he was gotten the better of because he had played by the rules and expected others to keep their promises and reward loyal service. That Walker and Vasquez broke their promise echoes Thrasymachus' contention that the unjust will almost always cheat on promises, at least when it suits them and furthers their own interests.[8] Frank certainly takes this to heart and never looks back, fully embracing prudence and injustice.

A number of characters embody something like the virtues of conventional morality—the just life. Think of Lucas Goodwin, in many ways the paragon of virtue in the show. He is high-minded, out to expose corruption and malfeasance. His love for Zoe appears genuine, and his pursuit of truth is noble and virtuous. Lucas is completely dominated and destroyed by Frank.

Or take Donald Blythe. Whether or not we agree with his policy views, he comes across as an honorable man, true to his word, upstanding, and honest. Given how effortlessly Frank uses and gets the better of him, he indirectly illustrates a Thrasymachian view of justice: While justice might not be a vice, it is a "very high-minded innocence," a naivety about the world and its workings that sets its practitioners up to be dupes and suckers, ripe for a good fleecing.[9] In Thrasymachian terms, the unjust gets the better of the just and the life of the former comes out seeming best. And, if we're honest, we have to admit that our "realist" selves are more attracted to Underwood than to Blythe. Or at least we recognize that the virtuous characteristics we admire in someone like Blythe are something of a liability in politics. It proves expedient for Frank to make him his Vice President, but when the prospect of his becoming a candidate for the presidency is raised, the party power brokers without hesitation accept Frank's assessment that he lacks what it takes.

Heather Dunbar is also instructive in this regard. She begins her run for president committed to high-minded ideals about political campaigning, flatly rejecting, on presumably moral grounds, an offer from Stamper to expose political dirt on Claire. However, as the campaign progresses and things heat up, she changes her mind. She reaches out to Stamper to play the "abortion card," as if in the interim she had learned the cynical Thrasymachian lesson that nice guys finish last: If you want to win, you have to be willing to hit below the belt.

## Rings of "Power" and Myths

Frank's Sentinel class ring is not necessary to further the plotline, but it serves an important, symbolic purpose for both Frank and the viewer. Typically, when he bangs his ring, it is in the context of some new scheme. It's as though through this process he invokes a kind of power, a resolve to get the thing done. He even has a myth about its origins: that his father told him it both hardens the knuckles and knocks on wood—preparation and luck. It's unlikely that this origin story is true; we have already learned, through an aside during his sermon at the Gaffney funeral, that Frank has no respect for his father (a point that gets reinforced in Season 3 when he urinates on his father's grave). However, it does make for a good story that he can use to impress others.

In "Chapter 8," focusing on the new library at The Sentinel, we learn that it was at this formative military academy that Frank "learned his craft." The ring then, as a reminder of that place, may well be a token of his craft, representing his skill at manipulation and his ability to get the better of others through deception and treachery. For our purposes, the ring also links *House of Cards* to one of the greatest thought experiments in moral philosophy: the Ring of Gyges story in Book 2 of the *Republic*.

The character Glaucon introduces the story to sharpen the position of Thrasymachus (who by now has withdrawn from the dialogue in disgust) by showing that most people would choose the life of injustice if they knew they could get away with it. The story concerns a shepherd, who comes upon a magic ring that gives him the power to become invisible. It's not long before he puts the ring to good (or bad) use by gaining entry into the palace where he seduces the queen, kills the king, and usurps the throne. His ring makes him all-powerful and able to fully realize the life of injustice. Who among us, Glaucon argues, possessing such a ring, could resist the temptation to get all that we wanted, acting unjustly while appearing to the world to be just?

Obviously there are no such rings of power, and yet there are people who think they can (and often do) live the life of injustice and get away with it undetected. They have a kind of special ability to mask or hide their injustice, making it invisible to the rest of the world. Certainly Frank has such an ability, and he likely developed it at The Sentinel. But there's more. Frank not only has the ability to appear just while being unjust, he also has the ability to make others who are just appear to be unjust.

## Rings and the "Craft" of Perfect Injustice

The library dedication at The Sentinel is important for the development of Frank's character in the show. We have already seen that he has a *craft* or skill for injustice. He has told us that he is like the plumber whose "job it is to clear the pipes and keep the sludge moving," but to the school president he stands for and "exemplifies" all the values and virtues The Sentinel represents and tries to instill: "honor, duty, discipline, sacrifice, service, and respect." Frank's reputation, at least at The Sentinel, is that of the man of justice. All of this was anticipated in the *Republic* through Glaucon's challenge.

That challenge ultimately has us imagine two different characters: the perfectly unjust individual in contrast with the perfectly just individual. The former, Glaucon tells us, will "act like the *clever craftsmen*"[10] who will know what is possible and impossible to achieve, and should he "trip up he has the skill to fix things." While he will achieve the greatest of injustices, he will have "provided himself with the greatest reputation for justice." Perhaps most telling, "through words and deeds," he is able to persuade and to use force to achieve his ends. With his skill and cunning, the unjust person will "rule because he seems to be just," and he will be rewarded with riches and honors and will always get the better of others in both private and public affairs. In short, through being unjust while appearing just, he will have the best sort of life.[11]

Glaucon contrasts this characterization of the ideal unjust man with that of the perfectly just man. Such a person will actually have a reputation for injustice, lying, and deceit. He will be shunned and ridiculed. In the end, he will be made to suffer all manner of torment. He "will be whipped; he'll be racked; he'll be bound; he'll have both his eyes burned out; and, at the end, when he has undergone every sort of evil, he'll be crucified and know that one shouldn't wish to be, but to seem to be, just."[12]

*House of Cards* brings this contrast to life through the clash between Frank and Lucas Goodwin. Lucas, of all the characters in the show, is arguably the most just. He is honorable and pursues the truth about injustice and corruption. Led astray and entrapped by Frank's minions, he is made to seem like an unjust man. If all of the stories of the state of American prisons are true, he will be made to suffer the greatest of torments, what in the modern world might be comparable to the fate of he whom Glaucon describes as the "seeming unjust just man."

## Tyranny, Philosophy, and the Search for Meaning in a Cynical World

The model that Thrasymachus holds up for would-be politicians is the tyrant,[13] the perfectly unjust person who can do whatever he or she wants, a characteristic that Claire ascribes to Frank in discussion with their dying bodyguard. And in Season 3, while listening to a broadcast of a speech in which Frank extols the virtues of the founding fathers for their fight against tyranny, veteran *Telegraph* reporter Kate Baldwin, aware of his ruthless machinations, retorts that "*he* is the tyrant."

No doubt Frank is a tyrant, but the model of the tyrant that Plato sets up for purposes of his argument is the *perfect* tyrant. There are reasons to suppose that Frank falls short of this ideal. In this regard, it is useful to contrast Frank with Petrov, the Russian President, who appears to get the better of Frank in Season 3. Compared with Petrov, Frank comes across as being somewhat weak. The show drives this contrast home in a rather clichéd and stereotypical way by accenting Petrov's machismo (he downs vodka like water; he openly flirts with Claire), on the one hand, and attenuating Frank's (e.g., he cries and is sexually attracted to men) on the other.

Clichés aside, the main difference between Petrov and Frank is that Frank, at least as far as the plot has developed so far, seems to have a conscience and something in him that moves him to reflect on the meaning of his life and his actions beyond mere calculation. Petrov and Frank are both murderers, but we see no evidence that Petrov has any qualms about this. Frank, on the other hand, shows signs of having, and struggling against, a guilty conscience. We see him on two occasions in a church, as if being on the verge of prayer or confession, and seeking some kind of meaning to his actions and life beyond mere power and calculation. Visiting the church in "Chapter 30," echoing the question of the *Republic*, he tells the priest that he wants "to understand what Justice is." He does not like the answer the priest gives him, and dramatically rejects it by profaning a crucifix. Nonetheless, he is tortured by the question, and appears to remain so. One might say that Frank's weakness (from the standpoint of the "ideal" tyrant), is that, in part, his nature is irrepressibly searching and philosophical, a claim that some commentators have made of Thrasymachus.

This hint of melancholy that Frank begins to display in Season 3 points to at least one further connection between *House of Cards* and the *Republic*. In Book 9, as Socrates is coming to the end of his long defense of justice and the just life, he returns once more to a discussion of the tyrannical personality.[14] Such a person, we are told, lives the worst sort of life. The driving force of the tyrant is an endless desire for self-aggrandizement and the pursuit of self-interest. He can trust no one and can be really close to none. Eventually he pushes away all those he thought loyal. He lives in isolation, fearing to venture out. Those who stay steadfast are mere flatterers or sycophants. Of him, Socrates asks rhetorically,

> Isn't it necessary that he be—and due to ruling become still more than before—envious, faithless, unjust, friendless, impious, and a host and nurse for all vice; and, thanks to all this, unlucky in the extreme; and then, that he make those close to him so?[15]

As Season 3 ends, Frank is being abandoned by all those who had been his closest servants and partners, not least Claire. He is becoming almost pitiable in his isolation and his single-minded pursuit of power for power's sake. He is abandoned and alone. As Socrates would say, he is living "the worst sort of life."

## Can We Really Get Away with Injustice?

So, can Frank get away with it? *House of Cards* has not answered this question yet, though as Season 3 ends things don't look good. To be sure, if the final season follows the book or the UK version, Frank's injustice will not triumph in the end. The bad guy will not finish first, in the long run. He will be found out, and so he will not be the example of perfect injustice. Hollywood always tells the story that way: The bad guy loses in the end, but only because he gets caught (and therefore is not truly a super-crafty bad guy).

But the problem presented by the cynical view of politics transcends the question of whether or not Frank "gets away with it." Rather, that problem, for us as it was for Plato's characters in the *Republic*, and may well be for Frank himself, is "Why ought we choose the just over the unjust view of politics?" We want to know, in other words, even if the villain does win, is his life truly the best? Socrates, Plato's mouthpiece, ultimately argues that there is no getting away with injustice because injustice in the soul (our true selves) is like a disease in the body. The unjust person is out of sorts and cannot live with himself. It is much better to be a just person with a clear conscience because only in this way will our true selves, our souls, find harmony and balance. Certainly the cynicism of *House of Cards*, like that of the *Republic* before it, leaves us wondering whether this is true, and of course that's why it too is a brilliant portrayal of this age-old problem.

## Notes

1. Plato presented his philosophy in the form of a series of dialogues, and *Republic* is considered his greatest achievement. The dialogues are dramas and relate their message through the give and take of philosophical discussion and argument between the characters. Plato's main character was his teacher, Socrates, and in *Republic* at least it is safe to assume that what Socrates says is what Plato believes. When discussing the ideas of the dialogues, it is customary to do so as they are expressed by the distinct characters who present them. Just keep in mind that always in the background is the author, Plato. The translation we use is that by Allan Bloom: Plato, *The Republic*, 2nd ed. (trans. with notes and an interpretive essay by Allan Bloom; New York: Basic Books, 1991). All

modern translations have adopted the practice of using the same original page numbers in the margins. Thus, the accepted way to cite Plato
is via reference to these numbers. We follow that practice here.

2. The Greek term is *dikaiosune*. No one English term quite captures its
full meaning Traditionally, it has been translated into English as "justice." That can seem strange to modern ears because we often think of
justice in terms of political and social institutions and our relations to
them. However, in using the term, Plato has in mind something more
extensive, like morality, right and wrong, and virtue. It is in this moral
sense, concerning the "proper," "right," or "good" ways in which persons should conduct themselves, that the term is intended in Books 1
and 2. In Book 3, Plato proposes an important analogy relating justice
at the individual level of moral behavior and justice at the level of the
society—justice in the soul of the individual and justice in the city or
society. This analogy marks a significant transition in the book and is
central to its argument.

3. *Republic* 331–332.
4. *Republic* 332d.
5. *Republic* 336b.
6. *Republic* 338c.
7. *Republic* 343b.
8. *Republic* 343d.
9. *Republic* 348d.
10. Emphasis added.
11. *Republic* 360e–361e.
12. *Republic* 361e–362a.
13. *Republic* 344a.
14. *Republic* 571–592.
15. *Republic* 580a.

# Being versus Seeming
## Socrates and the Lessons of Francis Underwood's Asides

*John Scott Gray*

The very first moments of *House of Cards* communicate to the viewer that we are watching a different kind of show. After hearing only the sound of screeching tires and the whimper of an injured dog, we see Francis Underwood coming out of his home to investigate. After telling his security guard to inform the owners of the hurt animal, he begins to talk—to the dog? To himself? As his words about two kinds of pain—one that makes you strong and the other that is useless suffering—wash over us, we begin to realize that we are somehow involved in what we are seeing. He looks at the camera—at us directly—and we have our first Underwood aside. As Underwood declares that he has no patience for useless things and begins to suffocate the dog, putting it out of its misery, we begin to realize that this show and its asides are going to involve us, perhaps even implicate us as accessories, in the activities of its chief protagonist. Underwood does what he calls the necessary and unpleasant thing, and we somehow know deep down that this is not the only unpleasant activity we will be involved in.

Other forms of media have used asides, most famously Shakespeare and several motion pictures (including *Ferris Bueller's Day Off*). *House of Cards* is perhaps unique, though, in employing asides over multiple seasons of a dramatic show, allowing us to peer inside the protagonist's mind in a way that conveys philosophical lessons.

*House of Cards and Philosophy: Underwood's Republic,*
First Edition. Edited by J. Edward Hackett.
© 2016 John Wiley & Sons, Ltd. Published 2016 by John Wiley & Sons, Ltd.

## "Who the Hell Are You Talking To?"

Many television critics have discussed the way *House of Cards*, with its all-at-once release, may signal the movement away from broadcast and cable television to an on-demand streaming world of entertainment. Other critics have pointed to the combination of big-name Hollywood figures, with David Fincher as director and Kevin Spacey and Robin Wright as stars, as a sign of the continued rise of the small screen as an important artistic medium. The show has received widespread critical attention, even receiving a 2014 Peabody Award, describing Spacey's Frank Underwood as guiding "the viewer through a modern-day tutorial of Machiavellian politics" and "[f]or broaching new possibilities for television storytelling and investing them with characters and plot turns at once wildly exaggerated and yet as unsurprising as the evening news."[1]

Much of the buzz around the show, however, has been about Underwood's asides. His practice of breaking the fourth wall and appearing to interact directly with the viewers has garnered a great deal of attention, both serious and humorous, ranging from an article in the *New Review of Film and Television* by Mario Klarer titled "Putting Television 'Aside': Novel Narration in *House of Cards*," to Spacey's appearance at the 2013 Emmy Awards, where he turns to the camera during an argument on stage about who should be hosting the show, talking about how he had been promised the job but had been turned down "for someone more likeable."

Perhaps the most entertaining reference to *House of Cards* and its asides was offered by Julia Louis-Dreyfus, in a White House Correspondents' Dinner bit in which she played her character Selina Meyer from *Veep* alongside real-life Vice President Joe Biden. As part of this short film, Louis-Dreyfus turns to the camera and in a nice vocal and tonal impersonation of Frank Underwood states, "Yes, we can all look directly into the camera, Kevin—the point is, you're not supposed to,"[2] before offering a couple of plot-spoilers for *House of Cards*. Echoing a question asked by many fans, Biden asks her, "Who the hell are you talking to?" Critical of the asides, the *New York Post*'s Kyle Smith refers to them as "Hannibal Lecterisms addressed directly to the camera," adding, "This technique doesn't become insufferable immediately—it takes about 15 minutes."[3]

Critics of the asides aside, several theories have been formulated about the meaning of the asides. Spacey himself says that when he performed the asides, he actually had a specific person in mind. "Instead of thinking that I'm talking to lots and lots of people, I'm talking to my best friend.... The person I trust more than anyone."[4] Others have talked about how the asides are pedagogical, designed to teach us the art of politics "as though [former Speaker of the House] Tip O'Neill were sitting down to explain that all politics is local."[5] On this view, Frank's messages communicate his political strategy and help us understand the ways in which he is on top of the situations that develop around him, as well as how he deals with adversity. A third theory considers the asides as a tool for the manipulation of the audience, for "Frank's asides not only explain the plot but craft our impression of him. He's constantly making the case that Francis J. Underwood is a savvy political operator around whom all others gravitate."[6] On this view, Frank is playing the audience in much the same way he plays the other characters to get what he wants.

While these asides clearly play a role in the development of the narrative, taking part in a tradition that goes back to Shakespeare, this chapter will instead focus on some of the philosophical lessons that may be learned when contrasting Underwood's asides to us with his statements made to the other characters when he emerges from his private camera conversations. In particular, we will explore the ways in which Underwood and his relationship with the camera fit with his perceived attitude and behavior during the remainder of the series.

## Frank and the Ring of Gyges

Underwood's hidden agenda is revealed through his asides. The distinction between having knowledge and appearing to have knowledge is a central concept throughout Platonic philosophy. It also serves as a main identifier of the difference between Socrates (Plato's teacher, who serves as both the central character and primary inspiration for Platonic philosophy) and his arch-nemeses, the Sophists. The Sophists focused on the use of rhetorical tricks to manipulate people's beliefs, something that Socrates and Plato fundamentally rejected.[7]

Plato's philosophical texts provide us with many lessons in Socratic philosophy. One of those lessons, which dominates the *Republic*, has to do with the being-versus-seeming distinction. The example that begins the discussion is the Ring of Gyges, a myth that centers around a magical ring that allows the wearer to become invisible. This invisibility would give one the power to accomplish anything they desired, with the added bonus of being able to frame others for those crimes while appearing completely innocent. The wearer of the ring does not have to be a just man, but instead can simply have the reputation of being a just man. This may be what people most want anyway, for "they do not praise justice itself, only the high reputations it leads to."[8] This story of the Ring of Gyges raises the question of whether it is better to be a good man who is seen by the masses as bad, or a bad man who is seen by the masses as good. Is it better to in reality be a good and just person, or to just appear as one yet enjoy the spoils of a devious life? This question dominates the remainder of the *Republic*, as Socrates discusses with those around him how best to understand the nature of justice. The details of that discussion are not relevant for this chapter, but the importance of the distinction between being and seeming is, for it captures a conflict that many of us feel ourselves throughout our lives, because wanting to present a public persona that would be accepted, respected, and popular is a desire that we feel everywhere from how we dress to what we choose to post on Facebook.

Frank Underwood illustrates this dichotomy. His actions often seem to have one motivation, but his asides reveal his deeper, truer motivation. As a politician, Underwood is very concerned about seeming to be in control, even in moments when he admits to the viewer his uncertainty, his weakness, or his awareness of the risks that he is taking. Early examples of this include his manipulation of the White House Press Secretary and his attempt to get the Vice President to pursue the Pennsylvania governorship. We also see Underwood's concern for appearances when he travels home to South Carolina to try to disarm the situation surrounding the car accident near the Gaffney water tower. Public perception is the air that Underwood and all politicians breathe. Even more important philosophically is the degree to which Underwood challenges Plato's Ring of Gyges position—for *House of Cards* to this point teaches us that it is far better to be the bad guy who seems good. Frank enjoys the spoils of a life lived outside the bounds of morality (adultery, corruption, and murder), yet keeps on winning.

## Frank and the Examined Life

According to Plato, living a life consumed by opinion polls can be harmful because it places one in the position of being controlled by the whims of an uninformed population. Socrates was famously put on trial in Athens, found guilty of corrupting the youth and impiety, and sentenced to death. While awaiting his execution, Socrates was jailed and his friend Crito planned to break him out. Crito is concerned that if he does not plot to save his friend, people will say that he had the resources but did nothing. Socrates responds, "[W]hy should we care so much for what the majority think … they cannot make a man either wise or foolish, but they inflict things haphazardly."[9] In his defense at trial, Socrates discussed this theme again, talking about how it is the expert that has knowledge, not the untrained majority.

The real problem with knowledge, according to Plato, is that many people claim to have it, when in fact it's actually a very rare element. The Oracle at Delphi said of Socrates that no one was wiser, yet Socrates himself had a hard time accepting this. Thus he went about testing others who he and others thought were wise, only to be continually disappointed. "I am wiser than this man; it is likely that neither of us knows anything worthwhile, but he thinks he knows something when he does not, whereas when I do not know, neither do I think I know; so I am likely to be wiser than he to this small extent, that I do not think I know what I do not know."[10] At his trial, Socrates chastises the citizens of Athens, saying that they live in "the greatest city with the greatest reputation for both wisdom and power," yet instead of caring about wisdom or truth, they are eager for money, reputation, and empty honors.[11] The people of Athens are in a daze, and Socrates believes that he has been placed there by divine powers to help them wake up and reevaluate their existence. This reevaluation involved living what Plato and Socrates called the examined life—asking questions and seeking answers. The answers sought were not merely the ones that sounded correct or felt comfortable or convenient, but instead were true. Knowledge is thus true belief justified by the process of continual examination—not the whims of convenience.

Unlike Socrates, Frank Underwood is not living the examined life. He pushes full speed ahead seeking greater position and power, but to what end? Motivations and missions do not appear to be a large part of the conversation, so the viewer is left with a picture of Frank as the scheming and power-mad politician who has forgotten why he wanted power in the first place, save having it itself. When he is appointed Vice President, Frank comments that there are two types of VPs, doormats and matadors. He claims to be the latter, but in fact Underwood is the bull—raging in the china shop with little concern for the destruction he causes.

Underwood's asides may not show him examining his motives, but they do draw the viewer in—creating a personal relationship with Frank. We see how he is in the asides—his true self—and can contrast that with what he shows to others. What does our relationship with Frank, and the degree to which we root for or against him, say about us? Without the asides, we would still see the bad things that he does (killing Russo, killing Zoe Barnes, and misusing FEMA money to fund America Works), but with the asides we see that these actions are not simply spur-of-the-moment events done out of passion—they are actually premeditated.

The education bill storyline illustrates Underwood's tendency to say one thing yet do another. Underwood is tapped by the White House to help move an education reform bill through the Congress during the new President's first 100 days, with noted education advocate Donald Blythe given the responsibility of crafting that bill, much to Underwood's chagrin. Underwood uses his connections to have an early draft of the bill leaked, leading to a firestorm of criticism. When Underwood and Blythe meet to discuss their response, Frank offers to sacrifice himself to the media, take responsibility, and step away from the bill. Blythe stops him, and at this point Frank looks at the camera, telling us in a nonverbal aside that things are going according to his plans. Frank had said to Blythe's face that he was on his side—that Blythe was "vital to this process." But we know the truth because in an aside to us, Frank tells us that "what a martyr craves more than anything is a sword to fall on. So, you sharpen the blade, hold it at just the right angle, and then three, two, one." Blythe offers to take the fall and leave the bill in Frank's hands. Unbeknownst to Blythe, Frank had six aides in the next room already working on a new draft. To soften the blow, Underwood asks Blythe, "Can I still come to you for council?" Of course, Underwood's plan all along was to remove Blythe from the equation so that he could take full credit for the bill's eventual success. He shows care, compassion, and respect to Blythe's face, yet lets his contempt for Blythe and his ideas flow in his asides.

Frank's tendency to say one thing in ordinary speech while saying something else in his asides becomes even more prominent in the second season. "Chapter 23" features Underwood meeting with the President to discuss whether or not the administration should appoint a special prosecutor to investigate the Chinese money-laundering and political contribution scandal. Underwood and the President's lawyer both question the wisdom of appointing a special prosecutor, with Underwood even trying to get the President to wait a few weeks, and then suggesting waiting a few days, before making a final decision. President Walker has concerns about waiting until the scandal overtakes the public consciousness, saying that waiting to that point would constitute being reactionary instead of proactive. Underwood responds by pointing out that acting now "could seem defensive, like the suspect who screams I didn't do it before anyone asked." The President insists that he has made his decision on the matter, suggesting a nominee for the special prosecutor position.

At this point, Underwood turns to us and remarks that "the only thing more satisfying than convincing someone to do what I want is failing to persuade them on purpose. It's like a Do Not Enter sign—it just begs you to walk through the door." It turns out that Underwood wants the special prosecutor, in part to try to undermine the President's position. In the next few episodes, talk will turn to impeachment, with Underwood working behind the scenes to push the process forward. He even approaches the Majority Whip, Jackie Sharp, who owes her position as Majority Whip (Underwood's previous position) to Underwood's prior manipulation of the political landscape. When Underwood suggests that Sharp assist the process, she remarks that what is being suggested is just shy of treason, to which Underwood replies, "Just shy of treason—which is politics." Thanks to the asides, however, we are well ahead of Sharp in realizing the mutiny that is taking place, and we also know that Underwood is willing to sacrifice Sharp as well, caring little for how events impact her political career. Frank's willingness to use Sharp continues in the third season, as he gets her to run for President to take away support from Dunbar in exchange for a future position as a Vice Presidential candidate. Finally, Sharp wises up to the way she is being used, siding with Dunbar and nearly handing her the Iowa Caucuses in the process.

Earlier in the third season, Underwood, facing opposition, announces to the party leadership that he will not seek reelection. He turns to us and tells us, "Look, they're thinking it's too good to be true—and it is." He sells his not seeking reelection as an opportunity to drive his America Works program. The leadership resists, but he tells them bluntly, "Think forward ... present my program to Congress, and if it dies there, so be it, but I want us TO FUCKING TRY. I am prepared to vacate this chair. Meet me halfway."

## Playing the President to Play the President

As Vice President in Season 2, Frank manipulates the most powerful man in the free world when he suggests that the administration provide an unprecedented amount of cooperation by agreeing to release their travel logs, as a "gesture of cooperation." What the viewer already knows is that the President and his wife, at the suggestion of the Underwoods, have been taking part in marriage counseling. When the President begins to balk at the suggestion to release the travel documents, not wanting someone poring over his comings and goings, Underwood turns toward the camera and says, "He's worried about his marriage counseling, as he should be." While those words are lingering in our eardrums, he turns back to President Walker and says, "If you are worried about your marriage counseling, you shouldn't be."

Comedians and commentators have long remarked that it is foolish to trust politicians. The old joke asks, "How can you tell if a politician is lying?" and answers, "His lips are moving." In *The Prince*, Niccolò Machiavelli (1469–1527) talks about the importance of a ruler appearing strong, even when he isn't. Machiavelli is acutely aware of the being-versus-seeming distinction, for he talks at great length of the need for a successful ruler to use deception as part of leadership, telling us that "a prudent ruler ought not to keep faith when by so doing it would be against his interest.... But it is necessary to be able to disguise this character well, and to be a great feigner and dissembler."[12] This two-faced political philosophy of promising one thing yet doing another when it suits one's interests seems to be embodied in Underwood, a trait that Socrates would certainly criticize.

Socrates states in Plato's *Apology* that he is aware of his ignorance, and that the central problem that many people have is their blindness to their own shortcomings. Frank's cockiness demonstrates a self-confidence that may be a requirement for public office, but it also constitutes a potential weakness from the Socratic point of view. As we watch Frank manipulate the situation to increase his political standing, the audience cannot help but wonder what he might be overlooking. What piece of evidence might be the piece that brings him back down a few notches? While he claims that there is only one rule—"Hunt or be hunted"—his asides show us an Underwood perhaps too sure of himself.

As the second season comes to a close, Underwood's double life is laid bare in a letter given to President Walker to try to persuade him to call off Raymond Tusk before his testimony to the House Judiciary Committee regarding the Chinese money-laundering conspiracy. The letter was written in a scene that occurs after Claire tells her husband to seduce Walker—to "cut [your heart] out and put it in his fucking hands." In a scene that plays out over the next six minutes, Underwood crafts this seduction, even going so far as to put down the pen he initially began with, choosing instead to type the letter on an antique Underwood typewriter given to him by his father. He states that he has only written one other letter with the device, and it did not fail him on that occasion—at which point he turns to the camera and says out loud, "I hope it will not fail me now."[13] The next few moments seem half aside, as if the letter is being read out loud for our benefit, while the other half cuts to Walker at Camp David, reading the letter as he walks in the woods.

This letter will prove successful, setting up Walker's demise, yet the letter itself reveals a great deal about Underwood's personality. It is filled with pomp and circumstance, using grand gesture and the tools of rhetoric to manipulate the situation. The letter is theater, beginning with words that Underwood's father told him when he gave him the machine: "This Underwood built an empire ... now you go and build one of your own." Underwood admits that this advice has served to drive him to become who he is today. He next moves to address claims that Walker made during a previous confrontation—stating that he does not wish to diminish the President (which, of course, he does) or challenge the President in the next election. He does admit that he wants the Presidency for himself (something that his maneuvers will deliver to him by the end of the episode). He admits to coveting the President's desk, but does so within the context of saying that any politician would feel the same way.

Here we see Underwood telling just enough of the truth to try to throw Walker off his scent and regain his trust. He tells a story of walking in on his father in the barn when he was thirteen. His father was holding a shotgun to his head, unable to pull the trigger. He asked Francis to pull the trigger for him—and he wishes in hindsight that he had. He claims to want to save the President from having to make the choice of whether or not to pull the trigger, instead giving Walker a confession note in which Underwood claims full responsibility for the whole affair. Of course, this does not remove the burden from Walker's shoulders, as he still has to choose to call off Tusk, with whom he had made a secret deal to frame Underwood in testimony in front of the Judiciary Committee. This tactic also is reminiscent of Frank's tactics with Donald Blythe, as well as with the parents of the girl killed while texting by the Gaffney water tower (in that case, he offered to resign his position). He swears that his only aim is to fight for and beside the President, but, privy to the asides, we know otherwise. In all three cases, Underwood says one thing, but implies its exact opposite in his asides. In Season 3, Underwood freely admits to us that he is comfortable with his lies, telling us, "Imagination is its own form of courage."

The practice of political manipulation takes us back to Socrates and the problems that arise when we try to fake knowledge that we do not have. The Sophists were teachers who were willing to impart the skills of rhetoric for a fee. To show off their capabilities, they would often argue both sides of a debate, showing both sides to be convincing. The ability to manipulate opinion is discussed in a Platonic dialogue called *Gorgias*. The Sophist Gorgias had claimed that rhetoric was the greatest good because it allowed one "mastery over others … the ability to persuade with words judges in the law courts, senators in the Senate, assemblymen in the Assembly, and men in any other meeting which convenes for the public interest."[14] In the dialogue, this claim meets with a discussion of how knowledge differs from belief, and the agreement that rhetoric teaches the latter but not the former.

Because rhetoric simply creates beliefs (which can, of course, be true or false), it is not concerned with facts, for "[rhetoric] has hit upon a means of persuasion that enables it to appear, in the eyes of the ignorant, to know more than those who really know."[15] Because rhetoric misleads the ignorant, Socrates calls it an ugly and foul form of politics that is easily associated with a tyrant. In contrast to most politicians, who are concerned merely with gaining more personal power, Plato praises the true politician, who concerns himself with making other people better and more virtuous.[16] Underwood, of course, would not win Plato's praise.

## Real Problems

While the storylines in *House of Cards* may be fictional and overly dramatic, the problems revealed are real. Underwood's problem is certainly not his alone, and certainly not reserved for those with political status and power. We are all guilty to a degree of manipulating people and situations for the sake of public perception. Still, we should wonder, must politics be about special interests, or might our political process move in different directions? When he is sworn in as Vice President, Underwood remarks in an aside, "Democracy is so overrated." That very well may be true, but what is the alternative?

## Notes

1. http://www.peabodyawards.com/award-profile/house-of-cards-netflix.
2. Read more: http://www.rollingstone.com/movies/videos/veeps-julia-louis-dreyfus-makes-trouble-with-joe-biden-20140504#ixzz36CA ZSMVa.
3. Kyle Smith, "Will You Watch Kevin Spacey Be Vicious on Your iPad?" *New York Post*, January 31, 2013. http://nypost.com/2013/01/31/will-you-watch-kevin-spacey-be-vicious-on-your-ipad/.
4. Tim Mollory, "'House of Cards': Who Kevin Spacey Is Talking to When He Talks to the Camera," TheWrap.com, February 5, 2014. http://www.thewrap.com/house-cards-kevin-spacey-talking-talks-camera/.
5. Zach Seward, "House of Cards's Fourth Wall," Medium.com, February 10, 2013. https://medium.com/@zseward/house-of-cardss-fourth-wall-b54a60143519.
6. Ibid.
7. Scholars debate which elements of Plato's philosophy are drawn from Socrates' own ideas and which are originally Plato's. This chapter does not address those debates, instead choosing for the purpose of simplicity to see the two as interchangeable.

8. Plato, *The Republic*, trans. G.M.A. Grube (Indianapolis, IN: Hackett, 1974), 363a.
9. Plato, "Crito," in *Five Dialogues*, trans. G.M.A. Grube (Indianapolis, IN: Hackett, 1981), 44c–d.
10. Plato, "Apology," in *Five Dialogues*, trans. G.M.A. Grube (Indianapolis, IN: Hackett Publishing, 1981), 21d.
11. Ibid., 29e.
12. Niccolò Machiavelli, *The Prince*, trans. Luigi Ricci (London: Grant Richards, 1903), 70.
13. Ironically, his next letter from this machine, concerning the killed soldier during the covert Jordan activity against Russia, may prove his undoing in the future, as he lies, saying the death occurred during a training exercise.
14. Plato, *Gorgias*, trans. W.C. Hembold (Upper Saddle River, NJ: Prentice Hall, 1997), 452.
15. Ibid., 459.
16. This point is discussed in James A. Arieti, *Interpreting Plato: The Dialogues as Drama* (Savage, MD: Rowman & Littlefield, 1991).

# Part II

# IMAGINING POSSIBILITIES: AMERICAN IDEALS IN *HOUSE OF CARDS*

# 3

# Frank Underwood Gives the Ideal Society a Reality Check

*Brian Kogelmann*

Political philosophers like to think about what the ideal society looks like. Some political philosophers, like Robert Nozick (1938–2002), think that a libertarian society is ideal. Others, like G.A. Cohen (1941–2009), think that justice requires perfect equality. Occupying the middle ground are folks like John Rawls (1921–2002) who strike a compromise between liberty and a concern for the poor. When offering a vision of the ideal society, political philosophers of all stripes tend to make a pretty funny assumption: People living in the ideal society behave a lot better than people like us actually do. Since political philosophers are in the business of telling us what the ideal government looks like, they most frequently make this assumption about politicians. Politicians in the ideal society don't pursue self-interest. They only, so assumes the philosopher, pursue the public good.

This assumption stands in stark contrast with the image of politics presented in *House of Cards*, an image that, though certainly dramatized, resembles our society much more closely than the philosopher's utopian vision. Indeed, the series follows politician Frank Underwood pursuing everything *but* the public good. Scorned by being passed over for Secretary of State, as promised to him by President-elect Garrett Walker, Frank sets himself on a warpath that ends with him in the Oval Office, a warpath that causes much harm to those

*House of Cards and Philosophy: Underwood's Republic*,
First Edition. Edited by J. Edward Hackett.
© 2016 John Wiley & Sons, Ltd. Published 2016 by John Wiley & Sons, Ltd.

around him, little to the dismay of Frank and his equally ruthless wife Claire.

So there's a disconnect between the utopian theorizing of the political philosopher and the sobering reality depicted in *House of Cards*. Philosophers assume that politicians, in the ideal society, pursue the public good. But *House of Cards* shows us that politicians, in our actual society, pursue their own private agendas, resulting in the public bad. This chapter grapples with this startling contrast and argues that if political philosophers want to be taken seriously, they must keep in mind the political reality that *House of Cards* depicts when they theorize about the ideal society. Political philosophers must design the ideal society under the assumption that people like Frank Underwood run for Congress.

## The Ideals of *The West Wing* and the Reality of *House of Cards*

John Rawls articulated the most famous vision of the ideal society in the 20th century. In his monumental *A Theory of Justice*, Rawls proposed an ideal society that strikes a balance between liberty and concern for those worst off: The ideal society allows some inequalities to be present, but only those that benefit the poorest in society. In arguing for this ideal, Rawls proposed that we examine competing visions of the ideal society under the assumption that everyone in the ideal society knows and complies with what justice requires. He called this the "strict compliance assumption."[1]

Rawls has a few things in mind when he tells us to assume that people in the ideal society strictly comply with what justice requires. For one, he assumes that people living in the ideal society try to further what justice requires in their role as citizens. As an example, if a teacher is about to cast her vote on Election Day, then she might face a choice between two candidates. One candidate might clearly be the better choice for the country and might advance the public good. The other candidate might not be very good for the country but might've promised to support teachers' unions no matter what. Most would predict that the teacher would vote for the candidate who promised to back the unions. But in Rawls's ideal society, we assume that the teacher votes for the better candidate—the one who will do much to advance the public good, even if that harms teachers.

This assumption about how citizens behave in the ideal society contrasts with how people behave in *House of Cards*. The show depicts constituents asking their representatives to do things that aren't necessarily in the public interest, but are clearly in the constituents' personal interests. In the scene that introduces Congressman Peter Russo, we find a constituent complaining to Russo that he hasn't helped him change a zoning law preventing the constituent from building on an empty lot. The whole first season of the show features a story arc in which Frank battles the teachers' unions over a new education bill, led by hard-nosed lobbyist Martin Spinella. Members of the union fight hard against provisions in the bill that go against their own interests: performance standards for teachers and funding for nonunionized charter schools, to a name a couple. Such behavior, which is a regular feature of our *House of Cards* political reality, is assumed away in Rawls's ideal society.

Beyond assuming that citizens in the ideal society try to further the demands of justice, Rawls also wants us to assume that politicians in the ideal society only advance legislation that furthers the public good. If a politician is faced with a piece of legislation reducing corn subsidies, the politician examines the piece of legislation thinking only about how well the bill serves society from an impartial perspective. Politicians in Rawls's ideal society don't vote with an eye to whether corn farmers in their districts will withdraw their support and not vote for them in future elections.

Contrast Rawls's vision of how politicians behave in the ideal society with what we find in *House of Cards*. Politicians offer and withdraw support for various pieces of legislation based on whether the legislation in question advances their private agendas. In Season 2, "Chapter 16," Underwood tries to pass an omnibus spending package but meets resistance from Republican Senator Curtis Haas (among others). Though Underwood is willing to give Haas everything he wants in a deal that will avoid a government shutdown, Haas holds out for self-interested reasons. Haas is afraid of giving the Democrats a win, suffering in the next midterm election, and having his constituents think he's given in to the President's demands. In fighting for the same omnibus bill, newly appointed House Majority Whip Jacqueline "Jackie" Sharp encounters members of the House only willing to support the bill in exchange for political favors. By contrast, in Rawls's ideal society, politicians only vote for legislation insofar as the legislation advances the public good.

The image of politics that Rawls relies on in characterizing the ideal society is far from the political reality illustrated in *House of Cards*. Rawls's ideal society resembles much more closely *The West Wing*—a series following President Josiah Bartlett, depicted as a wise and publicly minded statesman, standing in stark contrast to Frank Underwood. Though Rawls's ideal society relies on the unrealistic *West Wing* model of politics instead of the realistic *House of Cards* model, one might ask: So what? Why does this matter? Even though Rawls's ideal society assumes that citizens and politicians are more selfless and less selfish than they really are, shouldn't we still try to work toward this ideal? The answer is no, and the reason has to do with what economists call the theory of the second best.

The theory of the second best says this: When one optimality condition fails to obtain in a model, other variables originally thought optimal might no longer be optimal. Imagine my ideal dinner is steak, A1 sauce, and a baked potato. If we remove one of the optimal conditions of my ideal dinner—say, the steak—it doesn't follow that my second-best dinner is just A1 sauce and a baked potato. In the absence of steak, my second-best dinner might be something completely different: perhaps lasagna and a glass of cabernet.

Now apply the dinner metaphor to Rawls's ideal society. In constructing his ideal society, Rawls assumes that people and politicians behave in a manner like that depicted in the *West Wing* rather than *House of Cards*. But when we remove one of the optimality conditions from Rawls's picture of the ideal society—the presence of selfless politicians, swapping them for selfish politicians—then other features of the ideal society might also change. Some ideal societies might work very well when governed by selfless politicians. These same ideal societies might work very poorly when inhabited by selfish politicians.

Since we're stuck in a world with selfish politicians like Frank Underwood and greedy lobbyists like Remy Danton, we should take this into account when thinking about the ideal society. If we're told that steak won't be available when planning the ideal dinner, then we need to start thinking about the second-best dinner. If we know that we're stuck with the political reality that *House of Cards* depicts, then we need to design the ideal society with this in mind. Anything else amounts to planning an ideal steak dinner when we know steak isn't on the table.

## Frank Underwood throughout History

Adam Smith (1723–1790) is widely considered to be the father of modern economics. Though Smith was primarily concerned with economics rather than politics, his approach to studying the economy reflects nicely the style of theorizing popular in his time. In thinking about the economy, Smith assumed that each individual was best characterized by "natural selfishness and rapacity," driven by "vain and insatiable desires."[2] But even though Smith was pessimistic about human nature, he showed that the free market was structured in such a way that self-interested individuals actually act so as to bring about the public good, though not by any intention of their own. To cite one of Smith's most famous examples, it's not "from the benevolence of the butcher, the brewer, or the baker, that we expect our dinner but from their regard to their own interest. We address ourselves, not to their humanity but to their self-love."[3]

Though Smith applies the *House of Cards* model of behavior to his analysis of the economy, his contemporary David Hume (1711–1776) advocated we apply the same behavioral standard when thinking about politics:

> Political writers have established it as a maxim, that, in contriving any system of government, and fixing the several checks and controls of the constitution, every man ought to be a supposed *knave*, and to have no other end, in all his actions, than private interest. By his interest we must govern him, and, by means of it, make him, notwithstanding his insatiable avarice and ambition, co-operate to public good.[4]

In telling us to assume that every man is a knave, Hume is telling us to adopt the *House of Cards* model of politics. We design our ideal society assuming that every man is like Frank Underwood, uncompromisingly pursuing his selfish agenda at the expense of the public good. But even though every man is a knave, Hume tells us that we must find a way to design our society so that the greed and ambition of all the Underwoods of the world actually contribute to the public good. Smith showed that the free market transforms the baker's selfishness into our delicious dinner. Hume likewise advocates that we figure out how to design government so that self-interested politicians end up inadvertently promoting our interests just as the baker does. James Madison, one of our country's Founding Fathers, did just that when he tried to design a Constitution so that "ambition must be made to counteract ambition."[5]

Though the *House of Cards* model of politics was popular in the eighteenth century, such a way of thinking fell out of popularity in the nineteenth and early twentieth centuries. It's not clear exactly when this shift occurred, but one might point to the developing field of welfare economics as a central fault line. The idea behind welfare economics is to identify and propose remedies for market failures—suboptimal distributions of goods produced by actual markets when compared to how we think markets should work.

In identifying market failures, welfare economists propose government remedies that, if enacted, would produce the desirable result that the market failed to achieve. As an example, imagine that Raymond Tusk's nuclear power plants produce a significant amount of pollution. This is a market failure because Tusk and those consuming Tusk's power don't take into account the costs of pollution for society as a whole in their transaction, resulting in smoggy air and difficult breathing. Politicians step in and fix this market failure by proposing regulations: They limit the amount of stuff Tusk's power plants can shoot into the air, or tax Tusk for doing so.

But, in proposing government remedies for market failures, welfare economists didn't consider (as Hume most certainly would have) the possibility of government failure. Welfare economists in the early twentieth century just assumed that government would get the job done, not thinking about the possibility of Frank Underwood manipulating the political process to do something besides what the economist says he should do. This bizarre assumption was finally targeted by Nobel Prize winner James M. Buchanan (1919–2013), who argued that the same self-interest we attribute to people in the economy should also be attributed to politicians if we are to compare competing ideals on equal footing.

In one of his most celebrated papers, Buchanan argued that we can't take seriously the welfare economist's policy proposal unless we analyze the proposal under the assumption that political actors won't selflessly carry out such proposals, but rather will carry out such proposals with their self-interest in mind.[6] We thus compare existing market failures to the possibility of government failures, a possibility that is only realized when we assume that politicians behave like *House of Cards* tells us they do.

Buchanan's emphasis on adopting the *House of Cards* model of politics didn't stop at welfare economics—he thought that we should think of *all* politics in terms of *House of Cards* rather than *The West Wing*. In Buchanan's words: "It seems to be nothing more than simple and obvious wisdom to compare social institutions as they might be expected actually to operate rather than to compare romantic models of how such institutions might be hoped to operate."[7]

So there we have it. The way of thinking about politics proposed in the last section has historical precedent in the roots of the Scottish Enlightenment, where Adam Smith and David Hume told us to think about politics employing the *House of Cards* model. James M. Buchanan ultimately revived the Frank Underwood–inspired way of thinking about politics in bidding us to examine politics without romance.

## A New Kind of Ideal Society

Having argued that we should take seriously the *House of Cards* model of politics when theorizing about the ideal society, and having shown that there is historical precedent for doing so, let's consider how we can design the ideal society to handle the possibility of people like Frank Underwood winning elected office.

One problem frequently faced in our *House of Cards* political reality is the problem of rent seeking. Rent seeking is not about landlords collecting money every month. Rather, it involves powerful individuals and corporations seeking favors from those in political power, often in exchange for campaign contributions. In capturing our political reality, *House of Cards* displays the rent-seeking process. Before he takes a job as Chief of Staff for President Underwood in Season 3, Remy Danton is a lobbyist for SanCorp, a fictional natural gas company. As a lobbyist, Danton pressures politicians into supporting legislation that favors SanCorp. As just one example of this, when SanCorp's drilling rights are threatened by Peter Russo's watershed bill, Danton offers campaign contributions to several Pennsylvania congressmen in exchange for withdrawing support for Russo's bill, making them reluctant to support the act as shown in the opening scenes of Season 1, "Chapter 9." As another example, in the very beginning of Season 1, "Chapter 2," Danton approaches Underwood, whose failure to be appointed Secretary of State threatens SanCorp's interests. An exasperated Danton warns Underwood, "Don't make me throw money at your challenger next cycle."

Because politics is frequently inundated with powerful rent-seeking interests, political philosophers ought to think about such problems when designing the ideal government. For example, the more power government has over the economy, the greater the government's capacity to deal out favors. A government prevented from regulating natural resources doesn't have to worry about lobbyists from Exxon-Mobil and Chevron buying politicians. As another way of dealing with the problem of rent seeking, publicly financed elections, instead of the current, privately financed system, would do wonders in preventing rent seeking. Such a system wouldn't allow Remy Danton to throw money at Frank's challenger in the next cycle. And, finally, some have argued for a constitutional amendment requiring that a generality constraint be satisfied, which prevents governments from passing discriminatory legislation favoring some groups at the expense of others.[8]

Another problem we face as a part of our political reality is the problem of politicians having what economists call high discount rates. Politicians don't care that much about the long-term future, but only care about the short-term here-and-now. The reason why politicians don't care about the long term is because they're always worried about the next election—why care about the next 20 years when you're up for reelection in two? Politicians are motivated to do things that are good in the here-and-now but that won't be good down the road, much in the same way that children want to do nothing but eat candy and play video games right now instead of focusing on doing well in school.

*House of Cards* accurately depicts the reality of politicians always focused on the next election. Consider an example from Season 3, "Chapter 27." Claire is trying to convince Senator Mendoza to confirm her for U.S. Ambassador to the United Nations. In doing so, she appeals to how Mendoza's choice won't affect him in the next election. If Claire is a disaster and Mendoza votes for her, then Mendoza can just attack Claire in a campaign ad. But if Claire is a success, then Mendoza can't be faulted for confirming her. Either way, the Senator's 2016 election won't be jeopardized. As another example, when debating the merits of Peter Russo's watershed bill at the beginning of Season 1, "Chapter 9," a member of the House objects: "I've already been approached by SanCorp with reelection funds." Another Congressman joins in: "I have too. They offered me a donation package from eight different drilling companies." Frank doesn't respond by appealing to the good the bill will do. Instead, he reminds the Pennsylvania congressmen that if Peter Russo doesn't win the governorship, then the Republicans will control redistricting within the state—which will put the Democrats' jobs at risk. *House of Cards* shows how politicians are always concerned with keeping their jobs, never with the long-term public good.

The good news is that there are steps we can take to make politicians more focused on the long term than the short term. For example, because politicians are always concerned with the short term, they tend to spend a lot of money—resulting in really, really big debts. Spending has a stimulus effect on the economy, and self-interested politicians don't want to be the ones who depress the economy when reelection is coming. We can prevent this problem by introducing a balanced-budget amendment that prevents politicians from spending too much money. Though politicians want to spend money on stuff to woo their constituents for the next election, a balanced budget would only let them spend money up to a limit. As another example, short-sighted politicians tend to inflate the currency too much (this means that they print too much money). They do this because inflation tends to decrease short-term unemployment, even though it leaves everyone worse off in the long run. Just as with spending problems, we can address our inflation problem with a constitutional amendment, one setting a rate of inflation every year so politicians can't print more money to make future voters happy. These are just a few ways of designing the ideal society with the *House of Cards* model of politics in mind.

## When John Rawls Embraces Frank Underwood

Many fictional depictions of politics prior to *House of Cards* depicted politicians as noble statesmen, selflessly pursuing the public good. But these depictions have always seemed wrong. We look at the news and see scandal after scandal; we see legislation that we can't make sense of; spending in elections continually increases; and we see high-profile Wall Street guys meeting with D.C.'s political elite. *House of Cards* shows us this side of politics. We may not like what we see, but what we see resembles the reality around us.

*House of Cards* may depict an ugly reality, but it can help us think about an ideal reality. We can't stop people like Frank Underwood from running for office. In large part, that's because politicians like Frank aren't radically different from folks like you and me. We're all self-interested. We all look out for ourselves, family, and community first—though perhaps not as ruthlessly as Frank does. We can't realistically hope for more virtuous politicians, but we *can* design our society under the assumption that people like Frank Underwood run for office. If we do so, the Underwoods of the world will do as little damage as possible.

## Notes

1. John Rawls, *A Theory of Justice* (Cambridge, MA: Harvard University Press, 1971), 8.
2. Adam Smith, *The Theory of Moral Sentiments* (Indianapolis, IN: Liberty Fund, 1982), 184.
3. Adam Smith, *The Wealth of Nations* (Indianapolis, IN: Liberty Fund, 1981), 26–27.
4. David Hume, "Of the Independency of Parliament," in *Essays: Moral, Political, and Literary* (Indianapolis, IN: Liberty Fund, 1985), 42–43.
5. James Madison, "Federalist 51," in *The Federalist Papers* (Indianapolis, IN: Liberty Fund, 2001), 268.

6. James M. Buchanan, "Politics, Policy, and the Pigovian Margins," in *The Logical Foundations of Constitutional Democracy* (Indianapolis, IN: Liberty Fund, 1999).

7. James M. Buchanan, "Politics without Romance," in *The Logical Foundations of Constitutional Democracy* (Indianapolis, IN: Liberty Fund, 1999), 47.

8. James M. Buchanan and Roger D. Congleton, *Politics by Principle, Not Interest: Toward a Nondiscriminatory Democracy* (Indianapolis, IN: Liberty Fund, 2003).

# 4

# "What Will We Leave Behind?" Claire Underwood's American Dream

## Sarah J. Palm and Kenneth W. Stikkers

An upside-down American flag. That is the icon that flashes across the screen with each episode of the Netflix series *House of Cards*. In military culture, an upside-down flag is the symbol for distress— an S.O.S. But as we watch Frank and Claire Underwood twist and pollute the very system that flag represents for their own personal gain, the insignia gains even darker connotations. It becomes a symbol of the inverted values to which Frank and Claire adhere—the American dream upended. And, as the title of the series suggests, it is a precarious and empty structure that they have built for themselves.

## "Burning the Barn to Find Our Penny in the Hay": Adams's American Dream and *Ressentiment*

*House of Cards* is the story of American dreams turned into nightmares, especially for its main characters, Frank and Claire. Historian James Truslow Adams first coined the term "American dream" in 1931 in his classic, widely read *The Epic of America*, describing it as "that dream of a land in which life should be better and richer and fuller for every man, with opportunity for each according to his ability or achievement." "It is not a dream of motor cars and high wages merely," Adams further explained, "but a dream of

*House of Cards and Philosophy: Underwood's Republic*,
First Edition. Edited by J. Edward Hackett.
© 2016 John Wiley & Sons, Ltd. Published 2016 by John Wiley & Sons, Ltd.

a social order in which each man and each woman shall be able to attain to the fullest stature of which they are innately capable, and be recognized by others for what they are, regardless of the fortuitous circumstances of birth or position."[1] It is a vision of "something nobler" than "material conquest" and wealth, and not just an ideal for America but "a hope for mankind." This American dream, however, Adams suggested, begged the philosophical question, "But what *is* better and what *is* richer?" The American dream thus rests upon "this question of values": "Unless we [Americans] can agree on what the values in life are, we clearly can have no goal ... and if we have no goal, the discussion of methods is merely futile."[2]

Adams feared that America had failed to answer this "question of values": it had failed to reach a consensus on what a "better and richer life" is, and thus the American dream had become perverted into a preoccupation with means, namely, material goods and instruments of power that serve no clear, intelligent ends. It thus was devolving from a dream of virtue into one of crass consumerism, taking with it the hopes for democracy in America: "We cannot become a great democracy by giving ourselves up as individuals to selfishness, physical comfort, and cheap amusements." "[U]nless we settle on the values of life," Adams warned, "we are likely to ... burn the barn to find our penny in the hay."[3]

*House of Cards* chillingly depicts the fulfillment of Adams's warning: Lacking a clear understanding of the values that make for a truly "better and richer life," Frank and Claire Underwood settle on a version of the American dream defined entirely by the selfish pursuit of power for its own sake. Throughout the series, however, there are intimations that underneath their projections of raw will-to-power, both secretly long for something "more" in life, for values that are not altogether clear to them and transcend what they are capable of achieving.

Frank Underwood, for all his disparaging of others' greed, is himself a slave to the pursuit of power, unknowingly caught up in this "American nightmare." The things he does in order to ascend the political ladder have robbed him of all integrity and decency, to the point where he hardly seems to have any humanity left in him at all. In his wake, he sucks countless others around him into the nightmare, including his wife, Claire, who has also been compelled to sacrifice many aspects of her humanity and her womanhood for the sake of her and her husband's political gain. Such sacrifices have made "ruthless pragmatists" of them both, undistracted by things like love and friendship, singlemindedly and furiously clawing their way to the top of the food chain. However, underlying the main characters' appearances of strength are feelings of weakness, stemming from their inability to achieve the "richer and fuller life" that they secretly and desperately desire. Such feelings erupt in vicious resentment against those manifesting the values of such a life and who thus painfully remind the Underwoods of their fundamental weakness and the spiritual poverty at the core of their lives.

Friedrich Nietzsche introduced the concept of *ressentiment* to philosophy. In his *Genealogy of Morals*, Nietzsche famously accused Christianity of being a "slave morality": out of an inner, vital weakness and hatred of life, it had elevated impotence—"humility," "obedience," and "patience"—into a merit, thereby disvaluing what it secretly craves but is too weak to achieve, namely, strength and power. Another German philosopher, Max Scheler (1874–1928), agreed with Nietzsche that the modern age was one filled with *ressentiment*,[4] but the source of that *ressentiment*, Scheler contended, is not Christianity but "the industrial ethos," or what sociologist Max Weber termed "the Spirit of Capitalism." In accord with that ethos, everything vital and alive is converted into dead fuel for the machinery of industry and politics: Life is made to serve the machine. Scheler describes the matter thusly: "everything living and vital is eliminated from this strange picture. This world is an accumulation of logicians standing in a huge engine-room—bloodless, emotionless, without love or hatred."[5] Does this not describe Frank Underwood's world, where political strategists coldly calculate their next move in their unlimited lust for power? Moreover, though, "*Ressentiment*," Scheler tells us, "is a self-poisoning of the mind.... It is a lasting mental attitude, caused by the systematic repression of certain emotions and affects which, as such, are normal components of human nature. Their repression leads to the constant tendency to indulge in certain kinds of value delusions and corresponding value judgments. The emotions and affects primarily concerned are revenge, hatred, malice, envy, the impulse to detract, and spite."[6] Furthermore, "It likes to disparage and to smash pedestals, to dwell on the negative aspects of excellent men and things."[7] Indeed, these qualities perfectly characterize Frank Underwood: His inability to achieve a loftier version of the American dream has turned "normal components of human nature," such as love and compassion, into hatred, malice, envy, spite, and an impulse to detract and to tear down what is noble, beautiful, and truly great in others.

That Frank once aspired to a loftier American dream than the one he has come to pursue is perhaps best revealed when he attends his college reunion at The Sentinel. In that episode, we learn that Frank once enjoyed true friendship, camaraderie, and the beauty of song. We are allowed a brief glimmer of the lost values for which he secretly longs and that drive his *ressentiment*. Moreover, this *ressentiment* is further revealed in his felt need, at the start of Season 3, to piss on his father's grave and to spit into the face of a crucified Jesus: Only a person of *ressentiment*, according to Scheler, would feel such a need to detract from better men.

Frank's *ressentiment* is subtle and fleeting. Claire's, however, is more clearly evident in the series, and it is the one on which this chapter focuses.

## Claire Underwood: The Resentful *Überfrau*

Dragged along with Frank in his pursuit of power is Claire Underwood. In many ways, the two of them seem cut from the same cloth—cold, calculating, and lacking in almost every facet of human decency. Claire, though, exhibits significantly more doubts about the choices she has made than her husband does. Opting for this life so that she "would never be bored," she could not have foreseen all it would end up costing her. She may have a "coat of armor three inches thick," but Claire's sacrifices for her husband's political career (and her resulting prominence) are still an endless source of regret and resentment for her.

The sacrifice that seems to cause Claire the most inner turmoil, especially as she enters menopause, is her potential motherhood. She reveals that she had three abortions—two while she was a "teenager and reckless," and the third a postmarital decision to avoid the "distraction" of children while she and Frank were on the campaign trail. To anyone who asks, she is quite convincing when she tells them things like "Francis and I wanted to devote our lives to public service" and "I'm perfectly happy without [children]." But when there is no one around to whom to lie, her resolve wavers. As she and Frank share a cigarette one night, he senses something is on her mind.

> CLAIRE: I was thinking about when one of us dies. Whether it's you first or me....
>
> FRANK: Well, if it is me, and I'm sure it will be, you won't be alone for long.
>
> CLAIRE: No. I mean, what will we leave behind?
>
> FRANK: We've accomplished a great deal. And I intend for us to accomplish a lot more.
>
> CLAIRE: But for whom?
>
> FRANK: For each other.
>
> CLAIRE: But if we're not.... Ah, I'm being silly. ("Chapter 13")

Here, Claire attempts to express not only her maternal void but also a desire for something else—that nebulous "more" to which Adams refers.

In the service of what ends or values do Claire and Frank want to put the power they relentlessly strive to amass? The query certainly never keeps Frank up at night: He seeks power without any clear, intelligent vision of the "better and richer life" for which power is, as Adams lamented, but a means. Claire, on the other hand, finds herself increasingly confronted by this troubling question throughout the series. Time after time, subconscious desires and fears bleed into Claire's daily life: She finds herself bonding with Peter Russo's children and later having a dream about them; she stares at her aging face in the mirror; she seeks out a pregnancy specialist without Frank's knowledge. But she catches herself, always, before it can go too far, before Frank suspects that she is not entirely like him and does not share his single-mindedness. She muses about the possibility of children, of a legacy, of leaving something worthwhile behind, but then she remembers to whom she is married and waves such thoughts away as folly. As Scheler warned, however, this systematic repression of human emotions and longings for enduring values—for something to "leave behind"—inevitably leads only to *ressentiment*.

Claire's *ressentiment* over her maternal void manifests itself most clearly in her treatment of her coworker Gillian Cole. Claire at first admires and respects Gillian's free lifestyle and her dedication to the cause, but that admiration quickly turns bitter when Gillian reveals her pregnancy. Having already denied herself all the things that Gillian has—children, integrity, and noble goals—Claire vents her *ressentiment* toward the woman by firing her. Gillian stands her ground, filing a wrongful termination lawsuit. When Claire comes to her apartment seeking an "amicable solution," Gillian grabs Claire's hand and puts it on her stomach, saying, "Do you feel that? The kicking? I won't let people like you fuck up the world my child has to live in" ("Chapter 13"). Claire's discomfort is palpable. She wrenches her hand away with a look of simultaneous revulsion and pain, unable and unwilling to connect this tactile experience to the abstract concept of motherhood she has given up.

When Gillian continues to fight her legally, Claire resorts to dirty tactics, making it her mission to destroy the woman she now sees as her enemy. Threatening to withhold healthcare from her and her baby unless she drops the lawsuit, Claire tells Gillian flat-out, "I'm willing to let your child wither and die inside of you, if that's what's required" ("Chapter 14"). Here we see in Claire, perhaps even more blatantly than with Frank, the need not only to overcome barriers to success but also to tear down and belittle those manifesting the very values for which she secretly longs. Gillian Cole embodies the values of altruism and motherhood that Claire has sacrificed in the pursuit of power—a sacrifice that has, indeed, led to "value delusions and corresponding value judgments." In her heart Claire knows that the values of power and control are not worth the sacrifice of the values of life and family, but because she is too morally weak to admit her mistake, she can only loathe and destroy anyone and anything that reminds her of it, thus running the gamut of what Scheler includes in his description of *ressentiment*: "revenge, hatred, malice, envy, the impulse to detract, and spite."

Claire's marriage to Frank itself can also be seen as a personal sacrifice, as her dalliance with Adam Galloway suggests, and one that leads to further *ressentiment*. Although there is genuine affection between them—one might even call them soulmates of a sort—Frank's and Claire's relationship is clearly more a political partnership than a union of love. What may have started out as a mutually beneficial arrangement seems to have slowly tipped in Frank's favor, with Claire constantly finding herself on the giving end, as her husband continues to rise in the ranks. She realizes this—is even constantly aware of it on some level—and confronts him about it on more than one occasion.

He always assures her that they make decisions together, decisions that benefit them both equally. "Yeah, well," she replies during one argument, "it hasn't felt like that. Not for the past six months. I don't feel as though I'm standing *beside* you" ("Chapter 9").

Because of this inequity, Claire soon finds the Clean Water Initiative (CWI) suffering for Frank's schemes. She tells him outright, "My career cannot keep taking hits on behalf of yours. It's more than an inconvenience" ("Chapter 5"). Indeed, this is her life's work, a nonprofit she started for a reason, seemingly an altruistic one. Those good intentions with which she started when she first conceived CWI have become eroded by Frank's power obsession.[8]

Claire begins to wonder how different things would be had she not married Frank and reconnects with her old flame, the photographer Adam Galloway. Adam in many ways embodies everything Claire gave up all those years ago—passion, love, creativity, freedom, independence, and selflessness—much like The Sentinel represented all those values Frank has sacrificed in his quest for power. When Claire leaves Frank briefly for Adam, we see an entirely new side to her, much as we did with Frank when he returned to The Sentinel. She is carefree, wearing Adam's jeans and button-up shirts (a far cry from her usual austere wardrobe). She actually *laughs*—something we never saw her do previously—with his artist friends, dancing with them and smoking joints into the wee hours of the morning. She and Adam spend their few days together making love and talking about life. She allows herself to wonder, to philosophize—"I think that sometimes, whether my life will add up." Then she catches herself, imagining Frank's reaction: "Francis would roll his eyes if he heard me talking like this" ("Chapter 11").

Eventually, Claire trades Adam and the life he represents for Frank and the power and wealth he can provide. The human desires she thought she could simply turn her back on, however, remain simmering beneath the surface, where they eventually vent themselves as resentment in Season 2. Upon learning of his new fiancée, Claire takes it upon herself to destroy Adam, much as she did Gillian. Through a series of lies and betrayals, she effectively destroys his career and credibility. Still resentful over the potential life with him that she sacrificed to be Frank's wife, Claire cannot abide Adam's happiness, particularly with another woman whom he admits to love more than he ever loved Claire. When she threatens to "bury him" if he doesn't cooperate with her and Frank's political scheming, he tells her, "I've never hated any-one before. Now I know what that feels like." She responds, "It's a ter-rible feeling, isn't it?"—finally admitting her hatred for him, for what he has and is, and for the repressed feelings and values he rekindles in her ("Chapter 9"). This is Scheler's and Nietzsche's *ressentiment* in its purest form, for "it likes to disparage and to smash pedestals, to dwell on the negative aspects of excellent men and things."

Claire manages to convince us for most of the series that she is as unfeeling and calculating as her husband. The façade first cracks, how-ever, after her interaction with fellow rape survivor Megan Hennessey. After convincing Megan to come forward about her rape and enlist-ing her help on a sexual assault bill, Claire ultimately abandons both Megan and the bill, citing "political realities we couldn't ignore." The betrayal sends Megan into a spiral. When Claire visits her after a sui-cide attempt, her steely resolve withers when confronted by the reality of what she has done to this girl in front of her—a girl who so closely resembles herself. When Megan compares Claire's violation of her to her rapist's, it hits home.[9] Hours later, back in her empty house, Claire breaks down on the staircase, ashamed of herself for what she has done, and mourning the loss of the person she once was—a person who adhered to loftier values than power and wealth, a person who would have fought for what was right. Never one to wallow, though, Claire quickly turns her shame and guilt to acid when Frank returns home. "You have to stop [Raymond Tusk]. . . . Trying's not enough, Francis," she tells him. When he responds with excuses, she is thor-oughly callous: "I've done what I had to do. Now you do what you have to do. Seduce him. Give him your heart. Cut it out and put it in his fucking hands" ("Chapter 26"). She has no patience for his fail-ure, not after all she has sacrificed. She has cut out her own heart and sacrificed it for him; now it is time for him to do the same. They are, after all, in this together, united by their *ressentiment*.

That ever-present question, "What will we leave behind?" contin-ues to haunt Claire more than ever after becoming First Lady. Per-haps the clearest instance of Claire being forced to confront that existential void is her meeting with the gay rights activist Michael Corrigan, who has been imprisoned by Russian President Petrov for his part in a protest. When her attempts to convince Corrigan to dis-tance himself from the cause and return home to the United States fail, Claire then resorts to her usual tactics of belittling his idealism.

He responds calmly, "You think you can shame me, but you can't." When she persists, he tells her, "I can't betray myself. Who would I be then?" ("Chapter 32"). She shouts at him to "be a fucking adult," to "learn to compromise," to let others take up the cause. But he is steadfast, even to his own demise. A few hours later, he hangs himself in his cell, rather than betray his cause. Whereas, in the past, she had always been able to force others to abandon their ideals once sufficiently threatened, in the face of Corrigan's unwavering sense of justice and his willingness to die for his beliefs, Claire is utterly powerless. Unable to drag him down to her and Frank's own moral level of political expediency and power, the *ressentiment* she carried for so long shatters. And while Frank and President Petrov are speechifying and lying to cover up the circumstances surrounding Corrigan's death, Claire tells the world the truth. It is her turning point. It is the wake-up call she needed to make her realize that her *ressentiment* did not stem, as she had always imagined, from the inequity of her partnership with Frank, but rather from the fundamental differences between herself and her husband. Though she remains unclear about what it is—what higher values—for which she longs, she knows that she must leave this empty life, and the last scene of Season 3 is of her walking away from Frank, away from the White House, away from the power she thought she had always desired, free at last from her *ressentiment*.

*House of Cards* might seem at first a cynical portrayal of the American dream gone wrong, but perhaps it is a more evolved one. America has matured somewhat since Adams's warning: We have taken that warning to heart, and maybe that is why we are so drawn to this series. Frank and Claire Underwood represent two aspects of and responses to this new, twisted American dream, but *House of Cards* offers an array of characters that embody many others, which is part of what makes the series so relevant. Indeed, it is beyond the scope of this chapter, but each character—from Zoe Barnes to Doug Stamper—aspires to and grapples with some version of the American dream. While previous portrayals of the American-dream-turned-nightmare in popular culture, such as *The Candidate* or *The Sopranos*, tended to focus more narrowly on one protagonist's or antihero's struggle, *House of Cards* depicts multiple experiences of the American dream, enabling us, the viewers, to identify with some aspect of every character's version of that dream and their struggle to attain it.

Frank Underwood has settled on material values of power. Claire, meanwhile, had settled on those same values, only to find herself constantly second guessing them and longing for "more." This makes her a fascinating foil to Frank's tightly wrapped enigma, and also makes her a character to whom we, the audience, can very much relate. Like Claire, we too feel trapped in houses of cards—perverted American dreams—that we have built for ourselves, caught between the hollow successes that we are told to want and the values for which we secretly, and too often resentfully, yearn. We applaud Claire's decision finally to leave Frank and the life he represents, and are perhaps inspired to confront our own distorted American dreams—our own *ressentiment*—and to gain the courage to leave our own houses of cards.

## Notes

1. James Truslow Adams, *The Epic of America* (Boston: Little, Brown, and Company, 1931), 415.
2. Ibid., 418.
3. Ibid., 422.
4. Scheler retains the French *ressentiment* because, he explains, it contains emotional connotations, specifically an intense "hostility," that are lost in translations. Max Scheler, *Ressentiment*, trans. William W. Holdhiem, ed. Lewis A. Coser (New York: The Free Press of Glencoe, 1961), 39.
5. Ibid., 164. Scheler identified the *ressentiment* comprising "the industrial ethos" as the perversion of life and utility values: According to that ethos, one no longer enjoys any "right to life," but rather one now must "earn a living" by making one's life useful for economic productivity and profit (158). Similarly, Weber described "the spirit of capitalism" as an "ethos," or value system, that turns life—human and nonhuman alike—into resources for endless capitalist profit making. Weber summarized that ethos with the words of Ferdinand Kuernberger: "They [capitalists] make tallow out of cattle and money out of men." Max Weber, *The Protestant Ethic and the Spirit of Capitalism*, trans. Talcott Parsons (New York: Charles Scribner's Sons, 1959), 51.
6. Scheler, 45–46.
7. Ibid., 47.
8. CLAIRE:   I fired half of my staff for us. I have turned down donations for us. I drafted Peter's bill for us. I diverted time and energy away from *my* goals for us.

FRANK:      Okay, I don't wanna have to say this, but maybe you need to hear it. CWI is important, yes, but it doesn't come *close* to what we are trying to accomplish! You must see that! I'm just being honest.

CLAIRE:     Then be honest about how you've been using me just like you use everybody else. That was never part of the bargain. ("Chapter 10")

9.  CLAIRE:     Your mom told me they found you in the lake.

MEGAN:      What do you care?

CLAIRE:     I care very much.

MEGAN:      No, you don't. You don't use somebody you care about. 'Whore.' 'Slut.' 'Bitch.' 'Traitor.' That's what they call me, in my mail, online. I wish I had never called. I wish I had never met you. I feel so stupid, believing what you told me, thinking that you did care. I was getting better. You did this to me (picks up pill bottle). Every time I take one of these, I think of him. And the next face I think of? It's yours.

CLAIRE:     I'm sorry that you felt used. You weren't. I just, um.... Like I told you, the political landscape shifted and we found.... Megan? ("Chapter 26")

# Part III

# CHARACTERIZING FRANK: ÜBERMENSCH OR THE PRINCE

# 5

# Underwood as Übermensch
## A Postmodern Play of Power

*Leslie A. Aarons*

We meet Francis J. "Frank" Underwood in the middle of the night, startled by the disturbing sounds of brakes screeching, glass breaking, and a dog yelping in terrible pain. Underwood bursts from his house with his trusted bodyguard, Edward Meechum. It was a violent hit and run that left the neighbor's dog mortally wounded. Frank Underwood sends Meechum to fetch the neighbors, but we quickly detect that it was only to gain a few precious moments alone with the suffering animal—and us. As the audience, we cringe at the sounds of the dog's obvious agony, but Frank remains composed and tells us, "There are two kinds of pain, sort of pain that makes you strong, or useless pain; sort of pain that's only suffering. I have no patience for useless things. Moments like this require someone who will act. Do the unpleasant thing; the necessary thing." We never see the dog, only Frank, kneeling over her, seemingly choking the pet to put her out of her misery. The dog's whimpering stops and Frank consoles us, "There, no more pain."

Frank Underwood is prepared to do many "unpleasant things" that he deems "necessary," never flinching as he orchestrates his ascent to the most powerful position in the free world. With ruthless pragmatism, driven and fixated on his mission, Frank Underwood should be a character who is easy to hate. He is viciously calculating and

*House of Cards and Philosophy: Underwood's Republic,*
First Edition. Edited by J. Edward Hackett.

remorseless; his machinations reach sociopathic heights as he becomes an invincible force that takes down anyone who stands in his way. He is perfectly comfortable in his villainous shoes, and yet many of us find ourselves hopelessly intrigued by him.

Philosopher Friedrich Nietzsche (1844–1900) theorized a figure much like Frank Underwood, a person insatiably obsessed with his own power. This character was so dissatisfied with contemporary values that he realized that he must create new ones to live at all. This Nietzschean character, called the Übermensch, was a new and better kind of human being, hell-bent on overcoming traditional moral and religious values. Nietzsche believed these mores render humanity impotent by destroying our brilliant capacity to create new, powerful ideals to achieve our highest potential and overcome despicable mediocrity. The Übermensch, which translates as "overman," detests Christian values that teach us to be merely obedient and submissive. Instead, as Nietzsche and his Übermensch see it, we should strive toward our highest calling, zealously pursuing victories for ourselves. This is what vitalizes us and makes us quiver with pleasure and excitement. The Übermensch, like Frank Underwood, craves power and wills himself to be the most powerful of men—beyond men.

## "Power Is a Lot Like Real Estate, It's All About Location.... The Closer You Are to the Source, the Higher Your Property Value."

In the very first episode of *House of Cards*, Frank Underwood is attending the inauguration of Garret Walker, the forty-fifth President of the United States. We alone are privy to his innermost thoughts when he says, "Centuries from now when people watch this footage, who will they see smiling just at the edge of the frame?" The camera zooms in on him—and wait—he's waving to us?!

The cinematic production of *House of Cards* utilizes a number of postmodern techniques that ingeniously enhance the nihilistic storyline and the dark character profile of Frank Underwood, connecting the viewing audience to him in unique, profound, and intimate ways. "Postmodernism" refers to a complex philosophical, aesthetic, cultural, and political movement that emerged as a rebellion against the largely optimistic worldview of the Enlightenment and its historical successor, modernism. Postmodernism represents a paradoxical rejection of modernist principles while it simultaneously parodies modernism.

> Postmodernism represents a decline of faith in the keystones of the Enlightenment—belief in the infinite progress of knowledge, belief in infinite moral and social advancement, belief in teleology—and its rigorous definition of the standards of intelligibility, coherence and legitimacy.[1]

Postmodernism embraces nihilism, a philosophy that rejects the idea that there is an objective reality or universal moral principles. In this way, it stops pretending that it can represent objective reality. Instead it *plays* with different perspectives, perceptions, and concepts, reveling in the irony and humor that *are* the purpose of the movement itself. "Postmodernism tends to use and abuse, install but also subvert, conventions, through the use of either irony or parody."[2] Postmodern filmography often uses nihilism by deconstructing, destroying, and distorting any and all traditional concepts, and *House of* Cards is a grand postmodern production.

Frank's notorious wave to us in "Chapter 1" is a cinematic example of metafiction. Here, the metafiction exposes itself as Frank Underwood acknowledges and addresses us, the viewers. We realize that we are watching a fictional work on TV. We also understand that in order to watch cinematic dramas, we have to suspend our disbelief—it's a story, after all, and we want to be transported by fiction, no matter how bizarre it may be. But when Frank Underwood waves to the television audience, he destroys our suspension of disbelief by directly revealing that the show is a fictional production. The use of metafiction here is meant to disconcert the relationship between reality and fiction, forcing the viewer to acknowledge that it is indeed a work that is not actually real. But, there's no denying that there's something inexplicably alluring when Frank turns to us, like the lure of a mythic siren beckoning us to rocky shores.

## "And Others Are There Who Are Like Eight-day Clocks When Wound Up; They Tick, and Want People to Call Ticking—Virtue."[3]

"Every Tuesday, I sit down with the Speaker and the Majority Leader, to discuss the week's agenda. Well, discuss is probably the wrong word. They talk, while I sit quietly and imagine their lightly salted faces frying in a skillet." In "Chapter 2," Remy Danton, Frank Underwood's former press secretary, hunts Frank down as he's dining with the house speaker and majority leader. Remy left his position with Frank to become a lawyer for Glendon Hill and a lobbyist for a natural gas company, SanCorp, which afforded him a much higher income. Frank is presently indebted to SanCorp as the company (at Remy's discretion) has given billions of dollars to Frank's caucus. Frank explains his deal to us by acknowledging his obligation to SanCorp as degrading, "but when the tit's that big, everyone gets in line." Obviously Frank feels somewhat betrayed by Remy having left him. He also feels it was a foolish move on Remy's part, telling us after their acrid dialogue:

> Such a waste of time. He chose money over power. In this town a mistake nearly everyone makes. Money is the McMansion in Sarasota that starts falling apart after ten years. Power, is the old stone building that stands for centuries. I cannot respect someone that doesn't see the difference.

Frank Underwood is a very powerful man because he is fearless, much like the Übermensch. Nietzsche conveys most of his thoughts about the Übermensch through the teachings of a fictional character named Zarathustra, a wandering sage. The Übermensch, as Zarathustra describes him, is fearless and intense, far surpassing ordinary human capacities. His vision and fearlessness gain him absolute self-mastery and ultimate power. Like Frank Underwood,

> the *Übermensch* is devoid of human timidity. The *Übermensch* aspires continually, to greatness, living a life of creative adventure. Zarathustra contrasts the *Übermensch* with "the last man," his caricature of a person who is too risk-averse to pursue any aim beyond comfort, to such an extent that even procreation is too exerting.[4]

Clearly, Frank Underwood is a man "devoid of human timidity," ferocious in his manipulation of others.

## "You Know What I Like About People? They Stack So Well."

Frank is interminably conniving as he plans his next move, flawlessly manipulating others. Consider "Chapter 2," in which Donald Blythe, a long-standing and respected representative, interferes with Frank's business and irks him. Frank wants Blythe to take the fall for the internal leak of controversial legislation, which Frank himself disclosed to Zoe Barnes, a reporter for the *Washington Herald*. Blythe is visibly upset over the article, and Frank uses this as an opportunity to further his mission, as he tells Blythe, "I'm on your side." Then he masterfully pretends to want to protect Blythe's reputation, and take the fall himself for the compromising leak. "You know, I'm of a mind to say screw it. I'll fall on this grenade myself, just to piss them off!" He goes to the phone and asks the receptionist to "get me John King at CNN." Using this reverse-psychology against Blythe works like magic. Blythe is extremely uncomfortable with Frank's seeming martyrdom. Frank turns to us and says, "What a martyr craves more than anything is a sword to fall on. So, you sharpen the blade. Hold it at just the right angle—and then three, two, one." Blythe utters, "It should be me. It was my bill." Blythe then relinquishes his management of a major piece of legislation, the Education Reform Act, to Frank Underwood—victory! But Frank is weaving many, many webs simultaneously, so there's no time to revel in this relatively small conquest.

Also in "Chapter 2," Frank has a clandestine meeting with Zoe to cause the next breach of White House information. Michael Kern, the President's pick for the position of Secretary of State, is out of the running after Frank sabotages Kern's reputation. Frank now wants to elevate Catherine Durant, a Senator from Missouri, to take the position as Secretary of State, no doubt to gain all kinds of advantages. Frank tells Zoe, "Say that name, Catherine Durant. Say it over and over. Tomorrow afternoon—write it down. Then watch that name come out of the mouth of the President of the United States. This is where we get to create."

The cinematic portrayal of this scene is deliberately murky. We have been accustomed to seeing Frank Underwood's face. But in this scene we are intentionally estranged from him, and denied the ability to see the face that has become so uniquely familiar to us. Frank faces the camera only once. He is sitting with his back to Zoe. We can only see the back of his head or his darkened profile, except when he turns to face us and Zoe to say, "Copaniac and Kern were appetizers, Miss Barnes, Catherine Durant is the meal." He then resumes his shadowy pose. The cinematography of this scene reveals Frank Underwood as a carnivorous monster, only showing himself to point out the carnage of his plot. As we will learn in future episodes, this merciless strategy will eventually win him the presidency.

## "I Will Make That Hypocrisy Hurt."

> *What belongs to greatness.*—Who will attain anything great if he does not possess the strength and the will to *inflict* great suffering? ... But not to perish of inner distress and uncertainty when one inflicts great suffering and hears the cry of this suffering—that is great, that belongs to greatness.[5]

In "Chapter 4," Frank Underwood pays a visit to US Representative Peter Russo, a Democrat from Pennsylvania's 1st Congressional District. Frank has been blackmailing Russo since "Chapter 1," when Frank "saved" Russo from being convicted of a DUI. In turn, as any good tyrant would, Frank immediately took to blackmailing Russo, eventually taking much more than a pound of flesh for the debt Russo owed him. Now, Frank comes unannounced to Russo's apartment, sits down with him on his living room couch, and with the cunning advance of a great white shark tells him dispassionately that they need to close the shipyard in his district. Frank is trying to garner favor with the Black Caucus and its leader, who has a shipyard in his own district that is scheduled to close, threatening the employment of 3000 people. In order to save the Black Caucus leader's shipyard, Russo's district will instead be the sacrificial lamb, resulting in 12,000 people losing their jobs. Russo is stunned by the attack. Much of his lobbying efforts and political success are synonymous with the vitality of this shipyard. His supporters and even his friends are employed there. Dazed, Russo responds, "I can't do that." Frank impassively responds, "Yes, you can Peter." Russo struggles futilely, as a fly inextricably caught in a spider's web. Dumbfounded, he asks Frank, "Why?" In Frank's classic monotone demeanor, he explains,

> Politics. This force is bigger than either of us at play here.... I'm not here to debate this Peter. The base—will—close. The only question is will you make it a swift death or a painful one.... I'm a powerful friend to have right now. Perhaps your only friend. So don't defy me.

And on that note, Frank exits the apartment, leaving Russo utterly broken and disenfranchised.

But, Frank is not done with him yet. As Russo spirals deeper into his addictions, desperation, and angst in the coming episodes, we will witness him cause his own political career to suffer an extremely "painful death," and Frank will be there to help him along.

The "will to power" (*der Wille zur Macht*) is one of the best-known concepts of Nietzsche's philosophy. This famous idea is also one that remains particularly controversial. Nietzsche uses the German word *Macht* for "power," signifying personal strength, as opposed to *Reich*, which refers to political might. Many scholars interpret Nietzsche's meaning as being that human life is "will to power," the passionate ambition to enhance one's capacity to act on the world, as opposed to merely reacting to it. Nietzsche states,

> [L]ife itself is *essentially* appropriation, injury, overpowering of what is alien and weaker; suppression, hardness, imposition of one's own forms ... it will have to be an incarnate will to power, it will strive to grow, spread, seize, become predominant—not from any morality or immorality but because it is *living* and because life simply *is* will to power.[6]

Nietzsche's "will to power," as exemplified by the Übermensch, is a psychological thesis about what drives human behavior. Frank Underwood has the best of both worlds. His "will to power" is both political and personal. His political rise to power *is* the fulfillment of his existential supremacy.

## "He's Got Power. He's Got a Lot to Lose. And Right Now He is Winning."

At the end of "Chapter 14," Frank is alone, looking at himself in the mirror, and says, "Did you think I've forgotten you?" In these first seconds, it appears that Frank is having a rare reflective existential moment, as he stands on the precipice of his newest conquest—the Vice Presidency. But—no! His reflection is talking to us! He continues, "Perhaps you hoped I had.... For those of us climbing to the top of the food chain; there can be no mercy. There is but one rule: Hunt or be hunted." He smirks, and tells us, "Welcome back."

We're used to Frank speaking to us, as he has done in so many scenes. This postmodern technique is described by Fredric Jameson as "self-referentiality." Self-referentiality occurs here when Frank refers to his own plot, revealing to the audience that he is aware that *he* is involved in a work of fiction.[7] In these powerful cinematic moments, Frank's self-referentiality accentuates the activity of the spectator—our experience. The plot thickens as our attention jumps between the fences of fiction and simulated reality. "Postmodernism is impure.... Tolerant of ambiguity, contradiction, complexity, incoherence.... Subjective and intimate, it blurs the boundaries between the world and self."[8]

## "When Has Your Help Ever Helped Me?"

Near the end of "Chapter 11," Peter Russo has drowned and snorted his life, family, and career into an irreversible state of dereliction. And to make matters far worse for him, his desperation has become an intolerable liability to Frank, who tells him, "Peter, this isn't *just* about *you* anymore. Alright, let me *help* you." Russo retorts, "I don't want your help." We witness Frank's black eyes, darting back and forth, ruminating about how rid himself of Russo. As we watch their shadowy faces in that dark car sitting in that unlit cement garage, we realize this will become Russo's tomb. The camera zooms in on Frank's unshaven, sweaty mouth for an interminable 12 seconds of footage. Disembodied, Frank Underwood transforms into the Angel of Death.

Russo was a hypocrite, parading as a family man and a good Christian, as he ruined himself with drugs, alcohol, and whores. Nietzsche loathed the principles of Christianity and regarded it as a "slave morality" that weakens the strongest spirit of individuals. Frank Underwood too, despises the hypocrisy of politicians in general, and those in the White House in particular, as they parade as good and decent Christian folks. Nietzsche writes,

> That lambs dislike birds of prey does not seem strange: only it gives no ground for reproaching these birds of prey for bearing off little lambs. And if the lambs say among themselves; 'these birds of prey are evil; and whoever is least like a bird of prey, but rather its opposite, a lamb— would he not be good?" There is no reason to find fault with this institution of an ideal, except perhaps that the birds of prey might view

it a little ironically and say: "*we* don't dislike them at all, these good little lambs; we even love them: nothing is more tasty than a tender lamb."[9]

In "Chapter 14," Zoe Barnes doesn't know that she is dealing with the devil himself. Her increasingly confrontational words and tone with Frank Underwood will be deadly. Her instincts as a reporter and her naivety will lead to her violent murder at the train station—a scene that is almost unbearable to watch. Frank strikes with lightning fast, deadly force. The camera has no mercy on us, as we to watch her petite, young body flung in front of the massive oncoming train—and that horrible sound of her body being crushed.... 

This depiction is purposely brutal. The scene could have merely suggested Zoe's obvious fate, without following her body with callously clear audiovisual detail. Here we witness another postmodern technique, "flattening of affect." Movies and television bombard us with images of violence that have a profoundly dehumanizing and desensitizing impact. And yet we watch, because we can. Viewers may have found themselves increasingly annoyed with Zoe's ignorant persistence in this scene, prattling on like a petulant child. And, as the camera followed Zoe to her death, how many of us were neither surprised, nor particularly upset, by her demise?

## "The Road to Power is Paved with Hypocrisy and Casualties. Never Regret"

Independence is for the very few; it is a privilege of the strong. And whoever attempts it with even the best right but without inner constraint proves that he is probably not only strong, but also daring to the point of recklessness. He enters into a labyrinth, he multiplies a thousandfold the dangers which life brings with it.[10]

Frank is not interested in having friends. Or perhaps he realizes that he can't afford them. Freddy is the closest thing to a friend Frank has. In "Chapter 22," after hearing that Freddy's son violated his parole, Frank decides to visit Freddy at his home. Claire protests mildly, telling

Frank, "Freddy is dangerous, because you care too much. When we care too much it blinds us."

Frank arrives and sits down with Freddy in his modest ghetto flat. The two have their usual brief, friendly, candid chat.

FREDDY:    Somebody's trying to take you out.

FRANK:    Appears that way.

FREDDY:    Whoever it is, they done stepped on the wrong mutha-fuckin' rattlesnake.

FRANK:    That's why I'm here Freddy. I have to distance myself from you. I need to make sure you're not going to play up what good friends we've been; that you've been to my office; that you've cooked dinner at my home, or that the president was there. We can't drag him into anything. And I won't be coming in for ribs anymore. With all that's going on, we can't add fuel to the fire.

Occasionally escaping to Freddy's BBQ Joint has been Frank's only satisfying respite in his relentlessly brutal daily life. But Freddy tells him: "You was a good customer, that's it. You ain't gotta pretend to be my friend." When the project is power, as it is for Frank Underwood, political theatre calls for the very best of treachery, deception, and the cool and masterful ability to sacrifice anyone and anything.

When victims are bitten by great white sharks, they often don't realize that an entire section of their body is gone immediately after the attack, due to the Shark's stealth and razor-sharp teeth. In the final episode of Season 2, Frank is talking on the phone with the President, who is now facing imminent impeachment. And, like so many victims before him, the President has not yet sensed that he has been mortally wounded by the very person he is talking to. Frank tells us, "He's in the darkness now. And I'm the only beacon of light. Now we gently guide him toward the rocks." Season 2 ends with Frank Underwood entering *his* Oval Office. He stands at his desk and slowly raises his eyes to look at us, and then with that notorious double-knock on the presidential desk, he pronounces his victory. But power is only valuable for as long as it lasts. Now that Frank Underwood has climbed to the summit, we cannot suppose that his hunger for more and more power will subside, and this leaves us eager to learn what's next.

## "I Will Win and I Will Leave a Legacy."

In Season 3, we realize early on that Frank Underwood's insatiable appetite for power is not curbed by being the current President of the United States. Frank has already set his sights on the 2016 presidential election. Inheriting the presidency by default is woefully unfulfilling compared to winning an election, and Frank needs to win. But the Party Leadership has established a united front to oppose his running for the presidency. What they fail to realize is that a powermonger like Frank thrives on such adversity.

As a wolf in sheep's clothing,[11] Frank convenes a meeting with the Party Leadership to respond to their warning that they will not endorse his nomination. In "Chapter 28," Frank stands before the Leadership seated across the table from him and states, "I've put a great deal of thought into what you've all asked of me. I challenged myself to keep an open mind. And my decision is: I will not run for President." Colluding with us, he turns to the camera and says, "Look they're thinking it's too good to be true—and it is." For Frank, their opposition is mere pabulum, an annoying and impotent inconvenience to his master plan. Like scraping gum off his shoe, Frank will pause to rid himself of them.

Despite his lust for power, Frank still sometimes has his moments of personal reflection. In "Chapter 30", we find President Underwood in the most unlikely of places—a church. Dissatisfied with the bishop's responses to his theological queries, Frank asks for a few moments alone, "to pray." The camera pans in on Jesus' merciful face for a moment, and then focuses closely on Frank's sneering face, as he stands menacingly close to the statue. Looking over his shoulder to make sure that he is alone, he speaks, "Love. That's what you're selling? Well I don't buy it." And glaring into Jesus' face, he spits in it.

Immediately, Frank looks over his shoulder again, and takes out a handkerchief to wipe the spit off the face of Jesus. This is not out of remorse but simply to erase the deed so there can be no evidence. To underscore Frank Underwood's malevolence, the statue of Jesus crashes to the floor, smashing into hundreds of pieces. As his bodyguard races into the sanctuary in response to the sensational noise, Frank claims, "I was praying and it just fell." Frank Underwood has no reverence for hallowed halls, whether those of the White House or a House of God.

Frank's salvation is bound up with power. In *The Antichrist*, Nietzsche writes, "What is good? All that heightens the feeling of power in man, the will to power, power itself. What is bad? All that is born of weakness. What is happiness? The feeling that power is growing, that resistance is overcome."[12] Frank would agree. Underwood embodies Nietzsche's irreverence as the episode ends with him picking up a piece of the shattered statue of Jesus—his ear, to be exact—and telling us, "Well I've got God's ear now." As Season 3 progresses and draws to a close, however, we see that Frank has alienated and underestimated the power of Jackie Sharp, Remy Danton, and, most importantly, his wife Claire. To effectively grow in power, Frank will need more than the ear of God.

## Notes

1. Tim Woods, *Beginning Postmodernism* (Manchester, UK: Manchester University Press, 1999), 11.
2. Ibid., 56.
3. Friedrich Nietzsche, *Thus Spoke Zarathustra: A Book for Everyone and Nobody*, trans. Thomas Common (Virginia: Thrifty Books, 2009), 79.
4. Robert C. Solomon and Kathleen M. Higgins, *What Nietzsche Really Said* (New York: Random House, 2000), 76.
5. Friedrich Nietzsche, *The Gay Science: With a Prelude in Rhymes and an Appendix of Songs* (referred to hereafter as *GS*), trans. Walter Kaufmann, (London: Vintage Books, 1974), sect. 325.
6. Friedrich Nietzsche, *Beyond Good and Evil* (referred to hereafter *BGE*) in *Basic Writings of Friedrich Nietzsche* (referred to hereafter as *BW*), trans. Walter Kaufmann, (New York: Random House, 2000), 393, sect. 259.
7. See Fredric Jameson, *Postmodernism, or the Cultural Logic of Late Capitalism* (London: Verso, 1991). This landmark text concerning postmodernism deals provocatively with film, video, art, economics, ideology, and cultural theory; it is for the more advanced reader.
8. Kim Levin, *Beyond Modernism: Essays on Art from the 70's and 80's* (New York: Harper & Row, 1988), 7.
9. Friedrich Nietzsche, *The Genealogy of Morals*, in *BW*, 480–81; essay I, sect. 13.
10. Nietzsche, *BGE* in *BW*, 231, sect. 29.

11. The phrase originates from a sermon given by Jesus that is recorded in the Christian New Testament: "Beware of false prophets, which come to you in sheep's clothing, but inwardly they are ravening wolves." (*Gospel of Matthew 7:15*, King James Version).
12. Friedrich Nietzsche, *The Antichrist*, trans. by Walter Kaufmann, in *The Portable Nietzsche*, ed. Walter Kaufmann (New York: Viking Press, 1968), sect. 2.

# 6

# Why Underwood Is Frankly *Not* an Overman

*Matt Meyer*

As the title suggests, this chapter is going to tell you about why Frank Underwood is not an *overman*. An over-what? To start with, the over-man is an English translation of *Übermensch*, one of philosopher Friedrich Nietzsche's (1844–1900) key ideas. The overman is one of three key types of people that Nietzsche identifies in his writing: the master, the slave, and the overman.[1] At least two of these types clearly appear in *House of Cards*. So first we'll look at these three types and how they fit into the Nietzsche's philosophy. Then we will look at why Frank, although a go-getter and a get-'r-done type of guy, is ultimately not what Nietzsche meant by an "overman."

## Inside the Beltway: Typology, Not Topography

Frank Underwood is a bad dude with few redeeming qualities. Per-haps the only reasons that we *could* cheer for him are that we see him as an underdog who was not fairly treated at the beginning of the series, or we are psychopaths. In seriousness, the picture is more complicated than that. Frank does some pretty *immoral* things, but *immoral* from whose perspective? Nietzsche imagines three "types" of people: the master, the slave, and the overman. There are at least two moral perspectives (really, though, there are as many perspectives as there are people): the perspective of the master, and the perspective

*House of Cards and Philosophy: Underwood's Republic*,
First Edition. Edited by J. Edward Hackett.
© 2016 John Wiley & Sons, Ltd. Published 2016 by John Wiley & Sons, Ltd.

of the slave. The master, according to Nietzsche, is "the one who is powerful, also ... one who has power over himself, who knows how to speak and be silent, who delights in being severe and hard with himself and respects all severity and hardness."[2] In contrast, the slave is uncertain and looks to the outside world, including the masters, as the cause of his misery. The master is active: she acts according to what she believes is right and useful to herself. The slave is reactive. That is, he must always first assert himself in reaction to someone else. The slave both envies and hates those in the position of the master, but— importantly—the slave is not in a position to do anything about it. In terms of our characters, we'll say that Frank exhibits multiple master qualities, and Peter Russo exhibits multiple slave qualities. But to clear the air: Frank's being a master, a slave, or an overman has very little to do with *our* perspective about what is right and wrong. As we will discuss more below, Nietzsche sees our ideas about what is "good" or "evil" as resulting from slave thinking winning over master thinking. As for what makes an overman, that gets a little more complicated, but it goes beyond these two basic perspectives and even combines elements of each.

## Master Frank: Doing What Is Necessary

There are several aspects of Frank's personality that reflect the master attitude. For one, Frank defines values according to his point of view: what is "good" is good *for* him.[3] Also, those of the master morality do not fear pain or suffering—they embrace it as a step to gaining more power. Frank captures both of these ideas in what he says in the opening monologue of the first episode when he has to put down a dog that has just been hit by a car: "There are two kinds of pain: the sort of pain that makes you strong or useless pain that is only suffering. I have no patience for useless things. Moments like this require someone who will act, who will do the unpleasant thing, the necessary thing. There no more pain." (One wonders if, to some extent, Frank is not putting down dying dogs throughout the whole series.) In addition, Frank's *view* about promises seems to reflect that of the more honorable master class: "The nature of promises, Linda, is that they are immune to change." There are other indications that the Underwoods belong to the nobler aristocratic class. For example, Frank's wife, Claire, also shows a healthy attitude toward action when she says, "My husband apologizes to no one, not even me."[4] So far, it seems as though Frank could be considered one of the noble ones.

Nietzsche also points out that masters have no allegiances to slaves.[5] We can see this when, in "Chapter 1," Frank first talks with Doug Stamper after he has found out that Vasquez and Walker broke their promise to him that he would get Secretary of State. Frank says, "They have done us a great favor Doug. No longer are we bound by allegiances."

Nietzsche argues that our current version of morality is essentially bunk. It came about, he argues, not as an expression of either reason or sympathy, but as the result of *psychological warfare*. That's right. As Nietzsche will frequently point out, things look very different in their origins than they do in their present form, much in the same way that President Underwood's rise to the presidency was not very presidential.[6]

Nietzsche speculates that originally there was a strong group of noble people, masters, who acted harshly toward inferior, unfortunate people, slaves. This acting harshly was not an expression of hatred or sadism. Instead, it was an expression of a natural order: The strong rule the weak. Frank thinks this way as well. For instance, in "Chapter 4," Frank uses the language of the wolf pack and the herd— the predator and the prey. Frank is a part of the wolf pack, willing to break away and attack the lambs. He asks us if his colleague is going to join the pack or stay with the herd. Nietzsche says it is natural for lambs to fear birds of prey and call them evil, even hate them. But, he says, the birds of prey would not see it that way at all: "we don't dislike them at all these good little lambs; we even love them: nothing is more tasty than tender lamb."[7] In other words, those who rule have no hard feelings against those who they rule, nor do they have a sense that their behavior toward them is somehow unjust or wrong.

Then something happens. The weak, slavish group gets fed up with being mistreated, but they don't have the physical strength to overcome the stronger nobler group. So what do they do? They attack *psychologically*.

If I were to enslave you, make you work for free, steal your spouse, and so on, what is the one way that you could quickly and effectively stop me from doing those things? To make me feel badly about doing them. To make me ask myself: Is this wrong? Am I an *evil* person?

Nietzsche points out that the idea of "evil" did not even occur to the nobler, master class until it was introduced to them by the weaker class.[8] Up until that point, they simply did what they had always done. Sure, it could have been dishonorable for one member of the masters to mistreat another member of that group. Indeed, Frank appears to have that type of mutual respect with his wife, Claire, who he rarely mistreats (the obvious exception being the final episode of Season 3). The dignity of being honorable largely prevented the masters from behaving toward their own kind in that way. But to dishonor a weak slave? No such thing was possible. One could have honor and duties only toward one's own kind.[9] Certainly, there were no universal moral precepts people had to follow. That would be as odd as calling a lion dishonorable for attacking a giraffe. Along these lines, Frank appears to honor those he considers his equal, such as Claire and Marty (the teachers' union rep about whom Frank says, "Friends make the worst enemies"), while caring less about those he considers lesser, such as Peter Russo.

## "Why Me?" Peter Russo, Slave Extraordinaire

In "Chapter 4," Frank convinces Peter Russo to close the shipyard. Frank's plan is to keep open a different shipyard and get the votes of the Congressmen of the Congressional Black Caucus for the Education Reform Bill. In "Chapter 4," we see Peter Russo falling apart. Already a "recovering" alcoholic and drug addict, the pressure of the blowback from not doing enough to keep the base open, in the form of hate emails and a visit from an old friend, causes Peter to spiral out of control. He winds up at Frank's house, supposedly because he intended to beat him up for what "you made me do." Peter shows all of the signs of being a slave in Nietzsche's sense: He cannot control his impulse to get stoned, and he cannot control himself or his life. In the interviews for his campaign for governor, it becomes abundantly clear that he cannot control his sexual urges either, thus leaving political time bombs everywhere.

Because Peter cannot control the forces within himself, he winds up getting arrested for soliciting prostitution and driving drunk. Given that Frank always wants a chip he can play later, he has Stamper work out a deal to get Peter out. Of course, Peter implicitly accepts this deal, which puts him in Frank's debt. Peter is slavish in his weakness. But he compounds this slavishness by not taking responsibility for his own decisions: to work with Frank, to close the shipyard, and to continue drinking. All of these are someone else's fault, as he sees it. Peter believes he must retroactively say "no" to what Frank has done because he cannot actually say "no" to Frank. This is *exactly* what Nietzsche means when he writes, "He who cannot command himself is commanded."[10] Whereas Frank may disregard others, especially those he considers inferior, he at least accepts who he is and takes ownership of it. Peter, by contrast, only regards others to the extent that he can blame them for his own mistakes. And when Peter really does have his downfall in "Chapter 10" and "Chapter 11", the only reason that he is so easily manipulated is because he cannot control himself. True, if you are like me, you probably hated to see him fail. But both Frank and Nietzsche would be like-minded on this point: Peter was constituted to fail. For what it's worth, Nietzsche does not fully endorse either masters or slaves, but he prefers the "innocence" and "good faith" of the simple master mindset over the slave mindset that turns not only against others but also against itself.[11]

## Will the Real Overman Please Stand Up?

We have seen what is meant by masters and slaves, but what makes an overman? Well, that depends on who you ask. In 1924, the great attorney Clarence Darrow gave a 12-hour speech to a sentencing judge on behalf of the cold-blooded killers Nathan Leopold and Richard Loeb. The essence of this speech was that the two men, who were just about 20 years old, could not have possibly *not* killed Bobby Franks given that they were raised in the cold environment of wealthy Gold Coast Chicago and that they had read the work of—you guessed it—Friedrich Nietzsche. The argument went something like this: Nietzsche's "overman" is so intelligent and so self-certain that he is above the law. He does not have to follow the mere "morality" of others; the overman creates his own morality (apparently one in which it is okay to kill for no good reason). Now, we should acknowledge that this thin notion of the overman as someone who is "above the law," for no other reason than that he considers himself to be, could per- haps include Frank Underwood. After all, consider all of the laws he breaks: murder, extortion, and bribery, to name a few. Never mind all of the moral norms he ignores: adultery, lying (profusely), manipulating, and all the more complicated ways in which he ruins the lives of Zoe, Peter, Freddy, Garrett Walker, Raymond Tusk, and many others.

Nietzsche doesn't help himself when he mentions Cesare Borgia and the overman in the same thought, but to suggest that Cesare Borgia *is* an example of an overman is a misreading of Nietzsche's point. Cesare Borgia was an Italian general and politician (the worst kind of politician) and was the model for Machiavelli's *The Prince*. It is rumored that he may have even had his brother poisoned to assume the role of general. Borgia wanted to be Pope (and was in line to be), not out of *religious* fervor but out of *political* greed. And, if you are not familiar with *The Prince*, then you may be familiar with the term "Machiavellian," which basically means an attitude in which the ends justify the means (like Frank's attitude). In order to make an omelet, you have to break a few eggs, and so on. Don't get me wrong: There are glimmers of this attitude in Nietzsche's thinking. But this is not the whole of his thinking on the overman. If this were the case, if Cesare Borgia *were* the epitome of the overman—without qualification—then most certainly Frank would qualify.

In *Beyond Good and Evil*, Nietzsche points out that it is absurd to consider someone who has *strong* impulses (presumably ones that he does not control) *less* psychologically healthy than someone who has *no* impulses, or, as he would put it, someone who is *emasculated*.[12] Nietzsche wonders whether our current state of morality is really something to be praised, if in fact we have lost all instincts to do so-called "immoral" things. For example, should I be praised for abstaining from alcohol if I have no interest in it whatsoever? Should I be praised for being celibate if I am asexual, or have no interest in sex?

For Nietzsche, being *moral* demands self-overcoming. It demands controlling our instincts and drives until the point that the new, considered position on something *becomes* our instinct. Think of Frank's relationship to exercise. At first, his instinct is to ignore the rowing machine, to think it ridiculous. His instinct is to play video games. But then he *overcomes* that undesirable instinct to play games and *creates* the instinct (now a habit) to row, and then later run with his wife. Back to the original point: It would be silly to praise Frank for overcoming his desire to play video games, if that was not a habit he had in the first place.

So what does this have to do with Cesare Borgia? Well, Nietzsche point is a simple one: In order to have a strong, disciplined, and interesting person who constantly overcomes himself, the person needs to have strong, even wild, instincts to hone and overcome in the first place. It is for this reason that Nietzsche says in *Ecce Homo* that, when we are looking for the overman, we should look "*even* for a Cesare Borgia rather than a Parsifal."[13] (Parsifal was the simple-natured "beautiful soul" and saint of Wagner's opera of the same name.) Nietzsche's point: We need something to work with. If a person has no instinct or impulses to overcome, then they can never go beyond what they already are. So, just for the sake of clarification: Cesare Borgia, the Machiavellian and ruthless politician who may have killed his own brother, is *not* an example of the overman. But he would be a much better starting point for one than some goody-two-shoes would.

So where does this leave Frank? Well, Frank has two things going for him that could make him overman-like. Firstly, he has strong drives. Secondly, he keeps them under control for the most part. What's more, he's gifted at manipulating others into doing what he would like them to do. (Though, he has met his match in Petrov, and we see how terribly Frank handled that challenge.) Here is a short list of his manipulations just from the first season: Peter Russo into closing the shipyard and into running for governor of Pennsylvania, Zoe into giving him information, Donald Blythe into taking the fall for the education bill, Marty from the teacher's union into accepting changes to collective bargaining, President Walker and Linda Vasquez into giving him more time, and so on. However, is the overman one who controls others, or one who controls herself? Consider the following point Nietzsche makes about the nature of the truly strong:

> I have found strength where one does not look it for it: in simple, mild, and pleasant people, without the least desire to rule—and conversely, the desire to rule has often appeared to me as a sign of inward weakness: they fear their own slave soul and shroud it in a royal cloak (in the end, they still become the slaves of their followers, their fame, etc.). The powerful natures *dominate*, it is a necessity, they need not lift one finger. Even if, during their life time, they bury themselves in a garden house.[14]

One who has reached the status of overman (if anyone ever has) need not be ambitious, need not rule. They only need to have a strong ability to mold themselves. They are driven by the desire to say yes to life and to create. Frank, in contrast, seems to be driven by a dual desire to prove himself and to attain what he believes he is owed. And, as Nietzsche predicts in the above quotation ("in the end, they still become the slaves of their followers, their fame, etc."), Season 3 sees Frank become a slave to his position.

The chances of Frank being an overman seem to diminish even further in the third season. For reasons that remain unclear, he anchors himself to one terrible idea after another: America Works, the Jordan Valley, challenging Petrov and Heather Dunbar. We never see him gain control of any of these forces. To some extent, these are the usual Frank-style "moves," only, unlike in previous seasons, in Season 3 Frank becomes the slave of his own machinations. Frank's own slavish attitude of helplessness becomes clear in "Chapter 36" after he has to tell Claire that Petrov is demanding that she resign as UN Ambassador when he says, "My decision. Sometimes I think the presidency is only the illusion of choice." However, we could interpret this as a variation of affirming fate. But we know that what Frank really means is: I have lost control, and I don't like it.

The overman is a synthesis. In fact, it is not so much a person as it is a worldview. It is a world-affirming view that begins with a combination of the "Yea-saying" of the master with the rich inner life of drives of the slave. But the overman does not negate, kill, or domesticate his drives; he sublimates them. This word "sublimates" is a difficult one to define. But it basically means to take something ugly and use it make something beautiful. Take anger and make grunge music. Take frustration and turn it into the drive to work out. In other words, the person in control of herself can take ugly drives and emotions and turn them into beautiful things. The master does not always control his own drives in this way. The master rules, and in ruling takes the wills of others and uses them toward his own end—this is the essence of the Machiavellian rule of Cesare Borgia. But keep in mind, Borgia was *not* the overman. Another possibility for the overman given by Nietzsche is Napoleon. Napoleon is to be admired because he offers great promise for uniting Europe. Ultimately, though, he is too much animal for Nietzsche; he was "corrupted by the means he had to employ."[15] Frank is also part animal: he kills Peter and Zoe without a second thought; he destroys an innocent man, Lucas Goodwin, just because he is a liability. If Frank has another more creative side to his character, we have not seen it yet.

## Don't *Übermenschen* It

The overman is the one who is so strong, so disciplined, and so in tune with her surroundings that she need not go out of her way to manipulate others. Consider what John Richardson says about the difference between the master and the overman: "Whereas the master affirms other wills as a means appropriated to his own end, the overman more nearly affirms them in themselves, as contributing to an overall process made not more efficient but richer for their distinctive presence."[16] There are two key points here. First, the overman demands richness over efficiency. Second, the overman affirms wills in themselves, not just for his own purposes.

Frank affirms the wills of others, to be sure, but always to his own ends, not theirs. He helps Zoe rise in her career, but only because she will write the stories he needs leaked. He appears to support Peter in his run for governor, but it turns out that this is all just an elaborate scheme to create an opening for himself for Vice President. When Frank asks the audience in Chapter 5, "Will he wither or will he thrive? Only time will tell," he is saying this in bad faith. Regarding his help in getting Meechum's job back, he says, "It requires very little of me and will mean the world to him. It's an inexpensive investment." Being an investment to Frank is the closest one can get to him. Once he is done with you he discards you, although at least he is man enough to admit this to Zoe. In the final episode of Season 3 it becomes clear that, despite his protest, Frank has more or less used Claire for the better part of his career. He knew all along that "there is only one chair behind [the] desk" in the Oval Office. Every investment, every confidence-building measure that comes out of Frank's mouth is in bad faith. Each is a duplicitous attempt to assert his own will.

In considering whether Frank is an overman, we must keep in mind the catalyst for his elaborate plan. Frank began to hatch his plan when he was passed over for Secretary of State. Most everything Frank does from that point forward is vengeful, spiteful, and duplicitous, not to mention illegal.

Nietzsche's overman would not have a need for this type of resentment or revenge; this scheming type of revenge is really closer to the slave's psychological warfare. Because Frank cannot react *immediately*, he unleashes an orchestration of epic proportions. Perhaps we could praise Frank for his uncanny ability to read people and bend them to his will, a sort of suggestive coercion. But of course to do that is to completely overlook the murder of both Zoe and Peter. It is to overlook the fact that Frank was poised to destroy Stamper if he exposed Claire's journal. Ultimately all of his relationships amount to destruction without creation.

## The Under/Over on Frank

Although Frank may have achieved his goal in becoming President, there are two aspects of his rise to power that disqualify Frank as an overman. Firstly, Frank could do much better in terms following one precept of the overman: *amor fati*. And, secondly, Frank is much more destructive than he is creative.

*Amor fati* means "love fate." It means essentially desiring that nothing change: "My formula for the greatness of a human being is *amor fati*: that one wants nothing to be different—not forward, not backward, not in all eternity."[17] Of course, this is difficult to apply in individual cases. Certainly, it does not mean being a lump on a log. But there is something too egoistic about Frank's drive. The purpose of being for Nietzsche is not "to become President," which is the endgame of Frank's long revenge, but rather to *create*. And what's more, once Frank attains the presidency, he seems to make a string of poor decisions just to survive. The overman does not survive; she thrives. In "Chapter 39," Frank says to Claire, "When we lose because of you there will be nothing. No plan. No future. We will be has-beens." By placing so much importance in what he has now, Frank is showing his lack of creativity and resourcefulness.

In "Chapter 14," Frank says, "There is nothing I despise more in life than pettiness." The irony is that the type of power that Frank seeks—influence, ruling over others—is the pettiest form of power there is. This is precisely why *masters* are not automatically *overmen*: they do not see beyond themselves and their own *desire* to dominate. The most desirable form of power for Nietzsche is not power over others, but rather power over oneself: controlling one's desires in the creation of a self, of beauty, and ultimately of the world. In *Thus Spoke Zarathustra*, Nietzsche has his character Zarathustra say, "Never has there been an overman. Naked I saw both the greatest and the smallest man. They are still all-too-similar to each other. Verily the greatest I found all-too-human."

In Frank's petty desire to rule other humans, and to seek revenge, he remains "all-too-human." Contrast this with Nietzsche's description of the great German artist Goethe: "what he wanted was totality ... he disciplined himself into wholeness ... the man of tolerance, not from weakness but from strength because he knows how to use to his advantage even that from which the average nature would perish ... he does not negate anymore."[18] Nietzsche's ideal overman was an artist who took everything in stride and was constantly committed to creating himself, his own style, his own vision, and his own world. The rules that the artist breaks are not morals or laws, but standards of creation. The Nietzsche scholar Walter Kaufmann stated this point well:

> The powerful man is the creative man; but the creator is not likely to abide by previously established laws. A genuinely creative act contains its own norms, and every creation is a creation of new norms. The great artist does not stick to the established code; yet his work is not lawless but has structure and form. Beethoven did not conform to the rules of Haydn or Mozart; yet his symphonies have form throughout: their form and law Beethoven created with them.[19]

This line of thinking—that of the genius who develops his own rules and style—is a far cry from Frank Underwood, whose entire person is devoted to assuming a role—a powerful role to be sure, but a role nonetheless. Once he achieves this role, it seems, he is lost.

"The Artist," a poem by Oscar Wilde, gives us a fine example of the creative drive that Nietzsche calls for in the overman. The poem depicts a sculptor who is so devoted to a new sculpture that he takes the only bronze he can find to melt it down. What was the bronze he melted down? His previous sculpture.[20] We have seen Frank do plenty of melting down. But, so far, he has yet to sculpt something new and interesting, something beautiful. Season 3 shows us that whatever Frank touches turns to dust. He is no overman.

# Notes

1. There are other types as well, such as the last man and the higher man, but we'll confine our discussion to these three.
2. Friedrich Nietzsche, *Beyond Good and Evil*, in *The Portable Nietzsche*, trans. Walter Kaufmann (New York: Viking Press, 1982), sect. 260, p. 395.
3. These ideas about master morality come from *Beyond Good and Evil*, mainly sect. 260, and from Friedrich Nietzsche, *The Genealogy of Morals*, from *The Basic Writings of Nietzsche*, trans. Walter Kaufmann (New York: Random House, 2000), essay 1, sect. 13.
4. Compare this to Nietzsche's idea in *The Birth of Tragedy*: "the noble human does not sin." Friedrich Nietzsche, *The Birth of Tragedy and Other Writings*, trans. Ronald Spiers (New York: Cambridge University Press, 1999), sect. 9, 47. Henceforth BT.
5. Nietzsche, BGE, 260.
6. "the cause of the origin of a thing and its eventual utility, its actual employment and place in a system of purposes, lie worlds apart." Nietzsche, *The Genealogy of Morals*, II, 12, p. 513.
7. Nietzsche, GM I.13, 481.
8. Nietzsche, GM II.16.
9. Nietzsche, BGE 260.
10. Friedrich Nietzsche, *Thus Spoke Zarathustra*, in *The Portable Nietzsche*, ed. and trans. Walter Kaufmann (New York: Viking Press, 1982), Pt. II, "On Self-Overcoming." Henceforth Z.
11. On this point, Kaufmann is clear in *Nietzsche: Philosopher, Psychologist, Antichrist* (Princeton, NJ: Princeton University Press, 1974), "Nietzsche was not 'endorsing' the will to power any more than Freud was 'endorsing' the sex impulse" (p. 246). In other words, Nietzsche's discussion of masters and slaves is *descriptive* not prescriptive, or telling us how things *should* be.
12. This account of Nietzsche's use of Cesare Borgia is taken from Kaufmann, chapter 7, "Morality and Sublimation," especially pages 224–227. Here he is referencing *Beyond Good and Evil*, sect. 197.
13. Again, I owe this point to Kaufmann, 224. Taken from *Ecce Homo*, III.1.
14. Kaufmann, 252, taken from *The Dawn*, sect. 412.
15. WP 1026, from Friedrich Nietzsche, *The Will to Power*, trans. Walter Kaufmann (New York: Vintage, 1968).
16. John Richardson, *Nietzsche's System* (New York: Oxford University Press, 1996), 70.

17. Friedrich Nietzsche, *Ecce Homo*, in *The Basic Writings of Nietzsche*, trans. Walter Kaufmann (New York: Random House, 2000), II.10.
18. Kaufmann, 281, taken from *The Twilight of the Idols*, sect. IX.
19. Kaufmann, 250.
20. This connection is also owed to Kaufmann, 248–49.

# 7

# American Machiavelli

## Greg Littmann

What does it take to achieve power? Through recorded history, ambitious people like Francis "Frank" Underwood have searched for the answers and fought for dominance. Conquerors like Alexander the Great, Julius Caesar, Genghis Khan, Napoleon, and Adolf Hitler have soaked the Earth in human blood to seize control. Like Frank, they were all experts in applied political philosophy, searching for the rules by which power can be taken and held. Not even you and I, mere individual citizens, can avoid searching for these rules. Any practical political views we hold must be founded on how we think power can be acquired and maintained.

Frank is someone who will do anything to take power. Breaking the law means nothing to him. "Of all the things I hold in high regard, rules are not one of them," he explains. He cares just as little about morality. He assures the viewer "For those of us climbing to the top of the food chain, there can be no mercy. There is but one rule: hunt or be hunted." To his mind, he's simply being realistic about what must be done to get ahead: "The road to power is paved with hypocrisy and casualties."

Television critics consistently call Frank "Machiavellian" and rightly so. Frank's rise to power is a beautiful illustration of Machiavellian principles in action. Niccolò Machiavelli (1469–1527) was a political philosopher in Renaissance Italy. In his masterpiece, *The*

*House of Cards and Philosophy: Underwood's Republic*,
First Edition. Edited by J. Edward Hackett.
© 2016 John Wiley & Sons, Ltd. Published 2016 by John Wiley & Sons, Ltd.

*Prince*, he lays out what he thinks are the secrets of becoming a dictator and holding on to power ("prince" being his term for an independent ruler). Of course, Frank is not a dictator. But Machiavelli's principles can be applied, to a greater or lesser degree, by any politically ambitious person.

For Machiavelli, Frank's actions are a model of intelligent ambition. Machiavelli believes that to take and safeguard power, you must be willing to do whatever is useful, regardless of whether it's illegal or even immoral. He writes,

> [I]f a prince wants to maintain his rule he must be prepared not to be virtuous, and to make use of this or not according to need [because] some of the things that appear to be virtues will, if he practices them, ruin him, and some of the things that appear to be vices will bring him security and prosperity.[1]

Machiavelli believes that there is no escape from the need to be wicked, since failure to be actively ambitious will invite disaster as you are overwhelmed by ambitious rivals. Frank agrees. He notes to reporter Zoe Barnes, "Treading water is the same as drowning for people like you and me." Machiavelli believes that it is vital to be bold and audacious, making your own luck rather than waiting for opportunities to present themselves. As Frank tells Secretary of State Catherine Durant, "If you don't like how the table is set, turn over the table."

## "We're in a Very Gray Area. Ethically, Legally. Which I'm Okay With."—Zoe Barnes

Politicians have been telling lies for as long as there have been politicians, but Machiavelli is the first known political theorist to recommend lying. He writes, "Princes who have achieved great things have been those who have given their word lightly, who have known how to trick men with their cunning, and who, in the end, have overcome those abiding by honest principles."[2] He would admire the way that Frank has achieved the presidency through lies and deception. In the first episode of *House of Cards*, Frank is enraged when President Garrett Walker breaks his promise to make him Secretary of State. But instead of expressing his bitterness, Frank keeps a calm exterior and plays the part of the President's loyal supporter, all the while plotting to take power from him. He deceives Congressman Peter Russo into thinking that he will support him to become governor of Pennsylvania, when he really plans to sabotage Russo's career. Later, he pretends to be helping President Walker to deal with the congressional committee investigating Chinese contributions to super PACs, when really he is just setting Walker up for impeachment.

Machiavelli would even approve of Frank's use of strategic murder. When Russo tries to come clean to the press about his addictions and his role in Frank's schemes, Frank kills him by gassing him in his own car. When Zoe digs too deeply into Russo's death, Frank kills her by shoving her in front of a moving subway train. In doing so, he's being less bloody than usurpers from history who Machiavelli holds up to be admired for their ruthlessness—like the Greek General Agathocles (361–289 BCE), who turned the republic of Syracuse into his dictatorship when he called the nobility to a meeting and then had them all butchered.

One criticism that Machiavelli would make of Frank is that he is too susceptible to taking revenge. For example, when Frank states that he wants billionaire Raymond Tusk "obliterated" for advising the President against making him Secretary of State, Claire objects, "More than that. Let's make him suffer," to which Frank replies, "I don't know whether to be proud or terrified. Perhaps both." But Machiavelli would say that Frank should be disappointed in her. Not only does the objective of making Tusk suffer distract from the objective of gathering power, but also it is liable to make an influential man bitter toward them. Machiavelli warns us to avoid hurting people we aren't going to kill, since they are liable to hurt us back. He writes that "men must be either pampered or crushed, because they can get revenge for small injuries but not for grievous ones."[3]

More sensible is the way that Frank finally deals with Tusk, making an ally of him. Likewise, Frank's final dealings with Walker are masterful in that he leaves him on such good terms when a less disciplined man would have used the chance to crow over his conquered enemy. To the end, Frank pretends to have been on Walker's side. "I can never fill your shoes, sir," Frank tells him just before being inaugurated as President, when he could have sneered, "I win!" There is no point in hurting Walker. As Frank notes after killing a suffering dog who had been hit by a car, "There are two kinds of pain: the sort of pain that makes you strong ... or useless pain—the sort of pain that's only suffering. I have no patience for useless things."

Another criticism Machiavelli would make is that Claire involves herself too much in charitable work. In the first season of *House of Cards*, Claire is CEO of the Clean Water Initiative, a nonprofit organization dedicated to providing safe drinking water in third world countries. Though Claire's real goal is power, she believes that it will be useful PR for her to seem charitable. Machiavelli thinks it is fruitless to try to develop a reputation for generosity. He writes, "If you want to sustain a reputation for generosity ... you have to be ostentatiously lavish; and a prince acting in that fashion will soon squander all his resources."[4]

Frank, in turn, might criticize Machiavelli for overlooking the importance of manipulating our enemies' images as well as our own. Frank leaks stories about his rivals to Zoe, and he appreciates that creating suspicion of wrongdoing is as powerful as demonstrating it. For example, Frank successfully associates Senator Michael Kern with an editorial that criticizes Israel, published in a student newspaper when he was an editor. Editing the paper does not mean that Kern wrote the editorial, and writing an editorial critical of Israel does not make one an anti-Semite, but Kern's connection is enough to get him tarred as an anti-Semite all the same and to lose his chance of becoming Secretary of State. Likewise, Frank breaks his association with Freddy Hayes of Freddy's BBQ Joint once Freddy's son is arrested for pulling a gun on a reporter. Frank has genuinely warm feelings for Freddy, who had nothing to do with the crime. But retaining his ties with Freddy would allow his rivals to paint him as a criminal.

## "Friends Make the Worst Enemies."—Frank Underwood

Machiavelli appreciates that one who wishes to rule needs allies. However, he warns that we should avoid making alliances with people more powerful than we are, since they are strong enough to break their promises to us when we are no longer useful. He writes "[I]f you are the victors, you emerge as his prisoner; and princes should do their utmost to escape being at the mercy of others."[5] Machiavelli would have warned Frank not to trust Walker to keep his deal to make him Secretary of State. After all, by the time Walker is president, he no longer needs Frank's support. Frank doesn't repeat the mistake. He refuses an alliance with Tusk because Tusk offers to help him in return for a favor to be named later. This open-ended commitment would make Frank the weaker partner. He explains, "I've … avoided a reputation for indentured servitude." Most of Frank's allies are less powerful than himself; people like Claire, Zoe, Durant, Chief of Staff Doug Stamper, and Congresswoman Jackie Sharp. As he reminds Claire, "Without me, you are nothing." Frank makes Russo the weaker partner in their alliance by threatening to expose his addictions, demanding his "absolute, unquestioning loyalty."

Machiavelli also warns that a politician "should restrain himself from inflicting grave injury on anyone in his service whom he has close to him in his affairs of state."[6] People we have hurt make dangerous allies because they have reason to want revenge. Walker foolishly trusted Frank after cheating him. Perhaps he thought that he could win Frank over with new powers and responsibilities, but Machiavelli would regard this as futile. He writes, "He who believes that new benefits will cause great personages to forget old injuries is deceived."[7]

Machiavelli believes that we should work to disrupt our enemies' alliances and, if possible, win enemy allies over to our side. He would approve of the way that Frank drove Walker and Tusk apart by making Tusk seem responsible for the failure of negotiations with Chinese billionaire Xander Feng, and thus for the trade war with China that makes energy prices soar. By the end of season 2, both Walker and Frank bid for Tusk's loyalty with the promise of a presidential pardon. When Frank wins Tusk over, the presidency is his.

## "I'm a Good Christian, Remy, Like Your Mother." — Frank Underwood

Machiavelli believes that success in politics requires presenting a carefully maintained false appearance. While politicians should employ any dirty means to further their power, they must look squeaky clean in order to get people to trust them. Machiavelli writes that one who wishes to rule must appear "compassionate, faithful to his word, kind, guileless, and devout ... a man of good faith, a man of integrity, a kind and religious man."[8] However, "He will be despised if he has a reputation for being fickle, frivolous, effeminate, cowardly, irresolute."[9] Fortunately, "Everyone sees what you appear to be, few experience what you really are,"[10] or, as Frank puts it, "We are nothing more or less than what we choose to reveal."

Frank agrees that image must be carefully managed in politics. He won't even allow Peter Russo to be interviewed by ordinary reporters, but uses Zoe to set up sympathetic interviews. Frank's own image is almost a complete fabrication. He's an amoral, callous powermonger, but presents himself as a warm, kindly, and public-spirited individual. Frank confesses privately that he hated his violently abusive dad, to the point that he wished he had killed him. In public, though, Frank pretends to have had a close relationship with his father, and relates inspiring things his father supposedly said to him. Privately, Frank has no faith in God. Standing in a church, he confides, "There is no solace above or below. Only us—small, solitary, striving, battling one another. I pray to myself, for myself." Left alone in a church with a crucifix, he spits on it. Yet that doesn't prevent him from going to church so that he can be seen to be religious. Claire reminds him that he mustn't even tarnish his image by ever admitting to being wrong: "My husband doesn't apologize ... even to me." The public doesn't like politicians to apologize, admit wrongdoing, or change their minds.

Despite Machiavelli's insistence that a ruler must have a reputation for kindness, he believes that it is even more important to be feared. He writes,

> [I]t is far better to be feared than loved if you cannot be both. One can make this generalization about men: they are ungrateful, fickle, liars, and deceivers, they shun danger and are greedy for profit.... Men worry less about doing an injury to one who makes himself loved than to one who makes himself feared. For love is secured by a bond of gratitude which men, wretched creatures that they are, break when it is to their advantage to do so; but fear is strengthened by a dread of punishment which is always effective.[11]

Perhaps this is true for independent dictators, but no Western politician could dare to take this approach with the voters. If the voters fear you, they'll remove you at the next election. Still, the rule arguably holds between individuals out of the public eye. Frank makes sure that his associates fear him for the harm he can do them. When Russo refuses to cooperate, explaining, "You don't understand. I'm not afraid of you anymore, Frank," Frank replies, "Then you're misguided." In the original British series *House of Cards*, Francis Urquhart is even more blatant, periodically "putting a bit of stick about," that is, lashing out at colleagues just to keep them scared. Of course, being too feared is dangerous. Machiavelli notes, "The prince must none the less make himself feared in such a way that, if he is not loved, at least he escapes being hated."[12] Perhaps Frank should have thought of that before becoming so heavy-handed that he alienated his allies Jackie Sharp and Remy Danton, and even his wife Claire.

## Majority Whip Jackie Sharp: "Mr. Vice President, What You Are Asking Is Just Shy of Treason."

*Frank Underwood: "Just Shy, Which Is Politics."*

As Machiavelli reminds us, political theory is only as good as how well it stacks up against what goes on in the real world. Are his depressing conclusions about the road to power right? Is it all, as Frank claims, "just politics"? Certainly, the idea that politicians must act deceptively to get ahead is a popular belief. In fact, being completely open about your opinions is all but impossible for a professional politician. To receive the backing of a political party, politicians must toe the party line. While they need not express agreement on every point, they are expected to more or less vote as the party leadership decides. The job of Majority Whips, like Frank Underwood, is to ensure that they do. What's more, politicians who are voting in accordance with party policy must pretend that they are voting out of conscience. The public won't vote for a politician who says, "I think this education bill will do more harm than good, but I'm voting for it anyway."

Machiavelli is also surely right that maintaining an image is essential for political success. For example, in an age when most of us would be horrified by the idea of employers making hiring decisions on the basis of candidates' personal lives, the public does just that for candidates for high political office. One who seeks the presidency must be heterosexual and happily married to a spouse who is a successful professional or happy homemaker with no embarrassing quirks. Politicians' sexual activities are of particular fascination to voters, and sex scandals are a traditional way for politicians to fall from power. President Clinton was impeached because of his affair with Monica Lewinsky. He lied under oath about it, of course, but he was only being questioned in the first place because of Republican hopes of undermining his political power by exposing his sexual shenanigans. It can even be ruinous for a candidate if their spouse is caught in sexual impropriety. It is realistic for Tusk to be able to harm Frank by having Adam Galloway leak a photograph to the press of Claire in the shower, secure in the knowledge that if the public thinks Frank has an imperfect marriage, they'll hesitate to trust him. Indeed, the mere fact that Frank's marriage is on the rocks at the end of Season 3 should cause him huge image problems in his bid for reelection to the presidency.

Likewise, long after most Americans have given up on the idea that it is appropriate for an employer to base a hiring decision on the candidate's religion (at least for most jobs), a political candidate who expresses insufficient religious feeling is unlikely to be elected. The Pew Research Center estimates that 20% of Americans claim no religious affiliation, but only 0.2% of members of Congress.[13] What's more, no affiliated member of Congress will express doubts about God, or ambivalence about religion and religious communities, and no politician could hope to win the presidency without clearly expressing their strong commitment to Christianity. It is realistic that for Walker, the mere possibility that he and his wife went to see a marriage counselor who is *not* a religious counselor is scandalous enough to threaten his presidency.

Even the candidate's leisure interests must fit the ideal. In *House of Cards*, we see Frank throwing the ceremonial pregame first pitch at an Orioles game at Camden Yards, with a cry of "Go Orioles!" Perhaps he genuinely loves baseball, but every president must appear to love sports. A candidate who confesses that they don't, and especially one who admits to being bored by baseball, would be rejected by the voters. After all, voters tend not to support candidates who seem too different from themselves. How many times in a single speech can President Obama address us as "folks," just to make it clear that he's one of us?

In some ways, the deceptive skill of modern politicians out-strips even Machiavelli's imagination. For example, while Machiavelli thinks it is counterproductive to try to develop a reputation for gen-erosity, modern politicians have proved him wrong. They are often charitable and receive positive PR because of it, all without ruining themselves. When President Obama won a $1.4 million dollar Nobel Peace Prize in 2009, he gave the entire amount away to charities, with the lion's share going to Fisher House, which helps veterans, and to the Clinton Bush Haiti Fund, a charity founded by two previous presidents to supply disaster relief in Haiti. For all we know, Obama, Clinton, and Bush all have a genuine desire to help the people of Haiti and would have donated money regardless of the political advantages to themselves or their party. Nevertheless, they successfully cultivated a reputation for generosity to their political advantage.

Modern politicians also show a greater understanding than Machi-avelli of how to manipulate an enemy's image, as Frank's fictional but plausible exploits illustrate. For a real-world example, consider the attempts to convince the public that President Obama is now, or was raised as, a Muslim. In the first place, he isn't and never has been a Muslim, and, in the second place, even if he was a Muslim, that would be no evidence at all of criminality. Yet if he can be painted as a Muslim, he can be branded as a terrorist by sheer association. In a modern democracy, being able to ruin a politician's reputation can be all that it takes to defeat them. Even someone like Frank, who achieves the presidency without being elected to it, would be unable to keep the presidency if the voters despised him.

## "Moments Like This Require Someone Who Will Act. To Do the Unpleasant Thing. The Necessary Thing."—Frank Underwood

So far, so depressing, but what about Machiavelli's claim that to get ahead, one must be willing to throw the law and morality to the wind as Frank has done: betraying people, killing people, and indulging in any other vice, crime, and corruption that offers an advantage? It would be nice to claim that nobody has ever gotten ahead by play-ing dirty, but it isn't true. Nobody would ever engage in dirty politics if dirty politics never paid off. Bastards like Joseph Stalin and Mao Tse-Tung did amazingly well for themselves, and corruption in the United States has always been lucrative. It is important to keep Machiavelli's warning against being hated in mind, though, and how badly corruption can backfire if you are caught. If President Obama were ever to be caught on camera taking a page from Frank Underwood's book by shoving an inconvenient reporter in front of a subway train, it would be the end of his career. So the degree to which it is in politicians' best interests to do terrible things depends on how likely it is that the public will catch them and how seriously the public will take their crimes. As citizens, it is incumbent on us to keep an eye on our leaders and hold them accountable.

Likewise, how profitable it will be for politicians to rely on image manipulation over reality will depend on the degree to which we, the public, respond to images rather than reality. As Machiavelli says, "I believe also that he will be successful who directs his actions according to the spirit of the times, and that he whose actions do not accord with the times will not be successful."[14] Voters tend to be badly informed and to have listened to a narrow variety of opinions, a product of being able to choose to use only information sources that reinforce our preexisting beliefs. Rather than taking the trouble to question everything we are told, we tend to make simplistic judgments that render the world in black and white. Studying the facts and questioning our sources to make informed decisions are hard work. It's easier to pick politicians or movements on the basis of their image, and to trust them to look after everything for us.

It's probably impossible to have a democratic political system in which ruthlessly ambitious people like Frank Underwood will not rise to power. After all, since people like Frank will do anything to get ahead, they will adapt to work with whatever system is in place, acting "according to the spirit of the times." However, we can still try to make sure that the best interests of Machiavellian politicians are served when they serve the citizens well, rather than when they betray our interests. If we reward politicians best for genuinely producing positive results, then Machiavellian politicians will want to produce positive results. Frank doesn't care what his policies are, provided that he is given power and prestige. When he thinks he can further his career by starting a trade war with China, that's just what he does, despite the harm that skyrocketing energy prices will do to ordinary citizens. Yet a Frank Underwood in power could, in principle, be the citizens' benefactor rather than someone who cons them with a warm smile while selling them out to the highest bidder or the most politically useful lobby. So while much of what Machiavelli says about getting ahead in politics is depressingly right, the moral is not to despair and leave politics in the hands of the Frank Underwoods of this world. Rather, the moral is that we, the citizens, must do the hard work required to educate ourselves on the facts and to track results, rather than making simplistic judgments based on surface appearances. And you can trust me on that, folks.

# Notes

1.  Niccolò Machiavelli, *The Prince* (London: Penguin, 2011), 50–51.
2.  Ibid., 56.
3.  Ibid., 10–11.
4.  Ibid., 51.
5.  Ibid., 73.
6.  Ibid., 65.
7.  Ibid., 28.
8.  Ibid., 57–58.
9.  Ibid., 59.
10. Ibid., 58.
11. Ibid., 54.
12. Ibid., 54.
13. http://www.pewforum.org/2012/11/16/faith-on-the-hill-the-religious-composition-of-the-113th-congress/ (retrieved June 20, 2015).
14. Machiavelli, 80.

# 8

# Machiavelli Would Not Be Impressed

## *Don Fallis*

Francis "Frank" Underwood, the unscrupulous protagonist of *House of Cards*, lies, cheats, and even kills in his quest for political power. His behavior is in keeping with Niccolò Machiavelli's (1469–1527) infamous philosophy that, even though it is clearly wrong for ordinary people to do such things, it is permissible for politicians to do them in order to acquire and to maintain power. As a result, Underwood has been touted in the media as a "modern-day Machiavelli" and a "perfect Machiavellian figure."[1]

Underwood certainly follows Machiavelli's advice that "it is essential for a Prince who desires to maintain his position, to have learned how to be other than good."[2] To show this, I'll run through the devious and ruthless things that Underwood does in order to carry out *just one* of his projects. But, as we shall see, Frank does not fully follow Machiavelli's advice, and to that extent he encounters difficulties despite his ultimate ascent to the Presidency.

## Education Reform at All Costs

Throughout the first two seasons, one of Underwood's main goals is to increase his influence with newly elected President Garrett Walker. As he tells us in "Chapter 1," "Power is a lot like real estate. It's all

*House of Cards and Philosophy: Underwood's Republic*,
First Edition. Edited by J. Edward Hackett.
© 2016 John Wiley & Sons, Ltd. Published 2016 by John Wiley & Sons, Ltd.

about location, location, location. The closer you are to the source, the higher your property value." Toward this end, Underwood plans to get the very first item on the new President's legislative agenda passed by Congress.

To carry out this project, Underwood has to get himself in charge of handling education reform. The White House initially appoints Representative Donald Blythe to manage the task with Underwood merely assisting. Recognizing that Blythe's first draft of the bill is "very far left of center," Underwood leaks it to the press (in the person of Zoe Barnes). The resulting public embarrassment forces Blythe to step aside.

Next, Underwood has to produce his own education reform bill. He is not going to get much credit for a legislative accomplishment unless the bill "has teeth." So, despite having painstakingly gone through a draft of the bill "line by line" with the heads of the teachers' unions and their lobbyist Marty Spinella, Underwood changes the bill in "Chapter 4" (without telling them) to eliminate their right to collective bargaining.

| | |
|---|---|
| BIRCH: | Has Marty Spinella seen this? |
| UNDERWOOD: | Not the version I showed him. |
| BIRCH: | So you lied to his face. |
| UNDERWOOD: | No. I revised the parameters of my promise. |

This is right in line with Machiavelli's view that "a prudent Prince neither can nor ought to keep his word when to keep it is hurtful to him and the causes which led him to pledge it are removed."[3]

Next, Underwood has to get the bill voted on. The Speaker of the House Bob Birch (a Democrat) refuses to take it to the floor as long as it contains the collective-bargaining amendment. So, in "Chapter 4," Underwood conspires to get Birch replaced as Speaker by Majority Leader David Rasmussen. When he is unable to talk Rasmussen into cooperating, Underwood turns around and reveals the plot to Birch, blaming it all on Rasmussen.

| | |
|---|---|
| RASMUSSEN: | This was Frank's idea. |
| UNDERWOOD: | I told you he was gonna try to blame me on it. |
| RASMUSSEN: | Ask around. Talk to Womack. |
| BIRCH: | I did. He said you came to him. |
| RASMUSSEN: | He's fucking lying, Bob! I would never … |

Rasmussen is forced to resign his leadership position so that he can keep his seat in Congress.

RASMUSSEN:      And if I don't play along?
UNDERWOOD:      We'll cleave you from the herd and watch you die in
                the wilderness.

In exchange for his help in putting down the coup that Underwood himself devised, Birch agrees to bring the education reform bill up for a vote. Interestingly, in chapter XIX of *The Prince*, Machiavelli described how the Roman Emperor Severus pulled a similar stunt on his way up. But in that case, the falsely accused politician, Albinus, ended up dead rather than just demoted.

It is worth noting that the plot to replace the Speaker of the House involves bribery and blackmail as well as lies and conspiracy. In order to gather enough votes for Rasmussen to win the speakership, Underwood offers to keep the Air Force base open in the district of Representative Terry Womack, the head of the Black Caucus. But in order to do this, he has to get Representative Peter Russo to accept the closure of the naval shipyard in his district. Fortunately, Underwood has something on Russo, having bailed him out of jail after Russo was caught driving drunk with a prostitute in his car.

Finally, in order to actually get the bill passed, Underwood has to overcome the opposition of the teachers. In "Chapter 5," he is able to get the support of the National Education Association through intimidation ("Cooperate, we'll give your people protection and a place at the banquet. Fight us, we break you"). But, unfortunately for Underwood, the rest of the teachers still go on strike in protest. So, in "Chapter 6," Underwood deploys a devious three-pronged attack to discredit the teachers' unions and their lobbyist.

First, Underwood orchestrates the *brick incident*. While Claire distracts their bodyguard by inviting him in for coffee (which almost costs poor Ed Meechum his job), Stamper lobs a brick through the window of the Underwoods' home. Several talking heads then go on cable news, blaming the teachers and using the catchphrase that Claire has come up with ("It's *disorganized labor*, plain and simple. When you've got angry teachers throwing bricks through congressmen's windows, you've gotta blame the union leadership").

Second, Underwood and Stamper patiently monitor 911 calls until something bad happens to a small child who would have been safe in school were it not for the strike. When an "eight-year-old Washington DC boy is killed by a stray bullet in a gangland shoot-out," Zoe sends out a tweet blaming Spinella. Underwood then holds a press conference with the grieving mother to further embarrass him.

Last but not least, by calling Spinella horrible names (which I won't repeat here) and by admitting that he was actually behind the brick incident, Underwood is able to provoke Spinella into attacking him. Since "assaulting a United States congressman is a felony," Spinella is forced to end the teachers' strike so that Underwood will not press charges.

These are just the unseemly activities that Underwood engages in to get a single bill passed. Thus, it's pretty clear that he agrees with Machiavelli that "a Prince cannot observe all those rules of conduct in respect whereof men are accounted good, being often forced, in order to preserve his Princedom, to act in opposition to good faith, charity, humanity, and religion."[4] Even so, I want to argue that Machiavelli himself would not be impressed with Underwood's machinations.

## The Original Machiavelli

Niccolò Machiavelli was a politician and writer who lived in Florence, Italy, during the Renaissance. (He was buddies with Leonardo da Vinci.) Interestingly, he had essentially the same job that Underwood initially wanted for himself. Machiavelli was a sort of Secretary of State who traveled on diplomatic missions representing the Republic of Florence. But when the Medici family defeated the Florentine Republic and took over, Machiavelli lost his job. Shortly after that, he was (falsely) accused of being involved in a conspiracy against the new Medici government and tortured for several weeks.[5] When he was finally released, Machiavelli moved to the country (although not quite to the literal wilderness) and spent the rest of his life studying and writing about politics (and unsuccessfully trying to get his old government job back).

Machiavelli's most famous work, *The Prince*, is part of a literary tradition of instructing young princes on how to conduct themselves once they take power. Such books (aka "mirrors for princes") tended to promote familiar virtues such as honesty, patience, generosity, courage, kindness, and compassion. By contrast, Machiavelli took a more pragmatic approach. He wrote that "since it is my object to write what shall be useful to whosoever understands it, it seems to me better to follow the real truth of things than an imaginary view of them ... any one who would act up to a perfect standard of goodness in everything, must be ruined among so many who are not good."[6]

However, Machiavelli did not just claim *that* it is permissible for politicians to lie, cheat, and kill. He also had a lot to say about *how* and *why* politicians should do these things. A careful look at Machiavelli's advice in *The Prince* shows that Underwood does not measure up.

Late in the third season, Underwood actually starts being open with a few people, such as his wife Claire and his biographer Tom Yates. As Machiavelli could have predicted, this sort of honesty (especially when it involves speaking "the brutal fucking truth," as in "Chapter 39") makes it extremely difficult for Underwood to hold on to the Presidency. But even where Underwood does maintain his commitment to deception, Machiavelli would think that he often does so in the wrong ways and for the wrong reasons.

## Failing to Keep Up Appearances

While Machiavelli thought that it was fine for politicians to be deceptive, he emphasized that politicians must nevertheless cultivate the *appearance* of trustworthiness ("A Prince should be very careful that to see and hear him, one would think him the embodiment of mercy, good faith, integrity, humanity, and religion"[7]). This is something that Underwood clearly fails to do.

After having gutted Blythe's education reform bill in the previous season, Underwood can't get Blythe to vote for entitlement reform in "Chapter 17," because, as Blythe explains, "I don't hold grudges, Frank. I just don't negotiate with people who are fundamentally deceptive." Later on, in "Chapter 20," Underwood is unable to get the Chinese to stop funneling money to the Republicans until the Port Jefferson Bridge project is approved, because, as Xander Feng explains to Stamper, "The Vice President has lied to me before. I need proof of his commitment." And getting that very bridge project approved in "Chapter 21" is difficult, because White House Chief of Staff Linda

Vasquez is worried that Underwood has "ulterior motives." At which point, in an aside to the audience, Underwood asks, "Why does everything have to be a struggle?" Machiavelli would have been able to answer that question for him.

Underwood doesn't even try to cultivate the appearance of integrity. As he finally acknowledges to the President in "Chapter 26," "I'm a liar, sir. I lack scruples and some would even say compassion. But that's just the image that I present to the world because it elicits fear and respect." Now, Machiavelli could certainly get behind the idea that princes should try to inspire fear. He famously claimed in *The Prince* that "it is far safer to be feared than loved."[8] However, Machiavelli went on to emphasize that "a Prince should inspire fear in such a fashion that if he do not win love he may escape hate." By showing himself to be a liar and a deceiver, Underwood clearly fails to "avoid such courses as would make him hated or despised."[9]

Moreover, it is not just the movers and shakers in DC who do not trust Underwood. When he briefly returns to his hometown to deal with the Peachoid scandal, it becomes clear that many constituents from his district in South Carolina are pretty dubious of him as well. And by the time Underwood starts campaigning to stay in the White House, much of the American public doesn't trust him either. In "Chapter 37," one voter tells the First Lady, "I have trouble believing that your husband truly cares about people." In "Chapter 38," another voter complains about Underwood pardoning the ex-President and Raymond Tusk: "those were bad people, and he let them off the hook, and then he says he's not running and he does." So, he is not living up to Machiavelli's idea that "he who becomes a Prince through the favor of the people should always keep on good terms with them."[10]

The episode with Blythe is also an example of Underwood failing to follow the Machiavellian principle that "men are either to be kindly treated, or utterly crushed, since they can revenge lighter injuries, but not graver. Wherefore the injury we do to a man should be of a sort to leave no fear of reprisals."[11] Even so, I have to admit that Underwood sometimes does get this particular *how* right. For instance, at the end of the day, Rasmussen and Spinella are pretty much flattened. And unless there is a crossover with *The Walking Dead*, Peter and Zoe are not going to cause any more problems for Underwood.

## The Other FU Was Better

But *why* does Underwood do all these terrible things? All indications are that Underwood just wants power for its own sake.[12] In contrast, power is not an end in itself for Machiavelli. Even though the accumulation of political power is the central concern of most of his writings, he thought that it should only be exercised to ensure the stability and liberty of the state ("To slaughter fellow-citizens, to betray friends, to be devoid of honor, pity, and religion, cannot be counted as merits, for these are means which may lead to power, but which confer no glory"[13]).

Actually, the Italian Renaissance thinker would probably have been much more taken by the other FU, Francis Urquhart from the BBC's version of *House of Cards*. Francis Urquhart is every bit as devious and ruthless as Underwood. But he is much better at the *how* as well as the *why*. Unlike Underwood, Urquhart is careful to maintain a reputation for neutrality and integrity ("It becomes us to be humble and honest, good old Francis Urquhart still"). Also, he has a clear view of what is good for the nation and simply believes that he is the right person to secure it ("Britain must be governed, and you know who will do it best").

It is not terribly surprising that Urquhart is a better Machiavellian. While there is no evidence (at least through three seasons) that Underwood has read *The Prince*, we know that Urquhart has. When she is presented with a copy as a gift from one of Urquhart's co-conspirators, his wife says, "*The Prince*. Niccolò Machiavelli. What a lovely thought. Do you know that this is one of Francis's particular favorites?"

## Maybe Machiavelli Wasn't Serious

Surprisingly, even though Underwood does not do very well at following the advice given in *The Prince*, there may not be anything wrong with his behavior by Machiavelli's lights. It is possible that Machiavelli thought that politicians *shouldn't* follow that advice. Indeed, several scholars have argued that Machiavelli did not actually endorse what he wrote in the book.

The political scientist Erica Benner claims that Machiavelli was just being *ironic*. In other words, the book was actually intended to be "a biting *critique* of both ruthless *realpolitik* and amoral pragmatism, not a revolutionary new defense of these positions."[14] It is supposed to be obvious to readers that these are actually horrible ways for politicians to behave. On Benner's view, *The Prince* is much like *House of Cards* itself, just in a different medium. Despite making him the protagonist, it is not as if the creators of the show are seriously holding up Underwood as a model statesman.

The political philosopher Jean-Jacques Rousseau (1712–1778) also did not think that Machiavelli was Machiavellian. On Rousseau's view, like an investigative reporter for the *Washington Herald*, Machiavelli was simply trying to reveal to the public the nefarious techniques that politicians actually use.[15] Machiavelli didn't think that politicians *should* behave in these ways.

The problem with such interpretations, however, is that, unlike *House of Cards* or the *Washington Herald*, *The Prince* was not made for wide public consumption. Machiavelli dedicated the book to Lorenzo de Medici and sent a copy only to him. (*The Prince* was not officially published until several years after Machiavelli's death.) So, it certainly doesn't look like Machiavelli was trying to criticize the morality of princes or expose their techniques to the public. He appears to simply be offering his sage political advice as a gift to the young prince in order to ingratiate himself with the Medici (and perhaps get his old job back). In the dedication, Machiavelli writes that "I have found among my possessions none that I so much prize and esteem as a knowledge of the actions of great men, acquired in the course of a long experience of modern affairs and a continual study of antiquity."

In any event, even if *The Prince* were intended as a critique or as an exposé, this would not get Underwood off the hook. It *would* mean that Machiavelli did not really think that it is permissible for politicians to lie and to cheat in their quest for power. But it would *not* mean that he questioned the effectiveness of the various techniques described in *The Prince* as means of acquiring and holding power. Since power is what Underwood is after, it still looks like he is failing to use the best Machiavellian techniques for achieving his goal.

However, a few scholars have suggested that Machiavelli did not actually think that these *are* effective techniques for grabbing and maintaining power. But if that is what he thought, why would he so carefully lay out these techniques (and illustrate them with detailed contemporary and classical examples) and then send them to the young Medici prince? According to the political scientist Mary G. Deitz, Machiavelli was trying to fool Lorenzo into following bad advice that would lead to the downfall of the Medici, who had tortured him, and to the return of the Florentine Republic that he loved.[16]

So, maybe I am wrong and Machiavelli would actually be quite impressed with Underwood. Maybe it is not that he is ineptly failing to follow good advice for acquiring power. Maybe, if he read the book at all, Underwood cleverly saw through Machiavelli's duplicitous tract (that has pulled the wool over the eyes of all but a handful of scholars) and is doing exactly the opposite.[17] After all, Underwood has gone from simply being a congressional representative from the great state of South Carolina, to being the Majority Whip in Congress, to being Vice President, and now to being the President of the United States. Who am I to argue with success?[18]

# Notes

1.  See *Washington Post*, http://www.washingtonpost.com/blogs/style-blog/
    wp/2014/02/18/a-brutal-supercut-containing-all-of-frank-underwoods
    -political-advice-in-house-of-cards/ (retrieved June 30, 2015); and
    *Huffington Post*, http://www.huffingtonpost.co.uk/alexander-leivesley/
    house-of-cards-philosophy_b_4802499.html (retrieved June 30, 2015).
2.  Niccolò Machiavelli, *The Prince*, trans. Ninian Hill Thomson (New
    York: Bartelby.com, 2001), http://www.bartleby.com/36/1/chap. XV.
3.  Ibid., chap. XVIII.
4.  Ibid., chap. XVIII.
5.  The Medici at least seemed to sincerely think that Machiavelli was
    guilty. Miles J. Unger, *Machiavelli: A Biography* (New York: Simon &
    Schuster, 2011), 203–4.
6.  Machiavelli, *The Prince*, chap. XV.
7.  Ibid., chap. XVIII.
8.  Ibid., chap. XVII.
9.  Ibid., chap. XIX.
10. Ibid., chap. IX.
11. Ibid., chap. III.
12. If Underwood had any more laudable motivations, you'd think that we
    would know about them. After all, he shares his innermost thoughts
    with the television audience every five minutes or so. By the way, as

Selina Meyer, protagonist of HBO's *Veep*, wonders in her video for the White House Correspondents' Dinner, what's up with that? After sneaking into the editorial offices of the *Washington Post* with Joe Biden in the middle of the night, she turns to the camera and says in a thick Southern accent, "The headline I'd like to write is 'Selina Meyer sworn in as President.' But all in good time. Yes, we can all look directly into the camera, Kevin. The point is, you're not supposed to."

13. Ibid., chap. VIII. In his other great work on politics, the *Discourses*, Machiavelli defends (small r) republicanism, and it is even clearer there that power is not an end in itself.

14. Erica Benner, *Machiavelli's Prince: A New Reading* (Oxford: Oxford University Press, 2013), xxii.

15. Jean-Jacques Rousseau, *On the Social Contract*, trans. G. D. H. Cole (Mineola, NY: Dover, 2003), book III, chap. VI.

16. Mary G. Dietz, "Trapping the Prince: Machiavelli and the Politics of Deception," *American Political Science Review* 80 (1986): 777–99.

17. Of course, even if Machiavelli thought that what he advised in *The Prince* was not a good idea, that does not mean that the specific way in which Underwood deviates from this advice *is* a good idea.

18. I would like to thank James Mahon, Kay Mathiesen, Ken McAllister, and Dan Zelinski for extremely helpful feedback on earlier drafts.

# Is Frank the Man for the Job? *House of Cards* and the Problem of Dirty Hands

*Tomer J. Perry*

When Frank Underwood walked into the Oval Office, turned to the camera, and knocked on the presidential desk with a wry smile—we knew nothing good could come out of an Underwood presidency. Surely, Frank Underwood is the worst man for the job: a slimy, calculating, self-centered egomaniac with ruthless ambition, an insatiable desire for power, and absolutely no respect for the law, morality, or God (especially not God). Frank Underwood became president because he is singularly fixated on shamelessly promoting his self-interest. And, if you had any doubt about that, Season 3 showed that he would abuse and discard even his wife and partner—the one person he actually seemed committed to. Clearly, you wouldn't want him as your friend or neighbor. But as president? Maybe That job requires different qualities from those desirable in a neighbor, friend, or spouse. Along those lines, some philosophers argue that politics is a special vocation: It requires people who are capable of doing bad things when the job calls for it, people who are willing to get their hands dirty.

One of the most notorious advocates of dirty hands, Niccolò Machiavelli (1469–1527), advised the prince to "learn how not to be good" and even "enter into evil when forced by necessity."[1] Say what you want about Frank Underwood, but he is certainly willing to dirty his hands. Moreover, in this he is superior to his challenger, the

*House of Cards and Philosophy: Underwood's Republic*,
First Edition. Edited by J. Edward Hackett.
© 2016 John Wiley & Sons, Ltd. Published 2016 by John Wiley & Sons, Ltd.

seemingly perfect Heather Dunbar, a solicitor general who made her name fighting corruption. When Underwood faces the Russian president Viktor Petrov in the Jordan Valley, Petrov talks about the time he killed a man with his bare hands. Petrov is testing Underwood, deciding whether to trust him or not. Underwood does not blink. Eye to eye with a guy like Petrov, don't we want a president who can measure up to his inquiring gaze? Could Dunbar dance with such a devil?

Politics may be a dirty business, but that is not what the problem of dirty hands is about. The problem of dirty hands concerns the dirt that politics actually *requires*. The first season of *House of Cards* starts with a scene where a dog gets hit by a car. The dog is alive, we hear him whimper, but he's unlikely to survive. "Moments like this," says Underwood, "require someone who will act. To do the unpleasant thing. The necessary thing."

Frank kills the dog and wipes his dirty hands. You probably would not have been able to kill a dying dog with your own hands, yet you would agree that if a dog is dying in pain, killing him is the right thing to do. And Frank can do it. He's the right man for *that* job. But is he the right man for the job of the president?

## Avoiding the Problem

The problem of dirty hands is an ancient one, but the name and modern reformulation come from Jean-Paul Sartre (1905–1980), an existentialist philosopher who wrote *Dirty Hands* as a political drama for theater. In it, a good-mannered revolutionary leader confronts his secretary with a challenge that seems to follow Machiavelli's advice, saying, "I have dirty hands right up to the elbows. I've plunged them in filth and blood. Do you think you can govern innocently?"[2]

The contemporary American philosopher Michael Walzer presented the problem, adapting the name from Sartre's play.[3] Walzer and Sartre thought you could not govern effectively without dirtying your hands—right up to the elbows. And that means we need people who can deal with the dirt. Donald Blythe is not one of them, and that's why Underwood chose him as a vice president. When Bob Birch threatens to impeach Underwood, Frank notes, "Congress would get killed for malpractice. As crooked as you may think I am, you know I can handle the pressure, and you know that Donald can't." Birch hates Frank, but his approving silence signals that he sees the point.

There are at least two kinds of philosophers for which this tension of dirty hands—being right and wrong at the same time—does not exist. These are utilitarians and absolutists.[4] For utilitarians, there is nothing wrong with dirty hands. For absolutists, there is nothing right about them.

Frank, as we know, does not hold rules in very high regard; neither do utilitarians. But that's not because they are selfish or immoral. Quite the opposite. Utilitarians believe morality has only one rule: Act in order to maximize the greatest happiness for the greatest number. When faced with a situation, you must do whatever will create the most happiness.[5] For utilitarians, rules of morality (such as "keep your promises" or "thou shalt not kill") are merely rules of thumb, useful guidelines that you should *usually* follow. But if breaking a promise or taking a life would maximize overall happiness—that would be the right thing to do. It may *seem* or *feel* wrong, but when you break the rule for the greater good, you are doing the right thing.

By contrast, absolutists take their rules with utmost seriousness, and that leads them, surprisingly, to agree with the utilitarians that there is no problem of dirty hands. The absolutists argue that the rules of morality are sacred and therefore should not be broken. They hold that rules—"don't lie," "keep your promises," "don't kill the innocent"—are there precisely because breaking them is sometimes advantageous. For example, the bishop who Underwood meets briefly in Season 3 does not compromise the rules. "Two rules: Love God, and love each other. Period." Nothing past that period. For absolutists, there is no problem—only dirty hands.

## The Struggle for Power

What is it about politics that makes it so we have to do bad in order to do good? To win power, Walzer thinks, one has to play dirty. Frank agrees. When Jackie Sharp is shocked to hear Frank's plan to impeach Walker, she tells him that what he asks of her is "just shy of treason."

Frank calmly responds, "Just shy, which is politics." This is the image of politics that Walzer has in mind.

Walzer notes that politics tends to attract bad people. Specifically, political office lets you order people around and be responsible for organized violence. What kind of people tend to want a job like that? People like Frank Underwood. Since politics attracts bad people, the competition for power cannot be won by playing nicely. If you want to run for office and do good—you have to overcome the Underwoods, and they won't be playing nice And, as Machiavelli noted, you can't win if you play fair against those who play dirty. "No one succeeds in politics without getting his hands dirty,"[6] says Walzer, and that is certain what Frank means when he says: "For those of us climbing to the top of the food chain, there can be no mercy. There is but one rule: Hunt or be hunted."

Walzer worries that good people will never win in politics unless they play dirty. However, it's not clear that the people who win in this manner are *still good people*. When Dunbar refuses to use dirty methods against the Underwoods—namely, the diary offered to her by Doug Stamper, with evidence of Claire Underwood's abortion—we hold her in high regard. But later in Season 3, when she changes her mind about it, we feel let down. We think that she is being corrupted by the mere prospect of winning the Oval Office.

I don't think we want politicians to dirty their hands just so they could get into office. Walzer's own view on the matter evolved over the years, and he has come to the same conclusion. In later writing he restricts the notion of dirty hands to extreme cases, where "necessity" is understood not just in colloquial terms of gaining or staying in power—but also in terms of what he calls "supreme emergency."[7] Walzer restates his position in a later piece, arguing that "political and military leaders may sometimes find themselves in situations where they cannot avoid acting immorally, even when that means deliberately killing the innocent … dirty hands aren't permissible (or necessary) when anything less than the ongoingness of the community is at stake, or when the danger that we face is anything less than communal death."[8] This is a much more striking claim, and a more interesting one. And this is where Frank Underwood might start to shine; deliberately killing the innocents is not something he is averse to. But what might justify, or at least excuse, such radical measures? Clearly, only extreme circumstances.

## Facing a Catastrophe

In this formulation the problem of dirty hands is limited to a narrow set of cases where the entire community is in danger of extermination. There is quite a distance between the prospect of complete destruction and the threat of terror attacks, but both could justify use of force that leads to innocent casualties. We see Underwood dealing with situations of both kinds, and the logic of dirty hands works the same way in both.

Walzer provides two justifications for dirtying one's hands in the face of a supreme emergency. The first is one of professional ethics—politicians have, in virtue of their position, duties that we don't have as individuals, and that might clash with ordinary morality. This is a familiar argument—we all think that doctors and police officers have different rights and duties from the rest of us just because they occupy a certain role. The president can order an insanely hopeless military action in the Jordan Valley while most of us have absolutely no right to risk the life of Navy Seals, no matter how good our judgment is. The right to make that call is attached to the post of the president and whoever fills it.

Occupying a role certainly gives people permission to do certain things, but we should note that such permission is never without limits. Lawyers are required to promote the interests of their clients but they are not permitted to fudge the evidence, let alone kill the innocent if it would help their clients. Doctors are required to maintain the confidentiality of their patients, but not if keeping their secret would jeopardize the lives of others.[9] A psychiatrist is not allowed to keep the confidentiality of an airline pilot who shows suicidal inclinations.[10] The president cannot approve drone strikes that kill a disproportionate number of innocent bystanders. Absolutists in particular are not impressed by this argument from professional ethics—for them, it is quite clear that whatever the role may require you to do, it cannot require you to break the absolute rules of morality. Do what you need to do for the community, but do not torture and do not kill the innocents.

The second way to understand the requirements of supreme emergency is what Walzer calls "utilitarianism of extremity."[11] People have rights that ought to be protected, but when the consequences of protecting people's rights would endanger much of the community, we start making calculations. This position has been called "threshold deontology"[12]—a position between utilitarians and absolutists. Although the absolutists say that we should never break the rules and the utilitarians say we should always make the calculation of consequences, the threshold position says that we should usually keep the rules, *unless the consequences of doing so would really be terrible*. Not Blythe in the president's chair awful, but millions of deaths terrible.

## The Solutions

So there we have Sometimes, in cases of supreme emergency and terrible alternatives, we want our politicians to break the rules of morality. We want politicians to break the rules but only when it's really necessary. This is a precarious position: Achieving such a delicate balance seems a grand task even for the best of us, and politicians are not usually the best of us.

Walzer argued that politicians who dirty their hands should be punished publicly. That sounds a bit harsh: Why would we punish someone for doing the right thing? And why would anyone do what's right if they are to be punished afterward? Walzer isn't concerned about that. He thinks political positions are sufficiently attractive to so many people that paying this price is a reasonable professional risk. Jackie Sharp's habit of causing herself pain for the harm she does people can seem like a form of accepting punishment for her sins. Walzer wouldn't be satisfied with Sharp's private penance, though. Walzer wants punishment to be done by the public and out in the open.[13]

Walzer's solution becomes even more complicated if you consider what he thought would bring politicians to justice. Good politicians, he thought, would feel guilty for breaking the rules and would take responsibility for what they did. In fact, Walzer thought, if they did not admit wrongdoing we would have reason to suspect them. If politics regularly involves dirty hands, politicians who leave office should be confessing and repenting all over the place instead of going on book tours. The fact that they are not doing so, Walzer thinks, gives us evidence that they are not good people. Walzer concludes that "[a politician's] willingness to acknowledge and bear (and perhaps to repent and do penance for) his guilt is evidence, and it is the only evidence he can offer us, both that he is not too good for politics and that he is good enough. *Here is the moral politician: it is by his dirty hands that we know him.* If he were a moral man and nothing else, his hands would not be dirty; if he were a politician and nothing else, he would pretend that they were clean."[14]

Walzer's solution seems even more troubling than the problem he raised. First, we only know that a politician is good enough in retrospect by the fact that they admit they did what we all know they had to do—dirty their hands. Second, after they have taken the extraordinary measure of admitting they did wrong, we publicly punish them, even though we wholeheartedly agree that they had to do what they did and that it was the right thing. Alternatively, if they don't admit they did anything wrong, we suspect them and seek to punish them anyway. Hardly satisfying.

Yet Walzer's solution has the advantage of drawing our attention to a politician's character. From this perspective, the solution to our problem is to elect the people who are most reluctant to break moral rules so they would only do so when it is absolutely necessary,[15] assuming, of course, that they are capable of breaking the rules in the first place. A desirable leader's character exhibits these two features: They are capable of breaking the rules, *and* they are reluctant to do so. Which of them is more important? This is the question we would have to answer when we compare Underwood's character to that of Heather Dunbar.

## Frank's Dirty Hands: The Wrong Person in the Right Place?

Frank Underwood is an awful person and a terrible candidate in many regards. Yet he is not the kind of person who would have a problem dirtying his hands when the need arises. Can this count in his favor as a candidate? Is he preferable to Heather Dunbar in this regard? The answer is, probably not. Still, he does have some advantages that are worth considering.

In the first episode of Season 3, we see Frank ordering a drone strike that would most certainly involve killing children and innocent bystanders. Why does he decide to do it? It's not clear that ordering the strike contributes in any way to maintaining his position as a president. You might think that he ordered it just to put on a good show for his wife Claire and dissuade her from insisting on the UN job. Or maybe he thought it was important to approve the strike in order to keep on good terms with military and security leaders. Yet, drone strikes are a political nuisance for Underwood. Later in the season they come to haunt him, when an American citizen who was injured in one sues the government. Frank meets with Kaseem Mahmoud, the unfortunate guy who happened to be in the wrong place at the wrong time. Surprisingly, the meeting shakes Frank. Mahmoud reproaches Frank, saying "there's a fine line between duty and murder." Frank complains later that this encounter threw him off his game. Were those the pangs of his conscience making a brief appearance?

Mahmoud is probably right that the use of drones by the US government is more extensive than is justified. Be that as it may, it's plausible that Frank believed he was saving lives when he ordered the strike. The most compelling argument in favor of his decision is actually advanced by the solicitor general, Heather Dunbar. In front of the Supreme Court, she eloquently argues that the strike "was tragic, [but] it was not unlawful. It was legal. It was necessary. It was right."

For our purposes, the issue is not whether the strike was justified. The issue is whether Underwood is the kind of person who could order it when it is, and the answer is yes. Is Dunbar that kind of person? We don't know for sure, but her argument suggests she might be. Dunbar also has the advantage of minimizing the risk of authorizing unjustified strikes. Since she would be, we assume, more reluctant to approve a strike even when it is necessary, she has a better chance of not ordering it when it isn't necessary.

So far, Dunbar seems ahead, even from the perspective of dirty hands. But consider Underwood's dealing with the Russian president Petrov. They dance around each other throughout Season 3, each pursuing his own personal agenda at the expense of the other, his country's national security, and the rest of the world. At the height of the encounter, the two men had a staring contest in a Russian army camp in the Jordan Valley. Despite their acrimonious hostility and scarred history, they are able to cut a deal in that ludicrous tent, making a new covenant for world security. The deal is messy and ugly; it includes Petrov's demand that Underwood fire his wife from the UN. It also includes a massive scale-back of US missile defense systems in Eastern Europe. We don't know the details of the plan, and it is possible that it is recklessly dangerous. Yet it might not be. And the alternatives to the deal are not less dangerous, especially if the Petrov–Underwood relationship stays its course. In any case, the stakes are high: Millions of lives are on the line. Saving the lives of so many people could easily cross that threshold of dirty hands, constituting a supreme emergency.

Petrov and Underwood are playing a perilous game when they mess around with the deal, and they are both clearly willing to risk it for their personal gain. Underwood seems primarily motivated by the fact that foreign policy is a distraction on the campaign trail, pulling him off-message. But if we assume for a moment that a deal of the kind he reaches with Petrov is one that is likely to reduce military tensions between the two countries and their allies, it is quite possible that Underwood has done the world a great service.

All of this is speculative. We don't know much about the deal, and some would say that it won't matter for the prospect of peace anyway. What is important is that Frank is the kind of person who can deal with Petrov and get an agreement. That is the strongest thing anyone can say in his favor. Would Dunbar be capable of staring down Petrov and gaining his respect? Could she reach any sort of agreement with him? I doubt it. Would the world be less safe under Dunbar's presidency as a consequence? It's hard to tell.

The only advantage that Underwood seems to have over Dunbar is his capacity to dirty his hands. As we have seen, this can be a good quality in a leader. Sadly for Frank, even judged from that perspective his victory is at best partial: He may be capable of dirtying his hands when the need arises, but he lacks the scruples to avoid dirtying them when it doesn't.

Is Frank the man for the job? Probably not. Still, his capacity to dirty his hands counts in his favor, and that, I daresay, is the only thing that could be said in favor of an Underwood presidency.[16]

## Notes

1. Niccolò Machiavelli, *The Prince*, ed. P. Bondanella (Oxford: Oxford University Press, 1984), chap. 18.
2. Jean-Paul Sartre, *No Exit and Three Other Plays* (New York: Vintage International, 1989), 224.
3. Michael Walzer, "Political Action: The Problem of Dirty Hands," *Philosophy and Public Affairs* 2 (1973): 160–80; Walzer was also

influenced by the formulation of the argument in Max Weber's "Politics as a Vocation," in *From Max Weber: Essays in Sociology*, ed. H.H. Gerth and C. Wright Mills (London: Routledge and Kegan Paul, 1977), 77–128.

4. Most of the absolutists would classify themselves as deontologists.
5. Or welfare. Utilitarians disagree about the right measure of utility.
6. Walzer, "Political Action," 164.
7. Michael Walzer, "Emergency Ethics," in *Arguing about War* (New Haven, CT: Yale University Press, 2004), 33–50.
8. Walzer, "Emergency Ethics," 46.
9. C.A.J. Coady, "The Problem of Dirty Hands," in *The Stanford Encyclopedia of Philosophy* (Spring 2014 ed.), ed. Edward N. Zalta, http://plato.stanford.edu/archives/spr2014/entries/dirty-hands/ (retrieved July 3, 2015).
10. http://www.cbsnews.com/news/germanwings-co-pilot-andreas-lubitz-mental-health-likely-to-play-role-in-lawsuits/ (last accessed July 3, 2015).
11. Walzer, "Emergency Ethics," 40.
12. Coady, "The Problem of Dirty Hands."
13. Walzer, "Political Action," 176–7. Walzer advances his argument here against that of Weber (1977), who allegedly would be satisfied by the politicians' self-inflicted suffering.
14. Walzer, "Political Action," 167–8.
15. The most explicit formulation of this criterion comes from Bernard Williams, "Politics and Moral Character," in *Moral Luck: Philosophical Papers 1973–1980* (Cambridge: Cambridge University Press, 1981), 54–71, who says that "only those who are reluctant or disinclined to do the morally disagreeable when it is really necessary have much chance of not doing it when it is not necessary" (62).
16. I thank Tomer Ullman and Torry Castellano for helpful comments on an earlier draft.

# Part IV

# CLASSICAL LIBERALISM AND DEMOCRACY

# 10
# Frank the Foole, Upon a House of Cards

*Shane D. Courtland*

Imagine that you live in a world in which there is no expectation that others will obey moral principles. Moreover, in this world, there are no institutions that will enforce such obedience. If you lived in this world, then, you would expect that people would fail to respect your rights (of person or property), interests, and desires. Even if some tried to behave saintly and respect such things, there would be no guarantee that their kind behavior would be reciprocated. With a lack of enforcement institutions (police, judges, and the like) such saints would be quickly exploited—and, most likely, killed. This horrible world was described by the English philosopher Thomas Hobbes (1588–1679) as the state of nature. In this state, "[T]he life of man [is], solitary, poor, nasty, brutish, and short."[1]

Hobbes is the father of modern social contract theory. Unable to guarantee one's wellbeing in the state of nature, Hobbes argues that rational (guided by self-interest) individuals ought to agree to constrain their behavior to rules outlined in a hypothetical contract. This contract would construct rules (similar to what we would find in most moral systems) by which to live in peace, and it would empower an enforcement institution to ensure that the rules were observed. According to Hobbes, there are two reasons to abide by such a contract. First, it provides some modicum of security against predation from other agents. Second, by providing peaceful security, it allows

*House of Cards and Philosophy: Underwood's Republic,*
First Edition. Edited by J. Edward Hackett.
© 2016 John Wiley & Sons, Ltd. Published 2016 by John Wiley & Sons, Ltd.

individuals to garner the benefits of cooperation (a division of labor, a market economy, knowledge of science, etc.).

On *House of Cards*, we see countless examples of people reaping the benefits of the social contract. Take, for instance, Freddy Hayes and his BBQ restaurant. As Frank Underwood frequently attests, Freddy makes the best BBQ. This good (Freddy's BBQ) can only exist in a place that observes a social contract. If we were in the state of nature, Freddy's BBQ Joint would not exist. He would have no way to ensure that he would be compensated for his services. If people did not pay Freddy, it would be foolish for him to make ribs. Moreover, making ribs as good as Freddy's requires a time commitment. If he lived in a place where his security was under constant threat (the state of nature), it would be foolish to dedicate his time to mastering this skill. Freddy's time would be better spent ensuring that his person and property were secure from others. Devoting such time to BBQ, even as good as Freddy's, would be suicide in the state of nature.

This is true of anything that requires cooperation or a division of labor. Without a social contract, we would lack cooperative institutions—hospitals, schools, factories, fire stations, science labs, and so on. In addition, we would lack any field of knowledge that requires specialization—there would be no doctors, scientists, politicians (like Frank), or engineers. If an item required more than one person to construct, it would not exist in the state of nature. Without the general obedience to a social contract, our security would be in such peril that it would be foolhardy to engage in cooperative endeavors.

Since most of the things we value come by way of peaceful cooperation, it is, according to Hobbes, in our interest to live under a social contract. This ensures that our persons are free from violence (more so than the state of nature), and it also ensures that we are compensated for our cooperative endeavors (contracts are enforced by legal institutions).

## Frank the Foole

In *Leviathan*, Hobbes's most famous work, he addresses an individual he labels the "Foole." This person declares that injustice may "sometimes stand with ... reason," and thus it may be in a person's interest to behave unjustly. Hobbes writes,

> He does not therein deny that there be covenants, and that they are sometimes broken, sometimes kept, and that such breach of them may be called injustice, and the observance of them justice; but he questioneth whether injustice ... may not sometimes stand with that reason which dictateth to every man his own good.... From such reasoning as this, *successful wickedness hath obtained the name of virtue*, and some that in all other things have disallowed the violation of faith, yet *have allowed it when it is for the getting of a kingdom.*[2]

The Foole recognizes that the core of the social contract is enlightened self-interest. Sure, the Foole will agree to abide by the contract. When the other citizens' backs are turned, however, the Foole asserts that it is rational (prudent) to break the social contract. The Foole gains all of the benefits of being a part of a social contract (others are constraining their behavior) while avoiding the costs (not having to constrain one's own behavior).

Frank Underwood seems to be employing the Foole's strategy. He reaps the benefits of the social contract (security and the benefits of social living) while betraying those around him. Frank frequently makes pacts and promises, but he is willing to break them (*"successful wickedness"*) when it fits his ends (*"the getting of a kingdom"*). Take, for example, Frank's relationship with Peter Russo. Early in the series, Frank seemingly befriends Congressman Russo. Peter has substance abuse problems, and Frank attempts to help. With the aid of Doug Stamper, Frank gets Peter into AA. Afterward, Frank seems to groom Peter to run for governor of Pennsylvania. From all appearances, Frank is Peter's friend and mentor. Unfortunately for Peter, this is all a ruse. Frank is using Peter as a pawn in a bigger game. He wants Peter to be a somewhat successful candidate for governor in order to eventually clear the way for Frank to become vice president. With the help of Doug Stamper and the prostitute Rachel Posner, Frank is able to entrap Peter and tempt him to succumb to his old demons. Peter's "falling off the wagon" engenders a serious scandal, requiring President Walker to tap the vice president to be Peter's replacement (opening the spot for Frank). This, of course, is all contingent upon Peter quietly pulling out of Pennsylvania's gubernatorial race.

However, Peter tells Frank that he will publicly "come clean" with all of his problems. Frank, then, in order to preserve his plan, murders Peter Russo.

As another example, consider Frank's relationship with the journalist Zoe Barnes. Early in the series, she secretly cooperates with Frank. He feeds her stories that help her career, and she publishes stories that advance his political agenda. Zoe climbs the ranks of the *Herald* and eventually takes a key position at *Slugline*. All through Zoe's rise, she places stories at the exact right time, helping Frank advance to the vice presidency. Their collaboration unravels, though, when Zoe begins to pursue the truth behind Peter Russo's alleged suicide. With the help of Janine Skorsky and Lucas Goodwin, Zoe begins to suspect that Frank had a hand in Peter's death. As Zoe presses Frank for information, he seems to convince her that (1) he didn't kill Peter (but did cover up his DUI), and (2) their relationship, especially with Frank as vice president, is still to her advantage. Later, Frank meets Zoe at the subway station, and after he has ensured that Zoe has erased incriminating information from her phone, he pushes her in front of a train.

As yet another example, consider Frank's relationship with President Garrett Walker.[3] *House of Cards* starts with Walker failing to reward Frank with a cherished appointment—the Secretary of State. Frank, then, decides that he will take power, all the while exacting revenge upon Walker. To do so, Frank pretends to be a close confidant of Walker. He helps him pass an education bill. He helps him find a replacement for Russo's failed gubernatorial bid. He helps Walker's ailing marriage. He helps Walker navigate his toxic relationship to businessman Raymond Tusk. As we know, though, all this help was part of Frank's ruse. By gaining Walker's trust, Frank is better able to manipulate him. Frank persuades Walker to let Vice President Jim Matthews run for governor. In addition, Frank manipulates Walker to appoint him to Matthew's newly vacant position. Finally, Frank manipulates Tusk and Walker to incriminate each other. Ultimately, Walker resigns. Through Frank's cunning deception, Walker yields the presidency to the man who engineered his disgrace.

By now, the pattern should be clear. Frank's *modus operandi* is to befriend, then to betray. He has no problem breaking contracts, trusts, or covenants. Frank will pretend to cooperate, *only* to ensure that those he betrays are caught unaware. His "successful wickedness" applies even to the core of the social contract. Frank will outright murder those who stand between him and his ends. He robs them of even the basic security provided by the social contract—a protection from violent death. Frank is the Foole.

## Hobbes's Critique of the Foole

In *Leviathan*, after the Foole's objection, Hobbes provides a counter-argument for the Foole. He writes,

> He, therefore, that breaketh his covenant, and consequently declareth that he thinks he may with reason do so, *cannot be received into any society that unite themselves for peace and defence but by the error of them that receive him; nor when he is received, be retained in it without seeing the danger of their error*; which errors a man cannot reasonably reckon upon as the means of his security... *it is by the errors of other men, which he could not foresee nor reckon upon; and consequently [he has acted] against the reason of his preservation.*[4]

When describing the Foole's folly, Hobbes does not mince words. In the Latin version of *Leviathan*, he claims that the Foole "acts against reason and imprudently."[5] The Foole avoids disaster only by "the errors of other men, which he could not foresee nor reckon upon."[6] This lack of foresight is *always* "against the reason of [the Foole's] preservation."[7]

Gregory Kavka, in "The Rationality of Rule-Following," interprets the core of Hobbes's criticism as that of the Foole's overestimation of his abilities. Kavka writes, "[The Foole asserts that] it is good general policy to follow moral rules, but one should be willing to seize any 'golden opportunities' for immoral gain that happen to come one's way.... But, in reality, many of these apparent golden opportunities will turn out to be 'Foole's gold'—and the agent will seriously damage her interests by pursuing them."[8]

The problem, according to Hobbes, is that people naturally suffer from vainglory.[9] That is, they tend to overvalue their own self-worth and intelligence.[10] In particular, when the Foole thinks that he has a golden opportunity to successfully violate the social contract, it is often due to an overestimation of his own intellectual abilities.

Because of his excessive self-love, the Foole often thinks, *wrongly*, that he can successfully deceive his peers. Within the context of crime, there is some empirical confirmation of this tendency. Baumeister *et al.*, for example, write, "Aggressors seem to believe that they are superior, capable beings . . . . Violent and criminal individuals have been repeatedly characterized as arrogant, confident, narcissistic, egotistical, assertive, proud, and the like."[11]

The Foole suffers, according to Hobbes, from an epistemic shortcoming. He overestimates himself and thinks that he is smarter than his fellows. Does Frank Underwood suffer from the Foole's folly—vainglory? Although Frank frequently feigns humility, his soliloquies tell a different story. There is no doubt that Frank thinks rather highly of his skills and intellect. The true question, however, is the accuracy of Frank's self-assessment. As one of my former teachers once remarked, "It's only arrogance if it's unjustified." Thus, Frank is only committing the Foole's folly if he overestimates his abilities. To judge Frank's accuracy, let's look closer at his transgressions.

## Is Frank's Behavior Rational?

As we saw above, Frank has no problem participating in strategic betrayal. To fulfill his goals, he has lied, cheated, and murdered. If Frank finds it advantageous to break the social contract, Frank breaks it. He thinks that he has enough skill to evade detection from the various social institutions that enforce the contract. Let's examine for a moment, in greater detail, the murders of Peter Russo and Zoe Barnes.[12] But, before that, we should acknowledge the difficulties that are associated with the successful execution (pun intended) of an undetected premeditated murder. First, the perpetrator will want to insure that there are no witnesses. If someone sees him during the act or immediately prior, there is a significant problem. Of course, the perpetrator might try to silence actual witnesses. This, however, has problems of its own. If you murder the witness, then you have a reiteration of all of the problems that beset the first murder. If you threaten or bribe the witness, you then have to constantly motivate the witness to remain quiet—all the while keeping your influence undetected by the relevant authorities. So the perpetrator will want to be reasonably assured that there will be no witnesses.

In our modern age, the problem with witnesses has been compounded. We now have a variety of electronic witnesses. These include, but are obviously not limited to, surveillance cameras, webcams, cell phone cameras, listening devices, cell tower triangulation, and GPS-enabled devices. Electronic witnesses, unlike their biological counterparts, cannot be intimidated. The perpetrator will either need strategies to avoid such devices or have the undetectable ability to alter or destroy them.

A second concern associated with successful premeditated murder involves forensic evidence. A principle behind forensics is that people always leave something behind at the scene of a crime, and they always take something away. There are many things to consider—DNA, hair, fibers, fingerprints, ballistics, shoe prints, toxicology reports, blood-splatter analysis, forensic entomology, and the like. In order to evade detection, the perpetrator will most likely need a working knowledge of forensic science. In addition, it would be prudent for the perpetrator to conceal this knowledge.

A third concern is that one ought not to have a traceable motive. The first question a homicide detective will ask is "Who would stand to gain from the victim's death?" If the perpetrator is named as such an individual, then he should make sure that he is reasonably protected concerning other aspects of the case (alibi, lack of witnesses, and lack of forensic evidence).

A fourth concern is that one ought to have a plausible and defensible alibi. The second question detectives tend to ask is "Who had the opportunity to commit the murder?" If the perpetrator is named as such an individual, again, he should make sure that he is reasonably protected concerning other aspects of the case (clear lack of motive, lack of witnesses, and lack of forensic evidence).

A fifth concern is that the perpetrator should have the ability to be deceptive under extreme forms of interrogation. Think of all that is required to successfully engage in high-stakes deception. In "The Truth about Lies: What Works in Detecting High-Stakes Deception," Stephen Porter and Leanne Brink mention some of these difficulties: "While telling the tale, the liar must try to control facial expressions and monitor body language. This necessary 'multi-tasking' should reduce the level of conscious control over each channel, and increase the amount of relative 'leakage' from one or the other(s), depending on to which he/she is devoting relative degrees of effort."[13] Liars' rates of speech tend to be different than truth tellers', and liars have a general tendency to repeat phrases and details.[14] In addition, "[L]iars tend to move their arms, hands and feet less than truth tellers ... and liars make fewer gestures to illustrate their speech."[15] This is not even to mention "microexpressions,"[16] increased perspiration,[17] reduced flow of saliva,[18] and facial blushing.[19] When it comes to high-stakes deception, if you know what to look for, the "tells" are legion.[20] Given the difficulty of high-stakes deception, we should expect that the person who attempts to engage in such deception (the Foole) would have a difficult time concealing himself. [21]

Given all of these considerations, how should we view Frank Underwood's foray into murder? Let's examine Peter Russo's murder. Frank drives Peter to his home. During the trip, Peter tells Frank that he will confess everything. Hearing that his plans could be unraveled because of Peter's new sense of responsibility, Frank takes action. Upon parking in Peter's garage, he persuades Peter to imbibe more alcohol. Peter passes out, and Franks starts the car. He closes the garage door (with the car running) and lets Peter die of an apparent suicide. Frank walks home and tells an enquiring Doug Stamper, "Whatever happens in the next few hours, whatever you hear, we will never speak of it" ("Chapter 11").

This is not a well-planned murder. There are many contingencies, all of which are beyond Frank's control, that determine the success of his murderous plot. Here is a list of just *some* of them: (1) Frank's quick attempt at wiping his fingerprints may have left some behind. (2) Leaving Peter in the passenger seat implies that someone else was at the scene. (3) How could Frank ensure that he would not be observed leaving the scene of the crime? There may be video cameras, random pedestrians, and the like. (4) There are many loose ends. Doug Stamper (Frank's chief of staff), Rachel Posner (the prostitute hired to tempt Peter), and Barney Hull (chief of police) know too much. (5) Although no one has pressed Frank, it's not clear that he has an alibi on the night of Peter's death.

With all of these contingences, it's not surprising that journalists Janine Skorsky, Zoe Barnes, and Lucas Goodwin suspect foul play. This eventually leads to Frank's second foray into murder. Fearing that Zoe Barnes knows too much, he asks her to meet at a subway station. After agreeing to a "fresh start," Zoe tells Frank she has erased all incriminating evidence from her phone. Frank, then, lures her around the corner. As Zoe follows, he shoves her in front of an oncoming train.

Like Peter's murder, Zoe's murder is not well planned. There are, again, too many contingencies. Here are a few: (1) How can Frank be sure that Zoe has really erased all of the incriminating evidence? She is a journalist who has, in the past, employed less-than-honest means to get ahead. (2) How does Frank know, exactly, what her fellow journalists (Skorsky and Goodwin) know? (3) Again, how could Frank ensure that he would not be seen leaving the scene of the crime? The train station is a public place, and Frank is a highly recognizable public figure. His attempt at a disguise is *merely* a hat and glasses; it might easily prove ineffective.

Frank's murderous behavior is irrational. If he were to get caught, not only would his career be over, but also his freedom would be lost forever. Society is concerned with the fulfillment of the social contract. In particular, when bodily security is at risk, society will employ (with zeal) various institutions to detect and punish such wickedness. In a modern society, then, it is hard (if not impossible) to engage in a rational murder. Frank does not take these risks seriously. His attempts to play the Foole only indicate that he is foolish.

## Frank's Objection and the Hobbesian Response

At this point, Frank Underwood might not yet be convinced that he has engaged in foolishness. He might claim that he has been successful. After all, his treachery has secured him the presidency, and it has eliminated many of his enemies. Perhaps he does not suffer from the Foole's folly—vainglory. Frank could claim that he has evaded detection because of his great skill (intellect, manipulative abilities, political savvy, and so on). This is not the arrogance of a vainglorious fool; instead, Frank might claim that this is the appropriate self-esteem of a political super-genius. Perhaps, Hobbes is wrong and Frank is a counterexample—a nonfoolish Foole.

Not so fast! Hobbes has two strong responses. First, Hobbes might point out that Frank's story is far from complete. It is true that his treachery has gotten him the White House, but it is truly a house of cards (pun intended). It could fall down with the slightest breeze. Look at some of the loose ends that might destroy Frank: (1) Janine Skorsky is still free and has serious suspicions of Frank's guilt. She is a competent journalist and might decide to pursue Frank. (2) Gavin Orsay is alive, and he understands the extent of Doug Stamper's treachery. He could help show others (like Tom Hammerschmidt) that Lucas Goodwin's story is more than a mere conspiracy theory. (3) Raymond Tusk might change his story; he could decide to tell the truth. And, with the information he possesses, his story would be compelling. (4) Doug Stamper knows too much. If he were to betray Frank, there would be little Frank could do to avoid destruction. Moreover, Doug has recently fallen off the wagon. If someone were to discover that he murdered Rachel Posner, it might not take much to get him to betray Frank. One should also note that he has been less than honest with Frank in the past (i.e., keeping Claire's journal when he was instructed to destroy it, hiding the extent of his injuries, downplaying his relationship to Rachel Posner, etc.). (5) Most important, Claire Underwood leaves Frank at the end of Season 3. She may still feel betrayed by being forced to resign the UN Ambassadorship. In addition, Frank's attempt to dominate her ("Chapter 39") only results in her alienation from him. She is a powerful enemy—*one that will be too hard to kill*—and she has the information that can destroy him.

Second, and more importantly, it doesn't matter if Frank gets away with his treachery. His success may be due to luck. Hobbes, of course, acknowledges that the Foole might get lucky and remain undetected. Luck, however, is not the point; it is prudence. Hobbes makes this plain in the Latin version of *Leviathan*. He writes, "For first, in a state anyone who does what, as far as can be foreseen and understood by reason, tends to his own destruction, even though something unforeseen happens which makes the outcome fortunate, has nevertheless acted imprudently, because what happens is unforeseen."[22] Thus, the mere success of Frank's treachery is not enough to show that Frank acted with prudence. It needs to be shown that he could justifiably foresee that such actions would be likely to lead to success. Given all of the contingencies that we have noted, it's not clear that Frank could have reasonably predicted success. His success was based upon fortunate contingences. As Hobbes would add, "[I]t is by the errors of other men, which he could not foresee nor reckon upon; and consequently [he has acted] against the reason of his preservation."[23]

At this point, we can say that Frank Underwood is not the "poster boy" for the rational violation of the social contract. He frequently betrays (at times, to the point of murder) others when he thinks that it's conducive to his ends. The only thing preventing his complete destruction is luck. Such a reliance upon fortune is not wisdom when the consequences associated with failure are prohibitively high. Frank has procured "the getting of a kingdom" through "successful wickedness." Unfortunately, this kingdom is a house of cards. If Frank's story is meant to serve as an example, it is the shining example of the vainglorious behavior of a foolish Foole.

# Notes

1. Thomas Hobbes, *Leviathan: With Selected Variants from the Latin Edition of 1668* (Indianapolis, IN: Hackett, 1994), L, XII, 9, p. 76 (hereafter, *L* or *OL* [for Latin excerpts]).
2. *L*, XV, 4, p. 90 (emphasis added).
3. Of course, there are more examples. For brevity, I'll merely focus on these three.
4. *L*, XV, 5, pp. 91–2 (emphasis added).
5. *OL*, XV, 5, p. 91.
6. *L*, XV, 5, p. 92.
7. *L*, XV, 5, p. 92.
8. Gregory Kavka, "The Rationality of Rule-Following: Hobbes's Dispute with the Foole," *Law and Philosophy* 14 (1995): 26.
9. In *De Cive* (hereafter, *DC*), Hobbes claims that it is a "naturall proclivity of men, to hurt each other, which they derive from their Passions, but chiefly from a vain esteeme of themselves." Thomas Hobbes, *DC*, in *Hobbes: On the Citizen* (Cambridge University Press, 1998), I, 12, p. 29.
10. Hobbes writes, "Of the passions that most frequently are the causes of crime, one is vain glory, or a foolish overrating of their own worth, as if difference of worth were an effect of their wit, or riches, or blood, or some other natural quality" (*L*, XXVII, 13, p. 194).
11. Roy F. Baumeister, Laura Smart, and Joseph M. Boden, "Relation of Threatened Egotism to Violence and Aggression: The Dark Side of High Self-Esteem," *Psychological Review* 103 (1996): 26. For more information on the empirical connection between vainglory and miscalculating the chances of success in criminal behavior, see (1) Baumeister *et al.*, "Relation of Threatened Egotism to Violence and Aggression: The Dark Side of High Self-Esteem," *Psychological Review* (1996); (2) Diana Scully, *Understanding Sexual Violence: A Study of Convicted Rapists*

(New York: Routledge, 1990); and (3) Michael R. Gottfredson and Travis Hirshi, *A General Theory of Crime* (Stanford, CA: Stanford University Press, 1990)

12. Although I am a not examining, in greater detail, Frank's betrayal of President Walker, that is not to imply that his betrayal was rational. As with his murders, the success of this betrayal was largely contingent upon fortunate circumstances (like Raymond Tusk's false incrimination of President Walker). It was extremely risky behavior that had little to no guarantee of success.

13. Stephen Porter and Leanne Brinke, "The Truth about Lies: What Works in Detecting High-Stakes Deception?" *Legal and Criminological Psychology* 15 (2010): 63.

14. For more detailed information, see (1) Bella DePaulo, James Lindsay, Brian Malone, Laura Muhlenbruck, Kelly Charlton, and Harris Cooper, "Cues to Deception," *Psychological Bulletin* 129 (2003): 74–118; (2) Stephen Porter and John C. Yuille. "The Language of Deceit: An Investigation of the Verbal Clues to Deception in the Interrogation Context," *Law and Human Behavior* 20 (1996): 443–58; and (3) Siegfried Ludwig Sporer and Barbara Schwandt, "Paraverbal Indicators of Deception: A Meta-Analytic Synthesis," *Applied Cognitive Psychology* 20 (2006): 421–46.

15. Maria Hartwig, Pär Anders Granhag, and Leif A. Strömwall, "Guilty and Innocent Suspects' Strategies during Interrogations," *Psychology, Crime, and Law* 13 (2007): 213–14.

16. For more detailed information, see (1) Paul Ekman, *Telling Lies: Clues to Deceit in the Marketplace, Politics, and Marriage*, 3rd ed. (New York: W. W. Norton, 2009); (2) Paul Ekman, Richard J. Davidson, and Wallace V. Friesen, "The Duchenne Smile: Emotional Expression and Brain Physiology: II," *Journal of Personality and Social Psychology* 58 (1990): 342–53.

17. Robert H. Frank, *Passions within Reasons* (New York: W. W. Norton, 1988), 128.

18. Ibid., 129.

19. Ibid., 127.

20. I must qualify this statement. Of course, people are quite able to "pull off" a successful lie. All I am saying is that, given the above-mentioned "tells," it is hard for a deceptive individual to ensure that he will elude detection when the stakes are high and the consequences are dire.

21. In the *Elements of Law* (hereafter, *EL*), an earlier work, Hobbes explicitly mentions this problem. He writes, "Of these signs, some are such as *cannot easily be counterfeited; as actions and gestures, especially if they be sudden; whereof I have mentioned some for example sake in the*

*ninth chapter, at the several passions whereof they are signs*; others there are that may be counterfeited: and those are words or speech; of the use and effect whereof I am to speak in this place." In *Human Nature and DeCorpore Politico* (Oxford: Oxford University Press, 1999) (EL, XIII, 1, p. 73) (emphasis added).

22. OL, XV, 5, p. 91.
23. L, XV, 7, p. 92.

# 11

# Hobbes and Frank on Why Democracy Is Overrated

## *Steven Michels*

Thomas Hobbes (1588–1679) was the first philosopher to take seriously the idea that people are essentially equal. Not only do we want the same things, but also we think that we have an equal claim to them. Consequently, Hobbes envisioned a "state of nature," the period before the establishment of civil society, where life is "solitary, poor, nasty, brutish, and short."[1] As a remedy, Hobbes preferred a hereditary monarchy.

Frank Underwood is Hobbesian to the core. He wants to use the harsh and violent reality of political life to satisfy his desire for power and the glory that comes with it. Democracy, as he sees it, is little more than the state of nature with elections.

## The Fault in Our Democratic Stars

The purpose of government is to impose a modicum of order. For Hobbes, that meant centralization—in a single sovereign. Dividing powers and holding elections don't secure freedom in a limited government as much as they create inefficiency and risk a return to the state of nature. In that sense, democracy is an insufficient response to the problems of human nature. As Hobbes saw it, if life and liberty are your main concerns, then democracy is the last kind of government you should want.

*House of Cards and Philosophy: Underwood's Republic*,
First Edition. Edited by J. Edward Hackett.
© 2016 John Wiley & Sons, Ltd. Published 2016 by John Wiley & Sons, Ltd.

The problems with democracy are on full display in the first episode of *House of Cards* when Underwood introduces us to the main players and gives us the lay of his political land. He begins with then-President-elect Garrett Walker. As the recipient of 70 million votes, Walker should be at the height of his power, which is exactly why Underwood backed him. Yet the 45th president is marked mostly by his mediocrity and hampered by the nature of his office. Walker lacks the ability to get anything substantive accomplished on his own, has a habit of trusting the wrong people, and makes a serious mistake by passing over Underwood for Secretary of State. What's more, the President rarely has an original idea, and he is fearful of almost everything, especially appearances. At one point, the First Lady says the American people voted for him because of his faith in God and faith in families, but none of that is ever on display. He is more concerned about the pictures in the White House than about having a vision for the country. These are the kinds of presidents that democracies elect: unexceptional, cautious, and kind of whiney. Walker only does two interesting things: take Xanax and end his presidency. A real sovereign couldn't be taken down by some measly legislator.

Underwood's abilities as an executive are more formidable. When dealing with China and helping nuclear energy, he glibly notes, "We're dealing with a national crisis; we can't get sidetracked with public opinion." Walker would have it the other way, no doubt. "Presidents who obsess about history obsess about their place in it, instead of forging it," Underwood attempts to counsel him. Walker is so impressed by the logic that he thinks it must have come from a great historical figure. It's no wonder that Underwood is fond of playing chess with himself.

An outsider might think that people in Washington are obsessed with power. But Underwood shows us a city filled with futile bunglers who don't understand power enough to be trusted with it. Vice President Jim Matthews had a ludicrous notion that the vice presidency would be a promotion over Governor. Linda Vasquez, the President's Chief of Staff, should be the second most powerful person in the executive branch, and yet even the admissions office at Stanford gets the best of her. Underwood's only real compliment, which comes later, is reserved for Patty Whittaker, the DNC Chair. "Competence is such an exotic bird in these parts, and I appreciate it whenever I see it," he says. But then he plays her, too, in getting her to support Russo's candidacy for Governor.

Heather Dunbar, the special prosecutor, is really the only smart, tough, and ethical person we encounter. Her rise to prominence could only be the result of someone else's mistake. Walker was foolish enough to think that his innocence would inoculate him from prosecution. Dunbar starts off as a learned and earnest supporter of the Constitution, but the thought of losing the Democratic nomination to someone like Underwood makes her desperate enough to look to Doug to help her air the Underwoods' dirty laundry.

If Underwood has no use for elected officials, he has even less for his constituents. "I just hate this small ball crap," he says as he leaves Washington to head off a scandal that involves a dead teenager and a big peach. In addition to seeing a very gifted (read: slippery) politician with a home field advantage, we also witness what might be the most calculated eulogy ever given, in which Underwood misrepresents the relationship he had with his father, and for good measure throws in a mix of forced anger and feigned religion. President Walker's popularity might be a mystery, but Underwood's is not. While in South Carolina, Underwood tells us why he was elected 11 times: "What you have to understand about my people is that they are a noble people; humility is their form of pride. It is their strength; it is their weakness. And if you can humble yourself before them, they will do anything you ask." That was how he knew he could offer up his resignation to a grieving and hostile Mr. Masters, without worrying that it would be accepted.

Underwood disagrees with Tip O'Neill's notion that all politics is local—not if you're doing it right, that is. He is tasked with holding the far-left hand of Congressman Donald Blythe (author of the unfortunately titled treatise *Learning to Learn*) and moving him to the middle. Underwood's real objective is to get Blythe out of the way, so he can get credit for passing a bill on his own. Indeed, education reform is in many respects the opposite of running the State Department, where the stakes are high and the accomplishments are more immediate and tangible. He might have asked Linda for "absolute authority and autonomy" with regard to education, but really he wants it on everything. Underwood will later tap Blythe, one of the more likeable but naïve pols we encounter, to be his vice president. Underwood is cautious in his selection: he knows full well the damage a clever VP can do.

As president, Underwood attempts an aggressive domestic policy. His America Works program calls for the creation of 10 million jobs. Everyone who wants a job can have one, and it's a good thing, too, because everyone is going to need one. To offset the program's $500 billion price tag, Underwood is scaling back entitlement spending. "You are entitled to nothing," he tells the nation during an evening address. Underwood likes his country like he likes his tightrope walkers: working without a net.

Not surprisingly, he finds few backers in the timid humidity of the Capitol. The Democrats can't support such a brazen attack on FDR's New Deal legacy, and the Republicans won't support planks of their own platform if it means crossing party lines to do it. But Underwood finds a way around Congress (if not the Constitution) with the Stafford Act. Passed in 1988, it permits the national government to redefine agencies in the aftermath of emergencies and disasters. After getting the Mayor of the District to declare an economic emergency, Underwood uses FEMA funds for jobs.

"The language is sufficiently vague" but "completely unorthodox," his lawyers tell him. "No president has tried to reauthorize funds this way." Undeterred by the inevitable battle with Justice Jacobs and the Supremes, that is all the cover Underwood needs. The *Telegraph*'s Kate Baldwin, the best of the reporters we've seen so far, is the first to call Underwood what he is—a tyrant.

Underwood is even less enamored with the opinion of the public now that he is President. "We have to do the things that people won't like," he says on cutting social spending. He is, he later reminds us, the President, not a talk show host. Hobbes would agree: For him, a tyrant is only a king disliked.[2]

Congress might have spurned him, but Underwood finds common ground with Viktor Petrov, the vainglorious autocratic president of Russia. "None of them understand, do they?—what it takes to govern," Underwood asks him. The sovereigns commiserate and smoke cigars until they are reminded that they lack a common power between them to enforce the rules of the game. They are, as Hobbes would tell them, in the state of nature, which always brings with it the threat of war.[3] Underwood's troubles with Petrov come not because Petrov is a tyrant, but because he is behaving irrationally and not giving him what his power warrants.

# Hungry Like a Wolf

As Hobbes sees it, humans are interested only in maximizing pleasure and minimizing pain. All of human activity is either a motion toward something or away from it—an appetite or an aversion.[4] The only true goal of life is pleasure, however it may be defined. That is the essence of all morality, he contends. That's why he had no room for ancient philosophy ("that painted, chattering whore") and its practitioners, who never did anything but take what gave them the most pleasure and called it good.[5]

Power is not the only thing that gives Underwood pleasure, and he is not immune from enjoying some rather simple things. "My one guilty pleasure is a rack of ribs," he says. The ribs at Freddy's BBQ Joint are tasty, but they have the added benefit of reminding him of the poverty of his youth. Ribs were a luxury that no one could afford, but those days are long gone. "I'm feeling hungry today," he explains, before diving into a second helping.

But ribs are not the only physical pleasure that Underwood enjoys. He smokes on the sly with his wife, has a healthy (and inclusive) sexual appetite, and initially eschews exercise—till Claire buys him a rowing machine and gets him to take up jogging. Eventually, Claire makes him quit smoking, and he takes up e-cigarettes. She keeps him in line with exercise and diet, but enables him when it comes to what actually matters. By Season 3, Underwood has given up his extracurricular sexual exploits and any form of exercise. Apart from an occasional cigarette, he only has a taste for power now.

Although Hobbes thought we are greatly moved by the fear of death,[6] Underwood is not overly concerned with it. He tells Feng that he fears death "No more or less than any man." It's not the end of life that bothers him so much as the lack of activity. "I've always loathed the necessity of sleep," he says. "Like death, it puts even the most powerful men on their backs." His contempt for inactivity is evident when Walker makes him stick around the Oval Office while he takes a nap. He'd just as soon go bird watching with Tusk. To be considered second to a second-rate power is bad enough; to watch it idle is excruciating.

Even Underwood's recreation is active. Mostly it involves his PlayStation—an enjoyment that he hides from others. He says it's to relax, but it looks more like target practice. Painting the Civil War figurines is more relaxing, but of course that doesn't stop him from eventually knocking them over. Underwood also has no use for historical reenactments except maybe if they include his ancestors. He for the most part finds history valuable only to the extent that there are lessons to be taken from its losers.

The main storyline of Season 1 involves the rise and fall of Peter Russo. He has overpromised to important donors, is having an affair with an aide, and has a great fondness for alcohol and drugs—"Can a corporate sellout roll a joint like this?"—which does not stop when he's behind the wheel. Underwood comes to his temporary rescue, and in exchange he only wants Russo's "absolute, unquestioning loyalty." He warns Russo that he has a high bar for what he deems loyal. Unlike Underwood, who knows how to prioritize his pleasures, and Stamper, who has sense enough to serialize them, Russo is addicted to anything and everything and all at once. It was only a matter of time before he destroyed himself. The only question was whether something good was going to come of it. And, indeed, it did. The end of Russo's "fresh start" was an essential part of Underwood's Big Picture plan.

And in case you're wondering what Underwood means by loyalty: "Doug will be in touch." Indeed, Doug is everywhere. When he's not in Vegas or China, he keeps himself busy by digging through the Capitol's trash bins, faking vandalism, and bribing the Police Commissioner. He loves power, too, but his ambitions don't require the limelight. That's good news for him, but it's even better for Frank. Stamper too has an ethic, but it's one of addiction—first booze, then Frank, then Rachel. And when he couldn't quit her, she turns on him.

The major subplot to Season 3 is Doug's recovery—physically, emotionally, and politically. When he can barely walk and is of little use, Doug is left behind. Told to "respect your mortality" by Underwood, he is shrugged off and nearly bought off. Underwood and Seth, the new lieutenant, are more interested in what Doug will tell the police than with his health or wellbeing. They send flowers and stock his fridge, but won't always take his calls. Doug refuses pain pills and measures out his bourbon in needle-sized doses. He has a relapse when he hears word that Rachel has died. Determined to show his value, Doug turns to the opposition and makes good use of Dunbar's desperation. Season 3 ends with Doug back where he belongs—in full command and firmly at Underwood's side.

Once Underwood has attained the presidency, it's time for Claire to consider her position. She wants an ambassadorship and a big one—to the United Nations. Underwood is initially opposed to it because it will cost him politically, mostly with Durant and the State Department. Perhaps Claire would have more pull if she and Frank were not keeping separate bedrooms. Realizing that he can't afford to marginalize his best ally, he acquiesces. Claire has a rare stumble in her confirmation hearing but eventually gets a recess appointment, which lasts until she scuttles a deal with the Russians by taking a principled stance against Petrov's wrongful imprisonment of a gay American activist.

The self-interestedness of Frank and Claire is matched only by their self-awareness and self-assuredness. The Underwoods are both driven by a calculus of pleasure and pain. The most obvious aspect of what Hobbes considers pleasure is their ambition. And there is a lot of it. But there are other aspects, including hope, displayed in their undying belief that there is a way of getting what they want. Conflict emerges, Hobbes teaches, when equals want the same thing.[7] It was only a matter of time before their ambition drove them apart.

Season 3 ends with Claire leaving the White House for some undisclosed location. "We agreed to this before we ever set foot in this house," she reminds him. She has put his pleasure before hers for too long and now expects the debt to be paid. "Isn't that what marriage is about: accepting your partner's selfishness," Michael asserts from his Russian cell. "You of all people should understand." The final straw is Tom's book, which lays bare the difference between the rhetoric and the reality of the Underwood partnership. When even the color of your hair is subject to calculation and approval from your husband and his advisors, you know you have been thoroughly used.

## Money Changes Everything

*House of Cards* only seriously considers one other pleasure as a rival to power—and that is money. Hobbes recognized property as a complication to social life and politics. In fact, he recognized competition for gain, along with fear and glory, as the principle reasons for conflict.[8]

Underwood clearly favors power over the money he could make in the private sector. But the two are not mutually exclusive, and Frank

knows that even the President needs to get his bread buttered somewhere. "I've always said that power is more important than money,"
he offers while working the phones to bundlers, "but when it comes to
elections, money gives power ... well, a run for its money." A president can kill with impunity halfway around the world, but if he wants
to stay in office, then he also has to play the beggar.

Underwood is constantly challenged by those who favor money
over power, and with Remy Danton he even had a hand in creating one
of his strongest antagonists. We first meet Remy when he interrupts the
lunch Underwood is having with the majority leadership. The Speaker
of the House isn't interested in the young black man until he learns
that Remy is connected. Underwood later lays out the relationship he
has with Remy—and with money. "I don't give a hoot about natural
gas," he explains. "SanCorp helps me purchase loyalty, and in return
they expect mine. It's degrading I know. But when the tit's that big,
everybody gets in line." The divided nature of power in Washington
means that politicians are going to need some help from the outside if
they ever want to get anything done.

Season 3 finds Remy back in the seat of power as Underwood's
Chief of Staff. Remy, who is largely inconsequential to the action, has
more empathy for Jackie Sharp, his past and future flame, who Underwood is using and abusing on his way to the nomination. Remy and
Jackie have the last laugh, however: Sharp resigns her campaign and
endorses Dunbar, and Remy just resigns.

Unlike the wavering Remy, Raymond Tusk clearly prefers money to
power, and he has a great deal more of it to love. It makes him fiercely
independent and just plain fierce. Walker always takes his calls, and
when he does, Tusk calls him by his first name. "Tusk understands
the difference between power and money—precisely what makes him
dangerous," Underwood explains. "He doesn't measure his wealth in
private jets but purchased souls."

The clash between Underwood and Tusk is inevitable—not because
they keep score different ways, but because they both want the
President to themselves. When they do collide, neither pulls any
punches. Tusk crosses the line by eating at Freddy's. "I wanted a
place where you could feel comfortable," he claims. But really it's the
greatest violation. It doesn't take Underwood long to appreciate Tusk
for what he is: his only real obstacle. Going after him will be a full-on
attack. In the end, Tusk's billions are no match for Underwood's cool

machinations. Tusk makes the fatal mistake of letting things get too personal. He so wants to hurt Walker that he throws himself under the bus, too.

The saddest casualty of the war with Tusk is Freddy. "In a town where everyone is so carefully reinventing themselves, what I like about Freddy is that he doesn't even pretend to change," Underwood tells us early on. When the heat in Freddy's kitchen gets too hot, Underwood's immediate reaction is to come to Freddy's side. "I won't leave one of my own bleeding on the field," Underwood says. Then he does. In the end, Underwood loses his favorite food. But Freddy loses everything—his business, the joy he derived from doing what he was good at, and the potential for putting his family back together. "The road to power is paved with hypocrisy—and casualties," Underwood instructs. The only course of action is to "never regret." Freddy reemerges in Season 3 as a recipient of a job from the AmWorks project. When Underwood finds out, he offers Freddy a job in the White House kitchen. But Freddy is not interested: He wants to work outside.

Questionable ethics are not limited to the government or the corporate boardrooms; the nonprofit sector has its problems, too. Claire's Clean Water Initiative could possibly rise above Washington's petty and partisan politics, but instead she uses it for her own gain. The fact that she can make decisions unilaterally makes it an even more effective vehicle for her ambition. Evelyn, the Office Manager, was tasked with putting together a list of people to be fired. She spoke out in opposition, but she was not scrupled enough to refuse and not smart enough to see her own termination coming. Even Gillian, who is smart, tough, and actually dedicated to the cause of clean water, gets her hands dirty by filing a faulty wrongful termination suit against Claire.

"We are a charity, but not for our employees," Claire says. She is not the kind of enemy we want to make. Of course, she's not a very good friend, either.

## The Policy of Untruth

Now that we've seen how Underwood exploits the inherent shortcomings of democracy on his way to the presidency, we have to consider the ethics of that pursuit. Where does his understanding of right and wrong come from? And what do we learn about how the love of power can be challenged by the love of truth?

Part Three of Hobbes's *Leviathan* features an exhaustive treatment of the relationship between civil and religious power. Hobbes contends that civil power ought to be superior. Revelation is an uncertain guide for law; it's too personal, which is probably why there are so many sects. For Hobbes, there is no absolute foundation for justice and morality in the state of nature. We need a sovereign for that.[9] The most basic right of nature is self-preservation and the right to do whatever we think that requires.[10]

Underwood also has problems with religion as a source of power. It first comes up when Claire visits Steve in the hospital. "I've never seen him pray, not in eight years," he tells Claire. But Underwood's views of the Almighty are complicated. He is not a believer or a politician presenting himself as a believer. Like nearly everything else in his life, it's adversarial. "Every time I've spoken to you, you've never spoken back," he says to God in church. "Although given our mutual disdain, I can't blame you for the silent treatment." Underwood also speaks to the devil and to Peter's ghost, before he offers this grim conclusion: "There is no solace above or below, only us—small, solitary, striving, battling one another. I pray to myself, for myself."

Religion is even more on display in Season 3. After a Navy SEAL is killed during an operation, Underwood is so despondent that he heads back to church in search of justice. Unmoved by what the priest has to offer—love God, love each other—he spits in the face of Jesus on the cross. If nothing else, it answers the question of what could be worse than pissing on your father's grave, which is how the season begins. Thinking it might be too much even for him, Underwood tries to clean the crucifix, but not before it comes crumbling down on him. Not exactly known for his reverence, he uses the opportunity to take a souvenir. "Well, I've got God's ear now," he says as he departs.

Underwood doesn't get his ethics from his father or in church, and he didn't get them from his time in school, either. We get a glimpse of his education during a library dedication at The Sentinel, the military school he attended in Charleston. This is the place where he learned the value of "honor, duty, and respect," or so he says in his speech. But, as he will later explain, "No one is a boy scout, not even boy scouts." His marks were so low that he was almost expelled. The only thing he picked up at The Sentinel is his habit of making the bed every morning. Even so, Underwood does not credit or blame The Sentinel for the trajectory of his life. It might have been harmonious, but it was also temporary. "It was just the place that we spent four years of our lives," he says. He might have a library on campus named after him, but Underwood is quite content to leave the past where it belongs.

In contrast to Underwood's ethics of power, we see the journalists, who in a Hobbesian world might be our best shot at anything close to philosophy—a theme explored more in other chapters. But their idealism makes them targets for politicians and would-be sovereigns like Underwood. "I just want the truth," Zoe tells Christina. Then Underwood fulfills his promise to hurt her and discards her—in front of a train. Lucas will eventually follow his reporter's instincts and love for Zoe until he finds the Deep Web and Stamper finds him. The murder has the added benefit of getting rid of Janine (Skorsky), who not only flees DC for Ithaca but abandons truth altogether, in her class and in the false testimony she gives against Lucas. Unfortunately, the United States is a liberal democracy, complete with a constitution and that pesky First Amendment. Reporters can be useful when they repeat what they are told, but nothing more.

The most difficult part of being a journalist, we might imagine, is not so much finding the truth as sifting through all of the spin and lies that obscure it. When he is caught lying to Marty, the representative for the teachers' unions, Underwood first claims that he merely "revised the parameters of my promise." When that doesn't fly, he admits that he considers lying to be an essential part of politics. Politics is about power, and giving away information makes you vulnerable. Everyone lies; the goal is to get good at it. As Underwood tells Tusk, "The gift of a good liar is making people think that you lack a talent for lying." Underwood's most obvious falsehood comes in his AmWorks speech, when he announces that he is not running for reelection. No one believes him, but it is his only play. "Imagine what the voters would think if we started telling them the truth," he later reflects.

For Underwood, courage and truth are linked. In Season 3, he tells Tom about a story involving "a boy" who swam two miles to Fort Sumter. His aim was to emphasize that what is thought to be impossible is not always so—or at least not for everyone. Later, Underwood admits to the story not being true. "Imagination is its own form of courage," he tells us. In Frank's world, the strong say what they can, and the weak suffer from the truth.

Frank's boldest lie is also the final one he needs to complete his plan. He sends Walker a letter, taking the blame for what he pinned on the President. When Walker doubts his sincerity—at least he's getting wiser, if not wise—Underwood explains that his reputation for dishonesty and lack of ethics is a convenient contrivance on his part. And it works. Indeed, pretending to advise the President against resigning is dancing on a still-fresh grave. "I could never fill your shoes, sir," he offers. And, as Underwood becomes the 46th President of the United States, Walker announces that his successor "will bring virtue, experience, and courage to the Oval Office."

Walker didn't deserve his fate, but he didn't exactly deserve to be president, either. At the end of Season 2, Underwood pushes away the useless president's useless chair, sizes up the desk, and marks his new territory. A sovereign is born.

## The Advantage of the Stronger

Their aims could not be more different, but Hobbes and Underwood share a similar view of the political world. Frank does not follow Hobbes's philosophy as much as he exemplifies it. He is at once Hobbes's worst-case scenario and his best hope for order. Underwood is not a philosopher, but with a king like this, there might be no need for philosophy. Truth could only get in the way.

The petty partisanship in Washington has led to an Underwood administration, which quickly and not unexpectedly flouts the Constitution. But tyranny is just another word for getting things done. As Underwood puts it, "Democracy is so overrated."

In his Federalist 51, James Madison wrote of how our system of separated and checked powers created natural and unavoidable tension among branches and offices. "Ambition must be made to counteract ambition," he wrote. "If men were angels, no government would be necessary." The proper response is not to inform or moderate Underwood's ambition. It can only be contained by the ambition of others.

Good luck with that.

# Notes

1. Thomas Hobbes, *Leviathan*, ed. Edwin Curley (Indianapolis, IN: Hackett, 1994), 76.
2. *Leviathan*, 118–19.
3. *Leviathan*, 76.
4. *Leviathan*, 28.
5. *Leviathan*, 469.
6. *Leviathan*, 78.
7. *Leviathan*, 75.
8. *Leviathan*, 76.
9. *Leviathan*, 89.
10. *Leviathan*, 79.

# "Democracy Is So Overrated"
## The Shortcomings of Popular Rule

*Brendan Shea*

In some ways, Frank and Claire Underwood closely resemble the stereotypical villains that appear in a thousand books and films. Among other things, they combine the capacity for utter ruthlessness (as evidenced by Frank's brutal killing of Zoe Barnes, and his orders to kill Rachel Posner) with the ability to maintain a successful working relationship (at least for a while). When combined with their almost supernatural cleverness and luck, one might be forgiven for thinking they are a bit "unreal." After all, few real politicians have ever been caught attempting anything nearly so ambitious or well thought out. Instead, most real-world "plots" are nothing more than ill-thought-out attempts to obtain money, sex, or influence in cases where politicians think they can get away with it. The Underwoods, it might seem safe to say, are characters that could *only* exist in fiction.

In this chapter, I'll suggest that this view might be dangerously mistaken. In particular, I'll be looking at how the events portrayed in *House of Cards* might look to some historically important critics of democracy. According to these thinkers, the success of the Underwoods is not nearly as miraculous or far-fetched as many contemporary viewers would like to think. Instead, the Underwoods' success is guaranteed by certain structural features of democracy. On this view, *House of Cards* poses a significant challenge to those of us who want to defend or reform democracy, since it is our responsibility to say

*House of Cards and Philosophy: Underwood's Republic*,
First Edition. Edited by J. Edward Hackett.
© 2016 John Wiley & Sons, Ltd. Published 2016 by John Wiley & Sons, Ltd.

how (if at all) our real-world political institutions can be safeguarded against the sort of schemes that threaten the citizens of Frank and Claire's world.

## The Underwoods Visit the Kallipolis

> And so tyranny naturally arises out of democracy, and the most aggravated form of tyranny and slavery out of the most extreme form of liberty.
>
> —Plato, *Republic*, Book 8[1]

In *House of Cards*, viewers witness the perversion (and perhaps the eventual destruction) of a democratic government. Crucially, the danger comes not from an external threat, but from the democratically elected politicians themselves. Moreover, these politicians are, in at least some respects, "playing by the rules." So, for example, while Frank and Claire break many laws, they take great care to make sure all of their political maneuvering "looks" legitimate. So, laws that Frank favors are approved by legislative majorities and signed by the President, and the people he favors for cabinet posts are appointed by the President. The Underwoods are not, initially at least, some sort of all-powerful royal family who can enact policies based on their own whims.

According to the Greek philosopher Plato (429–347 BCE), the possibility of this sort of "destruction from within" is inherent in *any* democratic government. Plato's own experience in democratic Athens provided an excellent example of how this might unfold. Among other things, he saw Athens lose a war to its rival, Sparta, due to poor decision making by voters and betrayals by prominent citizen-politicians (including the infamous Alcibiades, a Frank Underwood–type figure). As a result of this loss, Athens had its democratic government temporarily replaced by the vicious "Thirty Tyrants." Finally, when democracy was restored, a jury of Athenian citizens voted to execute Plato's mentor Socrates (469–399 BCE), largely because prominent Athenians found his philosophically challenging questions unpleasant. Socrates—like Zoe, Lucas, and Janine—suffered the consequences for asking the wrong questions to powerful people.

As Plato clearly recognized, the political success of people such as the Underwoods owes much to certain structural features of democracy. So, for example, while ordinary citizens in Athens were legally allowed to do things such as serve on juries or hold elected office, not just anyone could realistically gain or hold power. Instead, success in democratic politics was crucially affected by factors such as the media (in Athens, playwrights played a major role in shaping public opinion) and one's skill with rhetoric and oratory. This feature of democracy was in clear contrast to governments such as hereditary monarchies, military dictatorships, or oligarchies, where one's position in society was strictly determined by one's parents, skill in combat, or wealth. A skillful politician such as Frank Underwood could have succeeded brilliantly in Athens in a way he could not have anywhere else in the ancient world.

With this in mind, it should come as no surprise that Plato was a forceful critic of democracy. In the *Republic*, Plato has the character of Socrates describe both the *kallipolis* (the perfectly just city) and the means by which this perfect city would inevitably decay into tyranny (the worst form of government). According to this story, democracy is the second-worst form of government and leads inevitably to tyranny, since a figure like Frank Underwood will eventually succeed in taking power.

The process by which the *kallipolis* degenerates to tyranny is a gradual one. In the beginning, all decisions are made by a group of philosophically skilled, perfectly benevolent "guardians," who have no personal interests aside from the wellbeing of the city. Socrates suggests, however, that this system is unsustainable in the long run, since it would be impossible to consistently select the *correct* children for the ruling class, no matter how careful one was with breeding and education. These problems would eventually lead the city to decay into first a *timocracy* (rule by the military elite), and then to an *oligarchy* (rule by the rich). The oligarchy, in turn, falls when a class of jealous, good-for-nothing "drones" instigate a revolt in an attempt to get their hands on the oligarchs' property. This event causes the establishment of what Plato has Socrates call the "second-worst" form of government—democracy. And, once democracy is founded, the time is ripe for a person like Frank Underwood—a *tyrant*, in Plato's terms—to take charge.

## Frank the (Unhappy?) Tyrant

> He who is the real tyrant, whatever men may think, is the real slave.... He has desires which he is utterly unable to satisfy, and has more wants than any one ... all his life long he is beset with fear and is full of convulsions, and distractions.
>
> —Plato, *Republic*, Book 9[2]

Frank and Claire's motives are, in some ways, relatively straightforward: They want to get as much political power as possible. All major decisions, from Frank's choice of which bills to support in Congress to Claire's choice to terminate her pregnancies, are made with this end in mind. Even their decision to stay together for so many years seems to be, in large part, due to their recognition that they *need* each other to achieve this goal, however much they (and, in particular, Claire) might dislike this dependence. It is this single-mindedness (together with a fair bit of intelligence and luck) that allows them to defeat their political opponents, many of whom are "distracted" by desires for sex, drugs, money, or love, or even by ethical scruples.

In the view of Plato's Socrates, the souls of would-be tyrants are something like miniature versions of the tyrannical state as a whole, with a single illicit desire serving as a sort of dictator. Something similar holds for the other governments and their potential rulers: The philosophers (like the *kallipolis* they would rule) are governed by reason, the militaristic timocrats by a desire for honor and victory, and the oligarchs by greed. Finally, the democratic person treats all desires "equally," and allows him- or herself to follow whatever passion happens to be strongest at the moment. For Plato, a person like Peter Russo (with his mix of moral and immoral behavior, and his widely ranging desires) would be something like the prototypical democratic politician, with a prototypical democratic "soul." On this view, democratic leaders are chosen not for any particular talents they have, but rather for the way they appeal to the temporary whims of the voters, and for their willingness to give the masses "freedom" to pursue whatever ends they desire. Unfortunately, according to Plato, this setup makes democracies perfect targets for tyrants such as Frank, who can use the democrats' love for freedom and equality to undermine and destroy the governments they create.

In the *Republic*, the inevitable collapse of democracy is described as having its roots in a conflict between the self-interested, politically powerful "drones" (which are in abundance on *House of Cards*) and the rich citizens whose money these drones want to take. These drones, in turn, justify their actions to the people at large by claiming they are defending them from the "oligarchs." Finally, in response to this, the richest citizens (such as Raymond Tusk) respond by becoming "oligarchs in fact" and using their economic power to try to dominate the masses. In Season 2, for instance, Tusk attempts to use his considerable power to force the reluctant President Walker (and, by extension, the people he represents) to bow to his demands.

According to Plato, this sort of conflict (which arises in *all* democracies) will eventually be exploited by potential tyrants such as the Underwoods. All they need to do is to present themselves as "protectors" of the people who are willing to protect them from the oligarchs. It helps if the tyrants-to-be can, like the Underwoods, offer "honey" to the various drones that dominate the democratic government, and can make vague promises to distribute the oligarch's wealth to the voters. When attempts are made to threaten or harm the rising tyrants (for example, when Claire's life is threatened), these attempts actually play into the tyrants' hands, convincing the democratic politicians and voters to grant the rising tyrants even more power and control. In reality, of course, a tyrant cares nothing for either the drones or the people at large, but is instead concerned only with satisfying his or her own tyrannical desire.

The Underwoods would presumably be thrilled with the predicted outcome of this process, which is the eventual success of the tyrant over the remaining democrats, and the replacement of democracy with an absolute dictatorship (Frank as President is unlikely to accept things like term limits or judicial checks on executive power). Socrates argues, however, that the structure of the tyrant's soul guarantees that he will be just as unhappy as the citizens he dominates. After all, successful tyrants must lead lives of continual fear and paranoia, can have no true friends, and can never dedicate a moment's thought to pursuing any pleasure except the (insatiable) lust that has driven them to become tyrants in the first place. And this, in fact, is precisely what happens to Frank when he finally achieves the presidency in Season 3. In his quest for *absolute* power, he tries to force his will on people such as Jackie Sharp, Remy Danton, Tom Yates, and even Claire. The results of these actions are all too predictable, and Frank is, in the end, left with no "friends" at all, but with increasing numbers of (powerful) enemies. On Plato's view, the more "successful" a tyrant is politically, the more he undermines any chance he has for a meaningful or happy life.

## From Hobbes to Hegel: Why Monarchs Rule

Now in Monarchy, the private interest is the same with the public.... For no King can be rich, nor glorious, nor secure; whose subjects are either poor, or contemptible, or too weak through want, or dissention, to maintain a war against their enemies. Whereas in a Democracy, or Aristocracy, the public prosperity confers not so much to the private fortune of one that is corrupt, or ambitious, as doth many times a perfidious advice, a treacherous action, or a civil war.

—Thomas Hobbes, *Leviathan*, Chapter 19[3]

While Plato's *Republic* provides a possible explanation for the success of the Underwoods, Plato makes it clear that he does not approve of tyranny, which he considers the worst of all possible forms of government (even worse than democracy!). Some later political philosophers, however, argued that Plato's characterization of tyranny was flawed, and that "tyrant" was just a word used to describe a monarch the writer disliked. Two of the most influential of these thinkers— Thomas Hobbes (1588–1679) and G.W.F. Hegel (1770–1831)—went on to argue that the ultimate destruction of democracy by a figure such as Frank Underwood was not only to be expected but also was actually desirable, as it solved many of the problems inherent in popular rule.

Thomas Hobbes lived through the decade-long English Civil War, which had disastrous effects for the citizens of the British Isles. In Hobbes's famous work *Leviathan*, he argued that this sort of war of "all against all" could be ended only when a single person—the monarch—gained absolute power. On Hobbes's social contract theory, the monarch is morally justified in wielding this power precisely because every rational citizen should consent to this arrangement, given the highly unpleasant alternative. Hobbes argues that democracy, by contrast, is an inferior form of government that, at best, might serve as a stepping stone to such a monarchy. Many of the problems that Hobbes identifies with democracy are apparent in *House of Cards*. For example, Hobbes argues that democratic politicians are likely to be both corrupt and ineffectual. This is because their personal success is disconnected from the long-term success of the state as a whole. Such politicians are also prone to arguing among themselves and to dividing the country. By contrast, he argues that a monarch's self-interest (who serves for life, and who will pass on the throne to a child or personally chosen heir) is much more tightly tied to the success of the state as a whole. Hobbes' idea here is a simple one: While the Underwoods might behave in ways that harm the country *now*, they would be foolish to continue doing so if, finally, they were to achieve the absolute power they seek. As a President who desires to keep his job, for example, Frank has a much stronger interest in making sure that America Works actually *works* than he would have when he was merely a congressional leader, or even a Vice President. The same thing might be said about his proposed Middle East peace plan, or his attempts to improve the relationship with Russia. The problem with merely "partisan" politics, in Hobbes' view, is that the sorts of politicians who engage in them can't really be "held to account" for the success or failure of their ideas in the way an absolute monarch can.

In his *Elements of the Philosophy of Right*, the German philosopher G.W.F. Hegel defended constitutional monarchy on somewhat similar grounds.[4] For one thing, Hegel thought that democracy demanded far too much moral "virtue" of its citizens and politicians. For related reasons, he also argued that a complex modern state required a degree of specialization and expertise that made it practically impossible for ordinary people to both help govern in a meaningful sense and also fulfill their responsibilities in their professional and personal lives. Finally, and most importantly, Hegel argued that the monarch allowed the people to express their will as a unified whole, and become something other than the "formless mass" that made decisions in a democracy. The basic idea here is that citizens identify with powerful leaders such as Frank and Claire, and it is this, more than anything else, that allows them to feel that they are all "part of the same nation." Hegel's admiration for ambitious, domineering (and antidemocratic) figures such as Napoleon suggests that he too might have found something admirable in the Underwoods' ruthless quest for absolute power, so long as it proved successful. Nor is Hegel alone in thinking this. Tom Yates astutely comes to realize that people's willingness to support ideas such as America Works is less a matter of them understanding the "fine details" (or even the constitutionality) than of their identifying with Frank and Claire as *people*.

## Are the Underwoods Marxist Revolutionaries?

The sum total of these relations of production constitutes the economic structure of society—the real foundation, on which rise legal and political superstructures and to which correspond definite forms of social consciousness.... It is not the consciousness of men that determines their existence, but, on the contrary, their social being that determines their consciousness.

—Karl Marx, *A Contribution to a Critique of Political Economy*, Preface[5]

Plato, Hobbes, and Hegel all agree that the "fatal flaw" of democracies has to do with the internal structures of their governments, and specifically the relationship between the voters and the politicians that are supposed to carry out their will. According to these thinkers, people such as the Underwoods attain power by exploiting certain *political* conflicts that arise in democracies. According to another famous critic of democracy, the German philosopher and economist Karl Marx (1818–1883), this is the wrong way of looking at things. In his view, both the initial creation of democratic governments and (perhaps) their eventual replacement by something else are merely side effects of the economic relationships between the various groups in that society. So, if we want to understand how someone like Frank Underwood could achieve power, we need to "follow the money" that makes this possible.

Marx thought that a society's social, political, and religious institutions could be analyzed in terms of the "modes of production" existing in that society, and that changes in these institutions could be explained by changes in the underlying modes of production. Here, *mode of production* refers to the methods of producing goods, which includes both technology (such as factories, railroads, computers, and phones) and the human labor used to operate this technology. It also includes the legal and social relationships that affect how the goods in question are produced and distributed. In *House of Cards*, for instance, Marx might well have been interested in the political influence wielded by corporations such as SanCorp and by wealthy individuals such as Raymond Tusk and Xander Feng.

Where the thinkers discussed earlier focused on describing the "political" transitions between democratic and nondemocratic forms of government, Marx instead focused on economic transitions based on changing modes of production. A simplified version of Marx's theory might go as follows. In the feudal societies of medieval Europe, a small group of aristocrats controlled the land, which was cultivated by much larger groups of serfs. Eventually, however, a somewhat larger group of nonaristocratic "bourgeois" acquired enough control over emerging industrial technologies (the new "capital") to make the old system unsustainable, and a capitalist system arose in its place. The sort of representative democracy founded in the United States (with its large numbers of voters and strong property rights) represented, for Marx, one of the most highly developed capitalist societies of the day. The world inhabited by the Underwoods, like our own, might be seen as a further development of this same sort of society.

While Marx clearly saw such capitalist democracies as an advance over previously existing forms of government, he predicted that they would ultimately be unsustainable for economic reasons. In particular, Marx predicted that over time the profits of the bourgeois capitalists would steadily decrease, and that the ownership of the capital itself would become increasingly concentrated in the hands of people like Raymond Tusk. Conversely, a larger and larger portion of the population would find themselves members of the *proletariat*—mere laborers who owned no capital, and who were at the mercy of the powerful capitalists (for example, think of the shipyard workers in Peter Russo's district who lose their jobs as a result of political maneuvering). This unsustainable situation would set the stage for the transition to *communism*, which would occur when the means of production were jointly owned by the members of society.

While Marx himself suggested that communism was likely to be brought about by a forceful revolution led by the working classes, it might also be caused by the actions of self-interested democratic politicians such as Frank Underwood. So, for example, while Frank himself is clearly not a communist, he is perfectly open to violating property rights if it serves his political advantage, as shown by his threat to nationalize Tusk's power plants or by his proposal to cut

Social Security and Medicare to provide jobs for the unemployed. On Marx's theory, this makes perfect sense—many self-interested politicians should certainly take the side of the (ever-growing) proletariat over the (ever-shrinking) bourgeoisie, even if this requires breaking the existing political and legal "rules" (as Frank is clearly willing to do).

Marx himself is somewhat unclear about what happens immediately after this initial communist "revolution," though he briefly discusses a transitional "dictatorship of the proletariat," in which the new government temporarily assumes control of producing and distributing goods, in an effort to keep the (still-powerful) bourgeois capitalists from taking back their former place.[6] While Marx suggests that this would eventually lead to a classless, fully democratic, communist society, one can also imagine the newly formed dictatorships (especially if they happen to include people such as Frank) holding on tightly to their newly found power.

## Are the Underwoods Unstoppable?

According to writers as diverse as Plato, Hobbes, Hegel, and Marx, the destruction of democracy by people such as the Underwoods is inevitable. Moreover, according to many of these thinkers, this was actually a good thing! In the face of such arguments, what can a defender of democracy say?

The English philosopher and economist John Stuart Mill (1806–1873) provides one possible answer. Mill, together with his wife Harriet Taylor Mill (1807–1858), was a strong supporter of democratic causes such as free speech, women's rights, and the abolition of slavery. In *Considerations on Representative Government*, Mill argues that antidemocratic thinkers underestimate the potential strengths of democratic governments *even if* the politicians occasionally turn out to be as selfish and ruthless as Frank Underwood.[7] In particular, Mill argues that the structure of democracies, unlike monarchies and aristocracies, guarantees that the leaders have to be somewhat responsive to people's interests (after all, there are elections to think of). He also suggests that democracies are likely to make better informed decisions than alternative forms of government, since even self-interested, powerful politicians such as the Underwoods will see the political value in consulting both their constituents and outside experts when trying to make difficult decisions. Finally, he notes that the citizens in democracies benefit from the mere fact of their participation in government—they feel more responsible for their fellow citizens, take the time to inform themselves about political decisions, and so on.

Another way of putting Mill's basic idea might be this: One main virtue of a well-functioning democracy is it will not *allow* a purely selfish and ruthless person such as Frank Underwood to succeed, at least in the long run. If Frank wants to have a successful presidency, he will need to establish and maintain good relationships with other *people*, including the press, judiciary, other politicians, his constituents, and even Claire. And this, in turn, will require that he take their interests into account.

On this view, the mere possibility of the events portrayed on *House of Cards* is not, by itself, a reason to abandon representative democracy. Instead, the Underwoods serve as a helpful reminder about the various things that we need to keep our democracy healthy, including fair elections in which all voters can take part, a free and strong press, and a political system that allows for effective checks against unscrupulous politicians such as the Underwoods. These are the sorts of important and realistic goals that we, as individual citizens, must keep in mind when we turn off Netflix and consider what *we* might do to stop the Underwoods.

## Notes

1. Plato, *The Dialogues of Plato: Republic, Timaeus, Critias*, trans. Benjamin Jowett (London: Macmillan, 1892).
2. Ibid.
3. Thomas Hobbes, *Leviathan* (Cambridge: Cambridge University Press, 1996).
4. Georg Wilhelm Friedrich Hegel, *Elements of the Philosophy of Right*, trans. H. B. Nisbet (Cambridge: Cambridge University Press, 1991).
5. Karl Marx, *A Contribution to the Critique of Political Economy*. Translated by N.I. Stone. (Chicago: Charles H. Kerr & Company, 1904).
6. For example, see section 4 of Karl Marx, "Critique of the Gotha Program," in *Karl Marx: Selected Writings* (Indianapolis, IN: Hackett, 1994).
7. John Stuart Mill, *Considerations on Representative Government* (London: Longman, Green, 1865).

# 13

# "Money Gives Power ... Well, a Run for Its Money"

## Marx's Observations on Why Capital and Not Frank Is Really in Charge of the White House

### Chris Byron and Nathan Wood

On several occasions, Frank Underwood has paused from his laborious scheming to inform the enraptured viewers that power is preferable to money. Frank isn't the only character in *House of Cards* to hold this preference. Doug Stamper turns down a job with the Congressman from Hawaii who is willing to pay Doug tens of thousands of dollars more than Frank, in hopes of returning to Frank's staff. And Frank's serpentine director of communications, Seth Grayson, breaks his lucrative contract with billionaire Raymond Tusk in order to join Claire Underwood's public relations detail. Of course, none of these carnivorous power seekers are poor or living paycheck to paycheck, but whenever they can decide between money or power, they always opt for power. Well, almost always. By the beginning of Season 3, Frank's unrelenting quest for power is finally consummated when he becomes President of the United States. Within a short period of becoming Commander-in-Chief, however, Frank is informed by the Democratic leadership that they will not back him for reelection. That evening, Frank spends hours drunkenly calling up the top 50 party donors hoping he can garner their monetary support and thus outflank the Democratic leadership. As he's seemingly violating his rule to opt for power over money, he informs the viewer that in the case of winning elections, "*Money gives power ... well, a run for its money.*"

*House of Cards and Philosophy: Underwood's Republic*,
First Edition. Edited by J. Edward Hackett.
© 2016 John Wiley & Sons, Ltd. Published 2016 by John Wiley & Sons, Ltd.

But why should it? After all, Frank is the most powerful man in the United States. The radical philosopher and political activist Karl Marx (1818–1883) would not be surprised by Frank's predicament. In fact, Marx said that "the executive of the modern state is but a committee for managing the common affairs of the whole bourgeoisie."[1] Marx isn't just pointing out that large amounts of money are necessary for running a viable election, and that capitalists have a lot of money to offer. That claim is obviously true, and no doubt the capitalists expect favors in return for their donations. Instead Marx is pointing out that the function of the state is to operate in the interests of the bourgeoisie, a class of people whose function is to act in the interests of capital. Capital is the flow of value through our economy that allows for the production of more commodities and the acquisition of more money. The role of the capitalist is to increase the flow of capital in society.

Marx's claim may sound extreme. After all, wasn't Karl Marx just a cantankerous nineteenth-century radical who would be incapable of making true statements about the modern state? Perhaps Marx was cantankerous; but Frank, his (temporary) allies, and his enemies show that Marx's claim is correct. Marx believes the *supposedly* democratic state is ultimately an instrument for sorting out the economic differences and conflicts faced by the bourgeoisie, which is the capitalist class. When Marx refers to the bourgeoisie, he has in mind people like Raymond Tusk and Xander Feng. These are the people who own the means of production, and the tools and raw materials necessary for production. These capitalists have lackey lobbyists like Remy Danton to do their political bidding. But Marx wants to argue that even our political representatives are ultimately the lackeys of the capitalists. At the very least, these representatives are not representing everyone equally. Rather, they are overwhelmingly concerned with representing the interests of the capitalists. Frank Underwood claims to represent no one but himself. So if it can be shown that even a man like Frank is conditioned by the will of capitalists, then we have serious cause for concern. Marx would be right after all.

## Marx's Method of Historical Analysis

Marx's theory of historical materialism explains the overwhelming influence that capitalists have over the state. In his 1859 preface to

*A Contribution to a Critique of Political Economy*, Marx explained his method of critical analysis:

> In the social production of their existence, men inevitably enter into definite relations, which are independent of their will, namely relations of production appropriate to a given stage in the development of their material forces of production. The totality of these relations of production constitutes the economic structure of society, the real foundation, on which arises a legal and political superstructure and to which correspond definite forms of social consciousness. The mode of production of material life conditions the general process of social, political and intellectual life. It is not the consciousness of men that determines their existence, but their social existence that determines their consciousness.[2]

This passage contains Marx's most succinct description of historical materialism, a theory that is popular for many reasons, including Marx's development of the base–superstructure model of societal analysis. The *base* is a metaphor for the *economic structure* of a society. By economic structure, Marx is referring to the forces and relations of production. The forces of production are composed of two primary components: labor power and the means of production. Labor power is our capacity to work in the most general sense, for instance Freddy's ability to make the best ribs in DC, or Zoe Barnes's ability to write a contentious article. The means of production are the instruments of labor, such as Freddy's smoker and kitchen equipment, and the raw materials that are incorporated into the operation (for example, BBQ sauce and electricity). These forces of production are organized by a particular social relation among the people interacting with them. Previous examples of social relations around the means of production have been master to slave, and lord to serf. Presently, they are capitalist to proletariat. In our society, the capitalists *privately* own the means of production, and members of the proletariat sell their labor power for momentary access to the means of production. This arrangement between the forces and relations of production constitutes the base or economic structure of society. Historically speaking, this form of economic organization is recent, unique, and by no means necessary, no matter how natural it appears to us. In past modes of society, one could engage the means of production without social mediation in order to produce sustenance. Presently the proletariat needs access to the means of production in order to receive the wages necessary to purchase sustenance goods.

Marx argues that the superstructure (for instance, the legal, political, judicial, and cultural institutions) arises from the base. The base *conditions* the superstructure.[3] More importantly, the base is a *necessary condition* for the existence of the superstructure. It's important to note what Marx means by conditioning here. Our political and legal structure, for instance, often espouses certain rights and duties that citizens have, which are always in conformity with the base of society (like the right to vocally protest Claire's abortion). It may seem that the very existence of legal rights contradicts the thesis that the state necessarily reflects the interests of the predominant economic system. After all, don't these same rights serve as constraints upon what businesses do? Not necessarily. Legal rights on paper only truly constrain the interests of capitalism if they can do so in practice. However, legal rights are largely a "pay to play" system, since enforcing them *requires* enough money to afford a lawyer and other costs associated with a lawsuit (not to mention affording competent counsel that can effectively combat the high-priced legal teams of corporations). Legal rights *seem* to give people the power of constraining capital, but that is only an effective reality for the bourgeoisie. Marx saw that a society cannot achieve social justice without first addressing its economic base.

Consider also that the right to property is the right to *bourgeois property*. The right to freedom is the right to freely maintain the present *social relations* that reproduce the economic structure of society. Frank Underwood, Garrett Walker, Jackie Sharp, and even Donald Blythe are members of the superstructure who are constantly conditioned by, and legislate in the interests of, maintaining the base (that is, the economic structure) of society. This is why it is true that the state merely sorts out the interests of the bourgeoisie. Since the bourgeoisie own the means of production and this economic arrangement conditions the structure and values of the state, the government inevitably ends up reflecting the interests of the dominant economic players.

## A Case Study in Historical Materialism: Frank for VP

One example of the base having vast conditional influence over the superstructure can be found in the first season of *House of Cards*. Frank consistently serves the interests of capitalists in order to climb from House Whip to Vice President. The primary reason Frank is gunning for the Vice Presidency is power. The President broke his promise to make Frank Secretary of State, and the reason the President went back on his promise demonstrates the veracity of Marx's claim. The capitalist Raymond Tusk—as the President's primary advisor—felt Frank would better serve their economic interests whipping votes in Congress favorable to their preferred market policies. The initial promise to let Frank be Secretary of State was offered because Frank was able to help President Walker fund his campaign via SanCorp dollars. SanCorp wanted to help put Frank and Garrett into higher echelons of government in return for future favors and legislation that would suit their business interests.

Throughout Season 1, Frank, Tusk, and Remy run things. Tusk reveals his hand in almost all of President Walker's policies, while Remy's agenda is even more explicit in furthering the flow of capital. Frank's repeated support of power over money quickly brings him into contention with Remy and SanCorp over the watershed bill that puts severe restrictions upon SanCorp's ability to drill for natural gas in Pennsylvania. Remy first approaches Claire to try to gain some influence on Frank, but she initially turns down the offer, after Frank insists they not be tied too closely to the interests of SanCorp. When Claire needs $200,000 worth of water filters brought back from Sudan, she initially seeks the assistance of Secretary of State Kathy Durant, who had been recommended for her diplomatic position by Frank because her diplomacy was favorable to SanCorp. SanCorp needed Frank to return a favor after they donated to many Democratic campaigns. Unfortunately, Durant is unable to come through in securing the water filters. Since Durant is unable to help Claire—due to rapidly declining relations between the United States and Sudan—Claire is forced to approach SanCorp directly.

Remy and SanCorp do not share Durant's problem. As Remy states, eerily echoing Marx's view of the state, "wherever there's a government we know people, even where there's only the illusion of a government." Knowing people in government extends to not only politicians but also those closest to them. SanCorp's willingness to support Claire's nonprofit organization is not an act of charity. Rather, it is an attempt to illicitly create a position of influence over Claire and, by default, make Frank beholden to their interests.

# AmWorks: Is Frank's Goal a Capitalist Goal?

The central aim of Frank's presidency, in Season 3, might appear to contradict Marx's thesis that the state is merely a sorting house for the bourgeoisie to resolve their market conflicts. If capitalism, and the bourgeois class as a whole, are always in some sense the winners when it comes to legislative changes, then how could Marx's theory explain bills like America Works, or a similar real-life analogue such as FDR's New Deal? These reforms appear to benefit the working class by guaranteeing them employment, and thus appear to contradict the thesis that the state always acts in the interests of the bourgeoisie. However, Marx's thesis that the state always acts to benefit the interests of capitalism and the bourgeoisie is not always in conflict with policies that give immediate benefit to the proletariat. There is only an actual contradiction of Marx's thesis when the interests of capitalism are harmed and the economic system gains no benefit from the legislation. In some cases, capitalism working in its own interest is mutually compatible with certain concessions to the working class. President Underwood's America Works plan is one such case.

AmWorks, the bumper-sticker nickname for Frank's key piece of legislation, promises to create 10 million jobs in order to end unemployment. The plan is fairly simple, as Frank puts it: "If you want a job, you get one." Those interested in getting a job simply need to enroll in the plan. However, AmWorks does not come without some significant costs. The so-called entitlement programs (Social Security, Medicare, and Medicaid) are essentially eliminated, and the money is redirected into creating infrastructure and construction jobs as well as guaranteeing up to $45,000, in yearly salary, for each person hired under the program. In one sense, it's clear how the proletariat *does not* benefit from this plan, given the elimination of those entitlement programs that help to keep much of the working class afloat.

The important question—for establishing Marx's thesis—is whether AmWorks constrains or contradicts the interests of capitalism. On that score, it seems very clear that it does in fact, *on the whole*, benefit such interests. Take, for instance, the fact that in order for a business to stay financially competitive, the amount of money it pays out to its employees must be as little as possible in order to maximize profit. This leads to the problem many businesses have, where a conflict exists between the wage paid to each employee and the number of employees necessary to efficiently run the business. Under the AmWorks plan, businesses can hire more employees without, in theory, incurring any extra costs for hiring the new employees (assuming that they simply offer the employee a salary of $45,000 or less per year, which the government will subsidize). Having more employees, with little to no extra costs, makes it possible for the company to increase its production, and by increasing its production it simultaneously increases its potential for profit. Even when this plan appears to be for the good of the working class, it ultimately ends up aiding capitalism and the bourgeoisie. After all, if it was really a threat to the totality of bourgeois interests, the candidates who would be willing to vote for AmWorks would rapidly lose funding and donations, and would be replaced by candidates more favorable to bourgeois interests.

## Capitalist versus Capitalist: AmWorks and Walmart

It may still seem possible to argue that not all legislation is in the interest of the bourgeoisie. Heather Dunbar, Frank's primary campaign rival for President, gives a speech to a crowd of supporters, explaining how Walmart takes advantage of Medicaid and food stamp programs to *underpay* their employees, and not provide them with decent health care and wages, knowing full well that the taxpayers will bear the costs. Dunbar convincingly argues that this is one of the ways in which the government subsidizes the costs of big business against the interests of the working class. In one sense, this shows how a working-class victory like Medicaid can still be exploited by the bourgeoisie to ultimately favor their market interests, but this raises a possible issue with Marx's thesis.

If Frank drastically cuts the social welfare state in order to fund AmWorks, then Walmart may have to start paying their employees more, or start hiring more full-time workers. Alternatively, Frank's bill could die, as the Democratic leadership desires, and Walmart could continue their policies unabated. In that case, though, full employment will not be obtained. There are multiple tensions here between various competing interests. Walmart is certainly a capitalist enterprise, and it is managed by capitalists. Therefore, they may want to defeat AmWorks, whereas many other capitalists may desire the passing of AmWorks in order to subsidize their hiring costs and increase productivity and profits. If capitalists are divided, can we really say the state always acts in their interest?

Marx's claim that the state is a committee for the bourgeoisie to sort out their conflicts is entirely capable of wrestling with the Walmart and AmWorks contention. Marx's claim is not that every capitalist will get what he or she wants all of the time, or that the state is conflict free. Instead, the claim is that the state is where the bourgeoisie sort out many of their affairs. In this case, if AmWorks is passed, although Walmart might lose, the capitalists will win overall, since an increase in the rate of profit and productivity *across* the United States is over-all better for capitalism. Thus, Frank's legislative agenda is ultimately conditioned by the wills of capitalists.

## Worker Victories: Class Warfare and Class Conflict

Marx argued that capitalism is a system that inherently involves class conflict. Overall, the interests of the working class are contrary to the interests of the capitalist class. For instance, when SanCorp and Raymond Tusk are engaged in mutual corporate takeover, the liveli-hoods and continued employment of their respective workers are never cause for concern. Under a capitalist system, more wages and benefits for workers hurt their employers' bottom line, and an improved bottom line for their employers often deprives workers of better compensation. Even if a capitalist wants to be beneficent and pay as much as he can to his workers, he still has to compete in an economic market driven by the profit motive, and any *overcompensation* runs the risk of losing market share. The capitalist needs to reinvest the profit he makes into growth and increased productivity if he wants to retain his market position; thus, he is constrained in how beneficent he can be toward his employees. This contradiction is best embodied in Raymond Tusk, who often appears as a down-to-earth unflashy business owner, but also a ruthless market competitor.

One may want to see capitalism as not involving class conflict but class cooperation. But, as Marx argued in *Capital*, the working class is consistently exploited.[4] In order for capitalism to generate more value, capitalists have to hire workers and purchase means of production. Once the workers engage the means of production and produce a commodity worth more than the initial capital investment, the capitalist then sells the commodity for a profit. Capitalists like to argue that the profit comes from shrewdness and cunning, but in fact it comes from exploitation. The capitalist *appears* to be paying the workers for their work, but he is in fact only paying them for *their ability to work* (their labor power). What the capitalist receives in return is their *actual labor*. For a portion of a work period, the worker produces enough value to reproduce his ability to come to work again (a wage is paid to reproduce his labor power). Once that amount of value has been produced, all the additional value goes into the hands of the capitalist. The workers are exploited, but they can also resist.

Because they can fight back via voting, there's one final way in which Marx's claim could seem dubious. Many fans of *House of Cards* may want Heather Dunbar to become President (even if they secretly love rooting for Frank). It is certainly not impossible for Dunbar to win, even if Frank is a ruthless and unscrupulous opponent. If Dunbar doesn't become president in the world of *House of Cards*, someone like her could *maybe* become President in the real world. People like Dunbar who are born into wealth can in some sense bypass the need to receive donations from numerous capitalistic organizations in implicit exchange for friendly legislation. So if someone like Dunbar became President, they could pass a minimum-wage increase, striking a blow against many capitalists and delivering a boon for the working class. Wouldn't *this* hypothetical event refute Marx's thesis?

In his *Address to the Central Committee to the Communist League*, Marx scoffs at the idea that progressive legislation could be wholly sufficient for alleviating the plight of the working class.

> The democratic petty bourgeois, far from wanting to transform the whole society in the interests of the revolutionary proletarians, only aspire to make the existing society as tolerable for themselves as possible.... As far as the workers are concerned one thing, above all, is definite: they are to remain wage labourers as before. However, the democratic petty bourgeois want better wages and security for the workers; in short, they hope to bribe the workers.[5]

Because capitalism is so class divisive, from time to time workers will rebel, and they will demand more. For as long as capitalism has existed, workers have rebelled (examples include the Railroad strikes of 1886, the Pullman strikes of 1894, the steel strikes from 1919 to 1920, and the 1981 PATCO strikes). Workers may want universal health care, improved wages, guaranteed holidays, and so on. So they could hypothetically organize and elect a Heather Dunbar figure, and she could hypothetically pass worker-friendly legislation. But this would not constitute a falsification of Marx's claim, if we recognize the state's role as an instrument for mediating the overall interests of the capitalists. Capitalism involves an ongoing class conflict, because its engine of profit is predicated upon continued exploitation. Thus, the bourgeoisie may begrudgingly lose a few battles in order to continue winning the (class) war, like they did during the New Deal.[6] If the working class ever becomes too rowdy, the capitalists could *squash* such rowdiness by force (for example, the Homestead strike of 1892) or by allowing Dunbar to win. Squashing the rowdiness may reveal the capitalist hand too explicitly, increasing the working class's awareness of their exploited position. By contrast, if the capitalists allow their representatives to support Dunbar's minimum-wage legislation, in return they will receive a complacent work force and stabilized markets. So even when the capitalists appear to be losing, capitalism as a whole continues winning, and working-class exploitation continues. The playing field of class conflict is never level as long as the capitalistic base continues to condition the superstructure.

## Liberal Democracy Is Overrated

The position we have defended in this chapter is that the state cannot help but serve the long-term interests of capitalism. Over the past few decades, many political scientists and theorists have considered Marx's work to be irrelevant for analyzing contemporary politics, but if the world of *House of Cards* mirrors our political reality, then Marx remains a powerful and relevant resource for examining our political landscape. The only time we see the working class depicted in *House of Cards* is when Frank suppresses the shipbuilders' and teachers' unions. According to Frank, the interest of Donald Blythe and the teachers' union is "left of Karl Marx." However, Marx's theory shows that a concession to the teachers' unions can still be strategically to the advantage of the capitalists, so long as we continue to reproduce the same economic structure of society. Most importantly of all, Marx shows that as long as capitalism flourishes, the idea that we live in a democracy of equal representation is false. Frank knows this too. When he's being sworn into office as Vice President, he turns toward the viewer and states with equanimity, "One heartbeat away from the presidency, and not a single vote cast in my name—democracy is so overrated."

# Notes

1. Karl Marx and Friedrich Engels, *The Communist Manifesto* (Brooklyn, NY: Verso, 2012), 37.
2. Karl Marx, *A Contribution to a Critique of Political Economy* (Ithaca, NY: Cornell University Press, 2009), 11–12.
3. Some readers of Marx argue that the base *determines* the superstructure. We disagree with that reading. For more, see Alex Callinicos's commendable book on the subject, *Making History: Agency, Structure, Change* (Boston: Historical Materialism, 2009).
4. Karl Marx, *Capital: Volume I: A Critique of Political Economy* (New York: Penguin, 1992).
5. https://www.marxists.org/archive/marx/works/1847/communist-league/1850-ad1.htm (retrieved June 30, 2015).
6. Sam Gindin and Leo Panitch, *The Making of Global Capitalism: The Political Economy of American Empire* (Brooklyn, NY: Verso, 2013), 45–67.

# 14

# Freedom and Democracy in a House of Fear

## Roberto Sirvent and Ian Diorio

*Democracy is not an institution, but essentially an anti-institutional force, a "rupture" in the otherwise relentless trend of powers-that-be to arrest change, to silence and to eliminate from the political process all those who have not been "born" into power.... Democracy expresses itself in continuous and relentless critique of institutions; democracy is an anarchic, disruptive element inside the political system; essential, as a force of dissent and change. One can best recognize a democratic society by its constant complaints that it is not democratic enough.*

—Zygmunt Bauman[1]

Frank Underwood is an example of excessive political ambition. He's also our go-to man for twisted leadership quips like "Power is a lot like real estate. It's all about location, location, location. The closer you are to the source, the higher your property value." So it's no surprise that when Frank is denied the Secretary of State post, he sets out to publicly disgrace and disempower his fiercest political enemies. In the first season, Frank orchestrates an elaborate plan to gain a cabinet position. Using his extramarital partner Zoe Barnes, a young and ambitious reporter, Frank leaks stories about his congressional opponents that lead to their eventual demise. His shrewd tactics do not

*House of Cards and Philosophy: Underwood's Republic,*
First Edition. Edited by J. Edward Hackett.
© 2016 John Wiley & Sons, Ltd. Published 2016 by John Wiley & Sons, Ltd.

end there. Frank is able to use everything at his disposal to acquire information about opponents, to gain insider information for political negotiation, and to harness the media in shaping "public truth" for his own aggrandizement. Frank also bolsters his political power in a far more significant—and philosophically troubling—way. He relies on surveillance (both man and machine) to manipulate, intimidate, and control anyone who tries to diminish his, shall we say, "property value."

## The "Property Value" of a Surveillance State

If Frank wants power, then he *has* to control others. Power and control—he can't have one without the other. By extension, if a government wants power, then it's going to have to control others as well. Thus, a highly technocratic society such as ours transforms democracy in ways that are both exciting and frightening. In highlighting the formation, limitation, and manipulation of public knowledge in an age of mass observation, *House of Cards* raises important questions about the role of power and surveillance in a democracy. In a surveillance society, what happens to privacy? And what about our other freedoms? What parts of democracy are threatened or sacrificed when its citizens are being watched? And since the study of politics is essentially the study of *power*, we'd be wise to ask how (if at all) government surveillance is addressing the all-important question: *Who* is in charge?

This seems to be the question troubling Zoe when she ditches mainstream media for the sidelined Internet political magazine *Slugline*. Zoe's internal moral shift is made under the assumption that *Slugline* represents a pure form of media transmission, different from the centrist power-based media channels tied to political and capital power. So who *is* in charge? Who *does* have the power? Is it the people? Or has the rise of government surveillance transferred power to someone, or some*thing*, else? And so what if it has?

The power relationship is not clear in surveillance societies because surveillance is more than political. As a society, we have slipped into a voyeuristic mood. We are watched *and* watchers of others in a world that social theorists Zygmunt Bauman and David Lyon describe as "liquid surveillance":

Surveillance is a growing feature of daily news, reflecting its rapid rise to prominence in many life spheres. But in fact surveillance has been expanding quietly for many decades and is a basic feature of the modern world. As that world has transformed itself through successive generations, so surveillance takes on an ever changing character. Today, modern societies seem so fluid that it makes sense to think of them being in a 'liquid' phase. Always on the move, but often lacking certainty and lasting bonds, today's citizens, workers, consumers and travelers also find that their movements are monitored, tracked and traced. Surveillance slips into a liquid state.[2]

The problem of surveillance, then, is not restricted to worries of how or why the *government* is watching us. Rather, Bauman and Lyon note how the society of liquid surveillance includes work, labor, commerce, and even the private realm of social media. The line between public and private—the political and the personal—is now blurrier than ever. Consider the show's text-message visualizations of Zoe and Frank's conversations. While these *private* conversations have drastic *public* implications in their own right, the political problem runs much deeper. In a moment of rare naivety, Frank asks Zoe to delete his contact information and text exchanges from her phone. This information may be deleted from her phone but not from her telephone company's hard drive. And certainly not from the NSA's. Though some of the forms of self-surveillance are convenient and enjoyable, they may also create a society where all people are held under the watchful eye of a mass network of systems, monitoring and charting almost every human impulse and decision.

## Prison of Cards

What does it look like when the personal becomes political? In his landmark book *Discipline and Punish*, Michel Foucault (1926–1984) draws upon the architectural imagination of utilitarian philosopher Jeremy Bentham (1748–1832). Among many other ambitions, Bentham sought to design the perfect power structure, the panopticon, a prison in which all the prisoners are visible while the guards watch their activity in darkness. The panopticon for Foucault is not a benign material invention. It is a prime example of a modern technology that allows a small number of guards to control a large group of others through the watching (and potential manipulation) of the prisoners' behavior.

If modern society were shaped by a single metaphor, for Foucault, the prison is that metaphor. When cameras are everywhere, when all actions are subject to being captured for all time, when the public sphere is no longer distinct from the private sphere, life becomes a prison where the warden remains anonymous yet extremely powerful. The panopticon's power is its generality, its ubiquity. It can be nowhere and everywhere at the same time.

*House of Cards* highlights the world of "panopticism" come of age. Peter, Zoe, Rachel, and others show us how paralysis and fear go hand in hand with being watched. Can we honestly say that Russo has any true freedom left? What about Zoe? How free is she in the exchange and publication of ideas when those "ideas" are being manipulated by none other than the House Majority Whip? And then there's Rachel, who has little freedom left after committing the unpardonable state sin of, well, being in the wrong place at the wrong time. Yes, that place and time involved someone powerful. But that's precisely the point. Even when Rachel wanted to escape the government's watchful eye, she couldn't. As long as she has a phone—or, for that matter, a pulse—she will be found.

Sadly, their experiences are no different from those of people in authoritarian states who are constantly being monitored by their government. Claire is perfectly aware of this on her visit to free gay-rights activist Michael Corrigan. "I'm assuming this cell is bugged," she asks President Petrov's chief of staff. "Show me where the bug is," she tells him. "If Mr. Corrigan and I are to speak privately, I would like to be assured that it is truly private." After being informed that the bug was removed, Petrov (rather irritated) tells Frank, "Your wife values privacy." Petrov's lost control—just a little bit. And it's enough to make him paranoid. Even Claire and Frank's private cell phone conversation later in the episode isn't really private. No surprise, really. Neither to Frank nor Claire. "Viktor, if you're listening to this," Claire says, "please know I'm advocating on your behalf." The surveillance victims in *House of Cards* provide a mere snapshot of what a culture of fear does to everyone involved. They're left fearing for the lives that, in any real and important sense, have already been taken from them.

The extinction of privacy does not necessarily imply a centralized mechanism of control, as with some of the most notorious expressions of authoritarian governments. What usually comes to mind are the atrocities of Soviet Russia under Stalin, with the systematic wiring of phones and monitoring of all levels of human interaction. Stalin's paranoia led him to infringe on the privacy rights of not only his enemies but even his closest allies. They, too, were under an umbrella of suspicion and surveillance, making Stalin's cabinet one of the most dangerous places to be in Soviet Russia. Today, we instantly think of North Korea when the concepts of "oppressive" or "dictatorial" forms of surveillance are mentioned. In this form, the violation of privacy rights is understood as a centralized evil because it is done not for the good of its citizens, but for the monopolization of power of the few, in this case the ruler and his aristocracy.

What *House of Cards* shows is that authoritarianism can and *does* exist in a democracy. All it takes is a group of people with unchecked ambition who crave unchecked power. Heck, all it takes is *one* person who fits this bill. Consider the trickle-down effects of Frank's devious actions. Sure, Frank might only intend to cause headaches, bruises, or public relations disasters to those *directly* in the way of his quest for power. But it's hard to ignore how Frank's sinister tactics affect the ordinary citizen as well. Such collateral damage is inevitable when someone drives down the road to absolute control. People are betrayed and people get hurt. Frank himself says, "The road to power is paved with hypocrisy and casualties."

Why else is Frank able to use an event like a child dying to his strategic advantage? The viewer might *want* to think that Frank feels some remorse for what happened. But when all you care about is power, then, to put it simply, *all you care about is power*. In this case, the tragedy helps him regain power; it's one of power's "casualties." Frank finds it difficult to care about anything *but* power. Just think of how Frank reacts to human weakness or failure. For him, Peter Russo isn't someone who just made a mistake or is dealing with the messiness of being human. Nope, Peter is just someone else Frank can control. It would be nice (relatively speaking) to say that for Frank, people are just tools. But he doesn't want to *use* people so much as he wants to *control* them. After all, Frank doesn't kill Peter and Zoe because he can no longer *use* them. He does so because he can no longer *control* them. "I understand the Old Testament God," Frank tells the bishop, "whose power is absolute, who rules through fear." Yes, Frank, you understand that all too well.

## "Open" House?

Okay, we're afraid of North Korea and Frank Underwood, and we'd prefer that they just leave us alone. So what? Can we ever have the "right to be left alone" in our day and age? *House of Cards* would seem to answer no. Politics and privacy are *both* public *and* up for grabs to those who want to gain power. The encroaching surveillance society can cause citizens who long for privacy and freedom to draw back in fear that democracy and the spheres it creates are wasting away under the omnipotent eye of the panopticon. Doug's hold over Rachel is an example of this ever-present eye. We can consider this in light of George Orwell's (1903–1950) fictional work *1984* with its "thought police" and ever-present eye of the state (i.e., "Big Brother"). Who is "Big Brother" today? It seems the Orwellian Big Brother as a centralized state that observes the masses has been exchanged for the subliminal watch guard of all social fields.

With the birth of the "all-seeing eye" of the panopticon, we have lost the distinction between the public and the private. The Greeks birthed the notion of democracy and how it should be structured. Their vision involved a distinct way to view the public and private spheres of life. Citizens were afforded the freedom to cultivate a private life that may not necessarily be *distinct from* public life, but nonetheless left available the *option* of self-concealment. It doesn't seem like our world, nor the world of *House of Cards*, allows for this option. So can the typical Greek distinctions of public versus private function in a society of surveillance? And what is the nature of privacy, of aloneness, in a world of surveillance?

The erosion of privacy in a surveillance society raises more questions than it answers. And perhaps we have a right to worry. We get that. But this is where the "ethics of surveillance" conversation usually ends. "This is a democracy!" we exclaim. "So leave me alone!" The problem of surveillance, however, runs deeper than this. A healthy democracy is not just a society where people are "left alone." And a healthy democracy is not just one where people are allowed to vote. Too often, this is what we think when we see news coverage of a country celebrating their first election. "They have a democracy now!" we exclaim. Well, not exactly. Democracy is about much more.

## Say Nothing

Democracy requires dissent. More specifically, it requires the *freedom* to dissent, to disagree, and to question those in power. This is why a free press is so important. And this is the problem with Frank getting so close to Zoe. As democratic citizens, we shouldn't want the press so close to the people in power—the very people they're writing about. Business reporters, for example, lack journalistic integrity when they get too cozy with the Wall Street executives they're paid to write about. After all, who's more likely to run a story about embezzlement and corruption in Fortune 500 firms? A reporter who has no personal ties to these bankers or a reporter who buys them shots at his local bar? But let's focus on what *House of Cards* asks us: What happens when the main obstacle to a journalist's objective reporting is not a close personal tie, but a paranoid fear of punishment?

With this in mind, we're able to see more clearly the real threat of the surveillance state. How exactly does a surveillance state get in the way of a critical and questioning society? For one, it makes people *scared* to question. Take the world of *House of Cards*. Would *you* feel comfortable talking freely there? Sure, they will ignore what you have to say if it's harmless. But in the world of *House of Cards*, all it takes is for me is to be at the wrong place at the wrong time, listening in on the wrong conversation. I now find myself watched and threatened for the rest of my life. What I know *privately* is now a matter of *public* concern. It poses a direct threat to state power.

At its best, democracy creates free spaces for citizens to talk, debate, and deliberate about the common good. And it's pivotal that these spaces also allow people to *freely* question those in power. *Freely* is the key word here. After all, what good is it if I can critique the government in a public space if I'm going to be punished for it later? This highlights the relation between freedom and fear. Where there is fear, there can't be freedom. And a culture of surveillance plays off this. When an authoritarian society tries to control and eliminate dissenting voices, like Michael Corrigan's, these "spaces" are no longer free.

What we see in *House of Cards* is a culture of fear. Those in power fear what people might say, and those who have something to say fear the people in power. The people in power, like Frank, do not view reporters like Zoe as critically minded citizens. No, Frank sees them as enemies of the state—or at least enemies of his pursuit of power. In the state's view, one cannot both bow down and raise a middle finger to it. Dissent is now seen as an act of disloyalty. When Frank says, "From this moment on you are a rock. You absorb nothing, you say nothing, and nothing breaks you," we learn exactly what an authoritarian state wants from its citizens. If you *do* absorb something, make sure it's what the nation-state wants you to believe. If you *do* say something, make sure it's the pledge of allegiance. And if something *does* break you, make sure it's not your unflinching loyalty to the Red, White, and Blue!

Governments and their defenders argue that surveillance and keeping secrets are meant to secure freedom, not take it away. So if any right to privacy needs to be violated, or if any information has to be stolen and publicized, then it is only done for the greater good of a free democratic society. In short, we must learn to balance security and freedom. If freedom is taken away, it's done to protect us! That's what we're told. But there are at least two problems with that solution. First, security must serve liberty, not the other way around. Second, it's dangerous to have the *state* be the one left to determine when we've reached this careful "balance" of security and liberty. If the state generally acts in ways that will preserve its *own* power, the citizen's appeal to liberty will almost always take a back seat. If this doesn't sound troubling, it should. With the state deciding how much freedom is *too much* freedom, or how much privacy we *really* deserve, or what information is *valuable* information, what could possibly go wrong?

## Nobody Can Hear You ... Except Us

Fear is used to control. What the state hopes to do is take something that's dangerous to the state—namely, the act of questioning and criticizing those in power—and make it dangerous to the citizen. Breaking the fourth wall, Frank tells us that Zoe simply got what she deserved:

> Every kitten grows up to be a cat. They seem so harmless at first; small, quiet, lapping up their saucer of milk. But once their claws get long enough they draw blood. Sometimes from the hand that feeds them. For those of us climbing to the top of the food chain there can be no mercy. There is but one rule. Hunt or be hunted.

Given what might happen to us, we're told, we should think twice before speaking up. Frank's words encapsulate this idea: "Nobody can hear you. Nobody cares about you. Nothing will come of this." This is what the surveillance state wants us to believe. It wants us to think that no one will listen to us. And if they do, they won't care what we have to say. Plus, we'd be crazy to think that our silly questions and criticisms will actually change anything. So don't even try, we're told.

Control and punishment are therefore linked. The state, then, resorts to a form of violence. Rather than use the typical methods of governance—public argument through dialogue, critical thought, reflection, and so on—the state relies on authoritarian means. The authoritarian process of surveillance essentially trumps the democratic process of public engagement and criticism. We only need Frank to remind us of how ineffective our "most deliberative body" has become when he says, "Every Tuesday I sit down with the speaker and the majority leader to discuss the week's agenda. Well, 'discuss' is probably the wrong word … they talk while I imagine their lightly-salted faces frying in a skillet." What's the point of talking and debating if change will only come through the threats and coercion of the state? What is left might still be a society. But it's not a democracy.

The dangerous nature of the surveillance state subverts the democratic principles at play. No longer do the people rule and decide. No longer must the people be wary and keep an eye out for the state, which is always assuming greater power. No, now it is the government who must keep the people in check, always making sure the people are governed into proper submission. It's the same charge made by Pussy Riot in their dinner toast to President Petrov, "who is so open to criticism that most of his critics are in prison." But if democracy is going to survive, it's the people in government who should stand trial, not its dissidents.

Checks and balances still exist, but they have been turned against the very ones they were created to protect. *House of Cards* speaks volumes to this. Yes, the show is a cynical take on DC politics. But it also forces us to ask where we fall short, where we are headed, and where we *should* be headed. Democracy calls us to wrestle with these questions. The *tough* questions. The questions that could get us into trouble. "The fear of an out-of-control executive," we're told by Heather Dunbar, "is exaggerated." If she's right, then pardon our paranoia. But what if she's wrong?

# Notes

1. Zygmunt Bauman, *The Individualized Society* (Cambridge: Polity Press, 2001), 54–55.
2. Zygmunt Bauman and David Lyon, *Liquid Surveillance* (Cambridge: Polity Press, 2013), 32.

# Part V

# INTRAPERSONAL RELATIONSHIPS, SEXUALITY, AND RACE IN *HOUSE OF CARDS*

# 15

# Under the Covers with the Underwoods
## The Sexual Politics of the Underwood Marriage

*Jason Southworth and Ruth Tallman*

Since the show's debut, no conversation about *House of Cards* has made it far without the discussion coming around to the topic of the Underwoods' marriage. While everyone seems to have an opinion, it has always surprised us that so many people's views of the relationship are so negative. What surprises us further is the strong connection people want to draw between the sexual choices of the Underwood marriage and its overall health. In this chapter, we will consider the various facets of the relationship that we have heard raised as critiques. Because the Underwoods' sexual openness is the aspect of their relationship most likely to be judged negatively, a defense of their nonmonogamy will be our primary focus. Although many instances of adultery are immoral, we will argue that there is nothing inherently wrong with an open relationship such as the Underwoods'. Additionally, in their case in particular, nonmonogamy appears to be a strength, rather than a weakness, of their relationship.

## A Frank Discussion of Adultery

So, what actually makes adultery wrong? Philosopher Richard Wasserstrom has given this question some thought, and he identifies three factors that cause adulterous acts to be morally impermissible: (1) Adultery often involves promise breaking, (2) adultery often

*House of Cards and Philosophy: Underwood's Republic*,
First Edition. Edited by J. Edward Hackett.
© 2016 John Wiley & Sons, Ltd. Published 2016 by John Wiley & Sons, Ltd.

involves deception, and (3) adultery often causes pain.[1] When adultery breaks a promise, it is because the couple has agreed to sexual exclusivity. This promise is often, but not always, a part of official wedding vows. That said, what constitutes sexual exclusivity is still something couples need to discuss in some detail. While there are some clear-cut violations, like penetrative sex, there are also some gray areas. When a couple fights over flirting or the discovery of a hidden porn collection, it's often due to a disagreement regarding what constitutes sexual exclusivity. If marital rules are built on the promises the couple has made to each other, breaking those promises is wrong. Each spouse is operating on the assumption that the other will behave in a certain way, based on the promises, so when those agreements are violated, the nonviolator feels cheated and betrayed. The wrongness of deception works basically the same way; we are unable to make rational decisions in the absence of accurate information, and when we are deceived, our decisions and actions might be guided by misinformation that results from the deception. The wrongness of both promise breaking and deception also boils down to Wasserstrom's third factor—they are wrong in that they often cause pain, and causing unwarranted pain, especially to one's spouse, is quite wrong. The question is, does adultery cause pain in a way that is different than other kinds of pain that arise in a long-term relationship, in which flawed humans will inevitably let one another down?

In identifying these factors, Wasserstrom is not arguing that all instances of promise breaking, deception, and pain are wrong. He is claiming that when we object to adultery, it is due to some combination of these factors. In bringing this clarity to what makes adultery morally wrong, Wasserstrom also presents an outline for how to practice moral adultery. If a couple can avoid these three pitfalls, then they can morally have sex outside of their marriage.

## A New Type of Marriage Vow

We can pretty quickly dismiss any concern that Frank and Claire are breaking promises with their dalliances. Although we do not know what promises they might have made to each other on their wedding day or before, we do know that they now have an agreement of nonmonogamy. The Underwoods speak openly and frankly with each other about their affairs. In "Chapter 23," Frank and Claire do not just discuss the content of their sexual experiences, but they also reflect on the nature of their relationship. In this conversation, the couple laments the fact that their political success has limited their ability to act on their nonmonogamy. Frank says, "There's just too much at stake now, no one we can trust. We don't have the freedom we once did." They talk about how it is in some ways regrettable, but that it's a choice they made, a necessary sacrifice for the other things they want. This intimate conversation offers good evidence that their relationship explicitly involves an open agreement of mutual, non-promise-breaking nonmonogamy. The Underwoods have a relationship in which previous agreements are not taken for granted, and marital terms can be renegotiated in service of their goals. This aspect of their relationship is the heart of Wasserstrom's view—the content of a couple's promises don't really matter (one couple promises full sexual exclusivity to the point where even pornography is off-limits, whereas another agrees to complete sexual freedom); what matters is that the promises are mutually discussed and freely agreed upon. Likewise, it probably doesn't matter what the Underwoods did or did not publicly vow on their wedding day; the important thing is what promises and agreements they are currently working under.

## Tell Me No Lies

Even if explicit promises are not broken, a common (and legitimate) concern is that adultery will involve deception. The two main candidates for deception are the other spouse and the extramarital partner. Frank is pretty upfront with Zoe about what he's offering, telling her in "Chapter 4" that, as an older man, he will use her and then discard her. Zoe is up for the challenge, claiming that he can't hurt her (turns out she was wrong about that). We do not witness any deception on the part of Frank to Zoe with regard to their sexual relationship. We see equal transparency with Claire. In "Chapter 5," Frank strolls into the kitchen after spending the night at Zoe's and Claire simply asks, "The journalist?" Frank responds in the affirmative. Claire is concerned about the affair only to the extent that she doesn't want Frank to jeopardize their goals by exposing sensitive information to a member of the media, but when he reassures her that Zoe can be controlled, Claire says she trusts him to know what he's doing. We learn later that Frank has told Claire specific details of his time with Zoe (like the spider incident), suggesting that she knew of the affair to whatever extent she desired, and her interest in meeting Zoe and positive response after reading her *Slugline* article suggest that she is unperturbed by the affair.

The issue of deception is a little less clear where Adam is concerned. In "Chapter 11," Claire is sitting in Adam's apartment, where she fled after an argument with Frank, but her mind is clearly back home. Adam is upset that Claire is using him as a little vacation from her marriage, suggesting that he does feel like he was at least somewhat deceived about Claire's intentions. Adam seems to believe Claire might be thinking of leaving Frank for him, but this does not appear to be something that was ever under consideration for Claire. She says, "I have a history with Francis, I have a future with him, and it's bigger than a moment." We don't have enough information to know whether Claire deliberately deceived Adam. Perhaps she was simply unclear, and he misunderstood, or believed what he wanted to believe. Regardless, this could be avoided by clear and open communication, and furthermore, even if Claire had outright lied to Adam about her intentions, and thus wronged him, her treatment of Adam wouldn't tell us whether or not she has a bad marriage.

## Do No Harm

Adultery can cause pain for each of the parties involved. One of the most poignant ways in which this pain might manifest is through the feeling that, in adultery, one's spouse is giving primacy of affection to another person, causing feelings of jealousy, betrayal, and fear of being left for the new individual. Many successfully nonmonogamous couples avoid this potential problem by taking care to always give priority to their spouse. In "Chapter 6," after watching Frank tell Zoe he'd come by her house later (presumably for sex), we see Frank screen a call from Zoe while sharing a cigarette with Claire. She asks if he needs to take it, but he tells her he's "done with work for the day," and we see them go off together, presumably to bed. In "Chapter 12," while sleeping in Adam's apartment, Claire gets a text from Frank telling her Peter Russo is dead. She immediately texts back "coming home."

Claire doesn't think twice about putting Frank before Adam, even though they have been fighting. When one of them needs something, differences are set aside. Perhaps Frank says it best, when speaking to Adam in "Chapter 22," "Do not mistake any history you may have shared for the slightest understanding of what our marriage is, or how insignificant you are in comparison." While Frank is clearly angry and trying to rile Adam up, his words also ring true. Claire smiles slightly as he says it.

Whatever extramarital adventures the Underwoods might have, they are first and foremost committed to each other. There does not appear to be much in-marriage pain generated by their nonmonogamy. Claire only gets upset about Zoe when she becomes a threat to their political goals, and we actually see Frank handle the Adam debacle in "Chapter 22" very gracefully. Claire tells him she knows it's demeaning, having the world believe he's been cuckolded, and he says, "Not another word. We'll put this behind us, like we've always done." However, what about pain to the extramarital partners? In "Chapter 12," Zoe tells Janine Skorsky that, despite having told Frank that he couldn't hurt her, "it does hurt." Adam also appears to be hurt by the fact that Claire prioritizes Frank over him. However, it's unclear that these heartaches are any different than the pain that is felt in any relationship where one party is less interested than the other, or has different expectations. Since Zoe and Adam both knew the score going in, the pain they felt does not appear to be the fault of nonmonogamy.

## God, Punzo, and the Case for Special Sex

Now that we've demonstrated that Claire and Frank are practicing moral adultery, at least according to Wasserstrom's criteria, we're left wondering what else might make their nonmonogamous marriage wrong. One possible answer is that they are violating a particular conception of a particular god's law. However, one doesn't get to that conclusion without accepting a whole host of theological assumptions that are unverifiable and hotly debated, even among believers. Thus, the fact that a prohibition on adultery might have been scratched on a stone tablet a few thousand years ago could act as a reason to keep believers' genitals inside their marriage, but that fact cannot possibly count as a reason for someone who doesn't share those theological assumptions.

Philosopher Vincent Punzo argues that sex is different from any other human activity because "the sexual encounter is a definitive experience, one in which the physical intimacy and merging involves also a merging of the non-physical dimensions of the partners."[2] Punzo calls sex "the most intimate physical expression of selfhood," and argues that casual sex attempts to merge bodies without merging selves, thus resulting in an incongruity between one's physical and nonphysical aspects. That may sound complicated, but it amounts to a view you have likely heard many times—sex is special, and when you do it outside the boundaries of a monogamous committed relationship you are doing something that is damaging to all parties involved. According to Punzo, adulterous sex is impermissible. Likewise, all sex with noncommitted partners is impermissible, and all sex with committed partners who lack sufficient feelings for each other is impermissible.

In a relatively concise argument, Punzo manages to make a significant number of controversial claims. Punzo accepts an account of the person known as dualism, so named because it posits the existence of two separate entities—bodies and souls—which are separate and distinct yet somehow joined together to form one person until death. Punzo believes that sex, done properly, involves a mingling not just of bodies but also of souls. Well, maybe dualism is true, and maybe it isn't. Our point is just that, for nondualists, Punzo's argument is a nonstarter. Set that issue aside, however. The idea that sex necessarily results in the merging of selves in a way other than the obvious is another questionable claim. To that end, we ask you to think about times you've had sex. Before you get too excited, ask yourself if you feel like you've merged selves/souls/spirits each and every time. Survey says—no. Punzo's response would probably be that those times when you've had non-soul-mingling sex, you've been holding back one aspect of yourself in your effort to satisfy your base bodily pleasures without the proper level of commitment and self-sharing openness. Okay, so now either Punzo is wrong, or he knows more about what is going on when you have sex than you do.

We're not denying that sex with someone you love can be a different, perhaps deeper experience than no-strings-attached sex, and we'd like to point out first that Frank and Claire do appear to have affection for each of their partners. Even so, clearly their extramarital affairs violate Punzo's standard, as do most people's sexual encounters.[3] Punzo's view of sex is actually damaging. It categorizes sex as this sort of mystical, transcendent experience. Really, it's this amazing-feeling physical activity that is sometimes better than others, sometimes goes wrong, and can be weird and embarrassing. If people believe that angels are supposed to show up and sing each time they have sex, their expectations are certain to be disappointed. Worse, people can be left feeling as if they've somehow done something wrong (more often to the detriment of women).

## Rethinking Sex and Commitment

Wasserstrom makes a much more modest claim than Punzo—adultery can be a morally permissible choice for those who are so inclined. Sexual nonexclusivity could be beneficial to more relationships than one might think. After all, much of the adultery-related pain Wasserstrom worries about could be curbed if we took monogamy off its pedestal. Being told that monogamy is the only way you can really love and be loved sets couples up for a lot of pain and heartbreak. Monogamy is hard, and contrary to our biological inclinations.[4] When an individual tries to be monogamous and fails, she often feels terrible guilt, guilt that she believes she must conceal, because society has told us that infidelity is the number one unforgiveable relationship sin. While the adulterer is feeling guilt and pressure to lie, the nonadulterous spouse feels he has been rejected, that it is impossible that his spouse could love him while having sex with another. This emphasis on sexual exclusivity pushes good relationships to dissolve after an instance of adultery; only a fool stays with a cheater. Think how different the situation would be if we could look at adultery more like everything else. We forgive our partners all the time—for cruel words said in anger, for lies, for costly mistakes—no one is perfect, and loving someone means recognizing their flaws and mistakes and loving them anyway. Why should this one physical act be so different, so unforgiveable, so permanently relationship altering?

We think promise-breaking nonmonogamy ought to be a candidate for marital forgiveness in the same measure as any other transgression. Better still would be agreed-upon nonmonogamy for couples who want it. You might ask, why would anyone add this complication to their marriage; aren't relationships tricky enough, without inviting more trouble? As Wasserstrom points out, couples don't need a reason to choose nonmonogamy, all they need is an agreement. You don't need a reason to watch television or play tennis or eat Thai food, but some of the same trivial reasons that can be applied to those activities—pleasure, relieving boredom, and craving new experiences—can be applied to a decision to open one's marriage as well.

There are also some more significant reasons why nonmonogamy can be a positive choice. Significant sexual incompatibilities, some of which might not manifest until well into the marriage, possibly brought about by health issues, can lead to situations in which monogamy means at least one member of the relationship is sentenced to a life of gross sexual dissatisfaction. For instance, if one spouse becomes unable to engage in sexual activity due to a chronic illness, an insistence on monogamy will force his partner to choose between unhappy abstinence, promise breaking and deception, or divorce, which is regrettable in situations where the couple has good nonsexual reasons to stay together.

In Frank and Claire's case, there appears to be a quite nontrivial reason as well—Frank's bisexuality. We know that he had sexual encounters with his close friend Tim Corbet in college, and he is delighted to engage in a threesome with Claire and Meechum. It is telling that the person Claire snagged as a little sexual gift for Frank was a man. If Frank's sexuality is such that he would be unable to feel satisfied with only heterosexual encounters, monogamy would ask a lot of him. It would require Frank to give up part of what it means to be Frank. Of course, most of life's choices involve some level of sacrifice; that fabulous Caribbean vacation you took last year necessitated missing *House of Cards* ... wait, no it didn't—isn't Netflix wonderful? ... but you understand the point. We give up one thing to get another all the time. If Claire were a more conventional woman, Frank might have had to choose to give up sexual encounters with men (and other women) in order to marry her. Or, he might have simply scratched his extramarital itches behind her back, breaking promises, deceiving, and causing pain. Isn't this way better? Frank is happier and more satisfied, and Claire also seems pretty happy and satisfied; nonmonogamy is positively contributing to the strength and longevity of their shared bond.

# The Underwood's Egalitarian Partnership

Claire's decision to undermine Frank regarding the watershed bill, which leads to a fight culminating in her going to Adam in New York, is evidence to many of a broken marriage. What wife purposely deceives her husband and sabotages his goals? Good partners don't run away from fights, certainly not into the arms of a lover. We see it a little differently. For one thing, the mere fact that they had a fight is not in itself evidence of a bad relationship. All relationships of any length involve disagreements, and relationships between ambitious, passionate individuals like Frank and Claire will likely encounter a good many points of disagreement over the years. Strong-willed people of conviction will not roll over when someone challenges them. To determine whether this particular fight is evidence of a bad relationship, then, we need to look closely at the content of their dispute.

Frank and Claire's relationship has been built on mutuality. They help each other. They keep each other in the loop. Every time we see Claire really angry at Frank, it is because he has left her out, failed to give her vital information, or failed to put her interests on an equal level with his own. This is precisely why Claire walks out at the end of Season 3. We learned this about their relationship way back in "Chapter 1," when Claire says, "When have we ever avoided each other? . . . We do things together. When you don't involve me, we're in free fall." When Frank confronts her about the bill, she tells him she did it for herself, because Frank wouldn't help her. He reminds her that they make decisions together, and she responds that for the past six months she's no longer felt like they were standing beside each other. When Frank stops working with her, Claire employs a tit-for-tat strategy, failing to work with him in return. This strategy causes Frank to see that working together is a preferable option, and if you watch carefully, you'll see that Frank does not leave Claire out of decisions for the rest of Season 2. Thus, rather than a betrayal, Claire's decision to act as she does is a strategy. She chooses the precise action that she knows will modify her husband's behavior. Frank recognizes through Claire's behavior that it was his violation of their mutuality agreement that caused Claire to in turn defect, and further recognizes what he needs to do to ensure it doesn't happen again.

Reasoning about one's marriage as if it's an abstract game theoretical problem might not be everyone's cup of tea, but it works perfectly for Frank and Claire. In a relationship in which both parties are pursuing goals that are very important to them, there will inevitably be times in which those goals run at cross-purposes. The watershed bill was an example of such a time. Some people might see this disagreement as manifesting a deep conflict within their marriage, but Frank and Claire view it as a road bump. In a way, it's no different than the sexual openness of their marriage. Sometimes they're working together, on the same project, and sometimes they're having sex with each other. At other times they're working independently, on different projects, and sometimes their sexual encounters are separate as well. Even when they are working at cross-purposes, as with the watershed bill, as long as they're open, communicative, and working toward a consensus, their marriage functions properly. The problem in the watershed case was not in having different goals, but in failing to talk them through and reach a compromise.

Obviously, the couple's marital disputes manifest in a more dramatic way in Season 3, but notice that things get as bad as they do because they stop employing their own strategy. After Frank takes office, they both begin neglecting their mutuality agreement, and we see the relationship go into the free fall Claire described. The failures manifested in Season 3 validate our point about the strength of their relationship in Seasons 1 and 2. Thus, if Claire and Frank were to once again employ their long-standing strategy of communication, consensus, and mutual compromise, it is likely their marriage would survive, provided it's mixed with some forgiveness over the mistakes that were made in Season 3. Even if the marriage ends at 25 years, however, this doesn't nullify its previous success.

## Incidental Objections

Another area where critics find fault in the Underwoods' marriage is in the fact that they spend a lot of time apart. Their house has a sort of "just visiting" feel to it, as their busy careers mean long hours and, especially for Frank, quite a bit of travel. This might be undesirable for some couples, but the Underwoods are two independent, goal-driven people, happy to be in a partnership where they have the freedom to pursue projects they value, even if it means their spouse will spend some nights at home alone. What's more, knowing their time together is scarce means they take seriously the moments they do spend together. Frank and Claire squeeze more quality intimacy into a shared cigarette at their window than do many couples during five hours of noncommunicative, nearly comatose television watching each night.

The Underwood's decision to remain childless is a recurring theme throughout the series. Claire tells their dying former bodyguard, known only as Steve, that when Frank proposed to her he said, "Claire, if all you want is happiness, say no. I'm not going to give you a couple of kids.... I promise you freedom from that. I promise you'll never be bored." This indicates that Claire entered the marriage planning to remain childless. We also know their relationship is one of discussion, negotiation, and compromise, so if she had decided she wanted children she could have asked Frank to reconsider. Furthermore, we know Claire had other options, so she could have chosen to leave Frank if he wouldn't agree to children. All of this evidence suggests that, even if she sometimes feels a tinge of regret, Claire autonomously chose against motherhood. The freedom to make that choice, and to be supported in it by one's partner, is something many women, even today, do not have.

While an Underwood-style relationship might not be for everyone, they stand as a strong model for couples that place a high value on intrarelationship equality. Rather than posing a threat to a good marriage, nonmonogamy, if practiced in an open and mutually negotiated way, can enhance a relationship by allowing each partner to acknowledge and satisfy their sexual desires without feelings of guilt, shame, or secrecy. The Underwoods are an example of the way this type of arrangement can work. Describing their relationship in the television interview in "Chapter 17," Claire says, "We're two very independent people who have chosen to live our lives together. I support him, he supports me." Sounds pretty good to us.

## Notes

1. Richard Wasserstrom, "Is Adultery Immoral?" in Robert Baker and Frederick Elliston, eds., *Philosophy and Sex* (Buffalo, NY: Prometheus Books, 1975), 207–21.
2. Vincent Punzo, *Reflective Naturalism* (Upper Saddle River, NJ: Prentice Hall, 1969).

3. For an impartial account of Americans' non-Punzo-like behavior, see this comprehensive analysis from the Centers for Disease Control: Anjani Chandra et al., "Sexual Behavior, Sexual Attraction, and Sexual Identify in the United States: Data from the 2006–2008 National Survey of Family Growth," in *National Health Statistics Reports*, no. 36, March 3, 2011.

4. For a really interesting read on this subject, see David P. Barash and Judith Eve Lipton, *The Myth of Monogamy: Fidelity and Infidelity in Animals and People* (New York: Holt Paperbacks, 2002).

# 16
# The Spice of White Life
## Freddy and Racist Representations

*Stephanie Rivera Berruz*

*You want them white folks to feel like they are slumming …
and I get to play the nigger.*

—Freddy

On *House of Cards*, Freddy Hayes represents what it means to be a black male with respect to US racial politics. His story functions as an African American stereotype that deploys themes of ghettos, incarceration, and violence, while constructing a narrative that aligns with the dominant US racial paradigm that equates blackness with criminality. We must wonder what we, as viewers, are called to assume about black life from narratives like Freddy's. As we'll see, Freddy's representation functions within an economy of racism that commodifies otherness (blackness) to the extent it continues to privilege and support white supremacy.

## "I Get to Play the Nigger": The Narrative of Freddy Hayes

Unlike Remy Danton, the accomplished SanCorp lobbyist and Underwood Chief of Staff, Freddy Hayes is portrayed as the stereotypical

*House of Cards and Philosophy: Underwood's Republic*,
First Edition. Edited by J. Edward Hackett.
© 2016 John Wiley & Sons, Ltd. Published 2016 by John Wiley & Sons, Ltd.

black male of contemporary US society. He is initially presented to the audience as Frank Underwood's "black friend." Underwood frequents Freddy's BBQ Joint for his consumption of "authentic" Southern cuisine. One of the most intriguing things about the relationship is the manner in which their encounters occur. Underwood is featured in black spaces without requiring invitation, but not vice versa. Consistent with the privilege that is afforded by whiteness in racialized spaces, there is no problem for Underwood roaming in black spaces. Nevertheless, Freddy's movement through white space is only ever a possibility when he receives an invitation to cater to white bodies. One of the most notable examples of this is found in "Chapter 6," when we witness Freddy's first visit to the White House, where he delivers some of his famous ribs to Frank Underwood. As he is leaving, he looks at Frank and states, "Twenty years you have been coming to my joint, and this is the first time I have been to yours… "

Freddy's narrative takes on its own dimensions in the show as he is approached to franchise his BBQ Joint. As Freddy is looking over the plans, he notes that the layout is set to make the linoleum on the counters look like it's peeling off. He is told that this is done in order make the restaurant "seem real" because "we do not want it to look too nice." In response, Freddy states, "You want them white folks to feel like they slumming … and I get to play the nigger." Freddy is told in response that the reason for this design detail has to do with making the restaurant feel like it has an "authentic atmosphere" because "they don't just want the ribs, they want the experience without having to leave the suburbs." Unfortunately, the deal falls through shortly thereafter. Freddy's son, who is on parole, waves a gun at a photojournalist, thus violating a morality clause in the contract and causing Freddy to lose out on the deal.

In Season 3, we are reintroduced to Freddy as a participant in the America Works program and as a depiction of menial wage labor. When Frank Underwood discovers Freddy's employment status, he calls him to the Oval Office. Freddy is accompanied by his grandson Deshawn, and Frank tells the boy that he can be president one day if he tries hard and gets good grades. The conversation that ensues between Freddy and Deshawn as they exit the Oval Office is worth noting since it poignantly reflects the situation of Freddy's life (and, by extension, black male life). In response to the exchange with Frank, Freddy says to Deshawn, "Listen up boy, he lied to you, the truth is you ain't never gonna be president.... This place ain't for you and me. It's good to have dreams just so long as they are not fantasies."

## The Situation of Black Male Life

Freddy's narrative in *House of Cards* consistently mirrors the experiences of contemporary life for black males. Tommy J. Curry notes that the lives of black men are "endangered by violence from birth."[1] Black men, Curry argues, have been and continue to be "at the bottom of the social structure of American society since its inception."[2] Moreover, the deep ties between black men and death and criminality continue to be the foil by which blackness is constructed in modern-day America.[3] It for this reason that Michelle Alexander has argued in *The New Jim Crow* that the racist processes that make up the mass incarceration system in the United States directly contribute to the symbolic production of race.[4] She argues, "Today mass incarceration defines the meaning of blackness in America: black people, especially black men, are criminals. This is what it means to be black."[5] The situation of black males in our society is one that is coded by criminality and violence to the point that blackness is defined in these terms.

None of this is an accident. The history of slavery tells us plenty about the contemporary symbolic production of race. Curry argues that "the enslaved African/Black body was not simply a commodity to be bought and sold, but commodified into what whites desired, feared, and sought to vacate from (white) virtue into (Black degradation)—creating the darkened/racialized Nigger."[6] The history of slavery in the United States, as is shown by both Curry and Alexander, continues to contribute to the disenfranchisement of black bodies, particularly black male bodies. What we see today is the regeneration of the relationship between blackness, commodity/desire, and criminality/fear. This is the "nigger" that Freddy sees himself playing in the imagination of the white life that comes to the "authentically black" BBQ joint. Moreover, the nigger that Freddy identifies himself with cannot be distanced from contemporary black life. Curry notes, "The nigger is not a representation, a mere phantasm; rather the/that Nigger (he) is the object; the thing, intended to be subjected to white violence, and dealt with through death, and incarceration."[7] In stating that he is playing the nigger, Freddy is very much displaying what it means to be a black male in our society. In this instance, it very much entails the death of Freddy's character as he signs himself into the role of the nigger when he franchises his business, a choice his life situation practically necessitates.

For many who watch *House of Cards*, Freddy's narrative is entirely consistent with what it means to be a black male in our society. He meets all of the standard criteria for blackness and maleness, and he in no way deviates from the presumptions of black life as associated with criminality, poverty, and death. Moreover, it seems to be the case that Freddy is aware of this fact, as he imparts this knowledge to his grandson as they walk out of the Oval Office by letting him know that the presidency is not "a place for you and me." In being consistent with the stereotypical associations of black male life in US society, Freddy's narrative may not seem problematic in the least. For many viewers, this may just be the depiction of the way things are. "Chapter 22" invites viewers to confirm the stereotypical tropes of black life. The episode opens by inviting the viewer to follow Freddy's morning routine, which begins with the death of a cockroach, a point that is symbolic to say the least. We follow Freddy out of his house and down the street, where we are witness to Freddy's neighborhood. We hear police sirens in the background, and a broader view reveals Freddy's BBQ sandwiched between a liquor store and an abandoned building.

In light of all this, let's consider the following questions: What are we as viewers invited to think about through Freddy's narrative? What does this representation of black male life really do to our general conceptions of white privilege and racism in US society? As we'll see, Freddy's narrative does nothing to challenge the problematic symbolic production of race that equates blackness (maleness) with criminality, poverty, and death. Quite to the contrary, it reinforces the notion that these concepts ought to operate in tandem with each other.

## Racial Capitalism and the Representation of Black Male Life

In order to advance the argument that Freddy's narrative does not interrupt, but rather reinforces, an economy of racism that commodifies blackness, let's consider the dynamics between race and representation. According to bell hooks, "Within commodity culture, ethnicity becomes spice, seasoning that can liven up the dull dish that is main-stream white culture."[8] The representations of ethnic or racial minori-ties in our commodity culture function for the consumption by white audiences in a way that does not elaborate the complexity of the lived experiences of these identities, but rather reinforces a one-dimensional spice that makes shows a little more interesting. If we think about Freddy's narrative with respect to hooks' claim, it becomes clear that the function of Freddy's narrative in *House of Cards* provides spice to a predominantly white narrative. The metaphor of spice, however, runs much deeper. The fact that Freddy is portrayed as the vehicle of "authenticity" through the consumption of food should not be forgot-ten. Freddy is relevant to the plot insofar as he disseminates authentic Southern culture through the consumption of a cultural product: BBQ ribs. Freddy's narrative is, in every sense of the word, a "spice" for *House of Cards*.

Furthermore, bell hooks notes that the representation of ethnic and racial minorities operates within an economy of desire. From the standpoint of white supremacist patriarchy, the desire for contact with the "primitive" is continually exploited and occurs in a manner that reinforces the status quo.[9] So, in Freddy's narrative, it should be no surprise that he is represented in a manner that continues to reinforce the status quo of contemporary black male life. However, there is more to it than just the reinforcement of a stereotypical narrative. hooks notes that "when race and ethnicity become commodified as resources for pleasure, the culture of specific groups, as well as the bodies of indi-viduals, can be seen as constituting an alternative playground where members of dominating races … affirm their power."[10] This is pre-cisely what we see happening with Freddy's narrative. He is a vehicle for an "authentic" (primitive) culture that is presented through food. In the realm of food consumption, white life can play on the desire for engagement with the "exotic" or "native" experience without losing access to the privilege afforded by whiteness.

The ability to move through the playground of the "native" is also what foils the layout plans for the franchise of Freddy's BBQ in Silver Springs. Recall that he is told that the plans are intended to make the restaurant seem "real" with an "authentic atmosphere" because "they don't just want the ribs, they want the experience without hav-ing to leave the suburbs." The racial spice that is black life in *House of Cards*, at least with respect to Freddy's narrative, exemplifies hooks' claim of commodification. In this instance, we have the commodification of black life for consumption by white culture, all the while preserving the status quo of the privilege afforded to white life. Furthermore, hooks notes that in commodity culture, approximating the Other is made possible by consumer culture.[11] It is precisely through consumerism that dominant culture can feel closer to the Other, without having to actually encounter them in any real intersubjective sense.[12] In the case of Freddy's narrative, the encounter would occur through the consumption of ribs at an "authentic" restaurant that makes "them white folks to feel like they slumming ... and I [Freddy] get to play the nigger."

For viewers of this narrative, there appears to be very little room for the articulation and representation of blackness (maleness) that interrupts the dominant stereotype. hooks argues, "Whether or not desire for contact with the Other, for connection rooted in the longing for pleasure, can act as a critical intervention challenging and subverting racist domination, inviting and enabling critical resistance, is an unrealized political possibility."[13] So, there is no room in this particular representation that allows intervention on the stereotype, and Freddy's character is very much aware of this insofar as he is aware of the role that he plays within white life—the nigger.

It is clear from hooks' contentions that the representation of black male life cannot be understood without an articulation of commodity culture and its uses of race. Nevertheless, Freddy's narrative requires further analysis. If the representation of black male life through Freddy's character is in fact the "spice of the authentic native life," it is important to consider the conditions by which the representation of black life becomes an instrument of white supremacy. Freddy's narrative adds more than just spice; it fits within racist paradigms of black life, and insofar as it does, it works in and through an economy of racial capitalism.

Nancy Leong defines racial capitalism as "the process of deriving social and economic value from racial identity."[14] Moreover, racial capitalism "requires commodification of racial identity by reducing it to another thing to be bought and sold."[15] Freddy's narrative is emblematic of racial capitalism. He represents the stereotypical story of black male life in the United States, associated with death, poverty, and criminalization. Moreover, his identity is commodified and sold as "authentic" for white consumption—a point the viewer is very much aware of as Freddy's character actively reflects on his situation as "the nigger" that white people get to consume as they "feel like they slumming." Freddy's narrative does not present itself as odd or out of place precisely because it plays into viewers' real-world experiences of racial capitalism whereby race—in this instance, blackness—is only understood as a commodity to be consumed in a manner that reinforces white supremacy (the status quo).

In further exploring the dimension of racial capitalism, Leong describes how race takes on value. Echoing hooks' claims that the status quo of US society is intricately bound to supporting white supremacy, Leong notes that "the value of non-whiteness is contingent on its worth to white people."[16] So, it is not just the case that blackness is commodified in our consumer culture, but rather that blackness is commodified with a value that is entirely contingent upon its relationship to whiteness. Our culture only values nonwhiteness to the extent that it supports and maintains systems of white supremacy. Leong argues, "Even when non-whiteness is highly valued, white people retain control over the assignment value, and may increase or diminish that value at will."[17] This situation creates an economy of racial capital whereby the value of nonwhiteness cannot be determined independently of white supremacist culture. Returning to Freddy, we need to consider how his entire narrative plays into an economy of racial capitalism as it not only confirms the black male stereotype, but also reinforces the claim that blackness (maleness) is only valuable to the extent that it benefits white people or white institutions. This appears to be the case within the narrative of *House of Cards*. Freddy is only valued as an extension of Frank Underwood, and as soon as that value is lost, Underwood devalues his presence and pushes him out of the narrative. This point is best illustrated in "Chapter 22," when Underwood comes to Freddy's home in order to inform him that he is going to distance himself from Freddy due to bad press. He tells Freddy, "I need to make sure you are not going to play up what good friends we have been ... and I won't be coming in for ribs anymore."

Another example that illustrates this point is found in "Chapter 20," when Freddy is invited to Frank Underwood's house to cook for the President. As the dinner comes to a close, Freddy is complimented on his excellent cooking by the President. Moreover, the President notes that he read an article that was recently published in *The Sun* (a Baltimore-based newspaper) about Freddy's joint. Before leaving the Underwoods' home, Freddy tells Frank that as a result of the article, "You not the only white person to show up there now." This scene shows that the interest and value of Freddy were entirely derivative from his associations with Underwood. Thus, as Leong's claims on racial capitalism indicate, the value of nonwhiteness is entirely determined by its benefit to white institutions.

Taking a step back, let's consider the effect that this representation of black male life has on viewers. Representing black male life in a manner that plays into an economy of racism and the commodification of black culture is deeply unjust. Freddy's narrative plays into the assumptions that we have of black male life in a way that does not disrupt or intervene on those assumptions. We need to wonder what the impact would be if Freddy were depicted as an accomplished business owner who lived in the suburbs of Washington, DC, with a stable family unit. What would we as viewers come to assume about black masculinity if the narrative did not meet our stereotypes? One of the wonderful things about representations is that they need not match the stereotype, and so they have the potential for getting us as viewers to rethink our assumptions about the world. Nevertheless, it remains the case that Freddy's narrative does not interrupt or challenge dominant US tropes of black masculinity. Freddy, after all, has a history of gang violence, imprisonment, and "failed" fatherhood (his son was born while he was incarcerated). As viewers of *House of Cards*, we are left with a rudimentary script for black male life, one that simply invites us to assume that this is "just the way things are." Unfortunately, "the way things are" simply reinforces the status quo that nonwhiteness only has value to the extent that it privileges white institutions and white people.

## Racial Realism and Harassing White Folks

Derrick Bell has argued that racism is a permanent facet of US society.[18] In other words, black people in US society will always have a subordinate status.[19] This tenet is known as *racial realism*, and Bell proposes it as a way to avoid the despair that comes with the long-standing failures of racial equity. In light of the position of *racial realism*, Bell offers the story of Biona MacDonald, a black civil rights activist in Mississippi whose fight for racial justice threatened her job, her home, and her livelihood. When asked where she found the courage to continue fighting, Mrs. MacDonald responded, "I live to harass white folks."[20] Bell notes that Mrs. MacDonald was not aiming for racial justice or racial equity, but rather found self-realization in the defiance of white supremacy.[21] This attitude, Bell notes, is the attitude that we should take when thinking about the fight for civil rights. It is not the case that racial equity will be achieved. In fact, that is impossible given his concept of racial realism. However, we should strive to be defiant of white supremacist culture to the best of our abilities, and in this defiance we will find true resistance without collapsing into a utopian vision of what the world could look like if race did not matter. This chapter has argued that Freddy in *House of Cards* sustains and reinforces a notion of black male life that does not interrupt white supremacy, but rather plays into its economy. My analysis presents a critique that harasses and resists this representation not with the hopes of changing the structure of racial capitalism, but rather to disrupt what we as viewers are called to assume about black life. This intervention demonstrates the problems with the representations of black male life through Freddy's character not with the hopes of achieving racial equity, but rather with the hope of highlighting the problematic features of the representation of blackness in the show, as I too live to harass white people.

# Notes

1. Tommy J. Curry, "You Can't Stand the Nigger I See! Kanye West's Analysis of Anti-Black Death," in *The Cultural Impact of Kanye West*, ed. Julius Bailey (New York: Palgrave, 2014), 131.
2. Ibid., 131.
3. Ibid., 131.
4. Michelle Alexander, *The New Jim Crow: Mass Incarceration in the Age of Colorblindness* (New York: New Press, 2010), 197.
5. Ibid., 197.
6. Curry, "You Can't Stand," 132.
7. Ibid., 132.
8. bell hooks, *Race and Representation* (Boston: South End Press, 1992), 23.
9. Ibid., 22.
10. Ibid., 23.

11. Ibid., 26.
12. Ibid., 26.
13. Ibid., 22.
14. Nancy Leong, "Racial Capitalism," *Harvard Law Review* 126 (2013): 1.
15. Ibid.
16. Ibid., 24.
17. Ibid.
18. Derrick Bell, "Racial Realism," *Connecticut Law Review* 24 (1992): 373.
19. Ibid.
20. Ibid., 379.
21. Ibid.

# 17

# Broken Friendships and the Pathology of Corporate Personhood in *House of Cards*

## *Myron Moses Jackson*

*House of Cards* appeals to the strongly held belief that politics is dirty and corrupt. Our leaders are not revered or looked up to as role models. It often seems that the farce of politics is choreographed and enforced by corporate elites motivated by greed, power, and control. *House of Cards* thus shows a well-oiled political machine in which the two parties are married and deserve each other. Like the Underwoods, Democrats and Republicans are enclosed in a circle of power and alliances crucial to their survival.

The philosopher Jean Jacques Rousseau (1712–1778) explored the tensions between our real and fake lives, highlighting the compromises that accompany the drive for public esteem. Rousseau called the will of the people as a whole, which favors the common good, the "general will." The "corporate will," by contrast, is the will of government, which Rousseau describes as "despotic, oligarchic," and pathological. On my interpretation of Rousseau, our corporate selves work on behalf of the company, institution, or government—not the community in general. Once the corporate will is established, it takes on a life of its own. The individual is viewed as a means rather than an end, and all friendships are subordinated for the sake of corporate personhood.

*House of Cards and Philosophy: Underwood's Republic*,
First Edition. Edited by J. Edward Hackett.
© 2016 John Wiley & Sons, Ltd. Published 2016 by John Wiley & Sons, Ltd.

## "You Ain't Got to Pretend to Be My Friend"

For a long time, Frank and Freddy enjoyed the time they spent together at Freddy's BBQ Joint. It was an escape from the social norms that reinforced their inequality and kept them on opposite sides of the track. Toward the end of Season 2, however, Frank and Freddy recognized the true nature of their friendship. They may have found a semblance of fraternity, but Frank was "just a good customer" and Freddy doesn't need his "guilt money." On a single-minded quest for power, Frank cuts all ties with his so-called friend once Freddy's criminal past and the photos of his gun-toting son go viral. Memory of their affiliations is to be erased. The Walkers and Underwoods can't be seen associating with ex-felons. That would go against the rules.

Aristotle (384–322 BCE) wisely said that true friends have no need for justice. Where there is mutual admiration, there are no pleas against wrongdoing or injustice. Frank and Freddy lack this *shared* admiration, and they symbolize the broken friendships that reveal the dark pathology of corporate personhood. The split between Frank and Freddy is a classic case of private wills being crushed under the yoke of the corporate will. Frank and Freddy have paid the price for civilization, and as Rousseau would see it, Freddy has paid less. This is why Frank envies him as "one who does not need to pretend." Freddy is under no illusions. Invited to the White House for a job as a part of Frank's America Works program, Freddy asks for a job *away from* the kitchen. Freddy seems as anxious to leave as when he retreated to the kitchen in order to be relieved from Frank's nonstop conversation at the rib joint. His grandson Deshawn, by contrast, is taken in by the prestige of the noble halls and decides, "I want to be President one day." Grandpa without hesitation offers a stern warning about the corporate will, "Well that's never gonna happen.... Naw, boy, this place ain't for you and me. It's good to have dreams, so long as they not fantasies. You let anybody sell you that shit, it's your own damn fault."

Rousseau's concern, on my reading, is *not* that corporations fail to be persons, but that they are sociopathic and highly destructive persons. Defective communities result from defective institutions, such as corporations, when they depersonalize us. There are no friends in Washington and corporate America. The essence of corporations and governments is to look secure, not weak or vulnerable. Our personal failings are mostly covered up or erased by the corporate ethos. When they are preserved, they become tools that can be used against us in the superficial relations that result when one must be cutthroat or else be destroyed.

## States and Corporations: What's the Difference?

Like states engaged in war, corporations directly compete against each other in ways that undermine moral personhood. When companies buy up patents because they can, or when automakers hide lethal malfeasance through confidentiality agreements, the difference between legal and personal responsibility is clear. Governments also enjoy the classified status that generates the mass conspiracy theories and overall cynicism and distrust of our elected officials. We witness in *House of Cards* how such legal maneuvering protects the sociopathic nature of corporate wills. Practices such as corporate espionage and the deliberate misuse of information are justified as "the price of doing business." Power and profits are the ends for which corporations exist. Thus, they justify their actions through legal *and* not moral means, regardless of the social consequences.

Such corporations generate institutionalized selves, who must be "forced to be free." Agents of corporate wills are forced into a trade of natural dignity for loyalty in which self-love (*amor de soi*) is degraded into self-interest (*amour-propre*). The "sentient being" of man is deranged into "an ingenious machine" with senses.[1] Rousseau considers this an act of impoverishing one's inner life, which eclipses personal relations for impersonal, generic ones. When it comes to friends, one of the things that attracts us is that they are irreplaceable and one of a kind. Part of their rare value comes from their individual uniqueness, but that is not the case for the corporate model. Corporate wills couldn't care less about the individual because they negate the inside-out processes of personal experience. One's use or value is seen only from the exterior and through the commercial expectations they envision. As I will argue in my reading of Rousseau, corporate personhood is all about appearances.

Thin yet well-veiled selves conflate the pursuit of happiness with power and success by a total devotion to corporate America, and such individuals are not in the business of friendship. Aristotle argued that true friendship is an end in itself. It is not to be treated only as a means to happiness as defined under the corporate dynamic of success, power, and privilege. Rousseau understood that corporate contractual relations are built on deceit and a lack of trust, which in turn leads to the kind of anxiety that makes Frank ask Doug, "Do we have any loose ends?" and add, "We can't afford any loose ends."

Under the corporate ethos, we can only have what Aristotle called friendships of utility or pleasure, but not true friendship. Frank and Freddy enjoyed a friendship of pleasure for a time, and Frank and Zoe enjoyed a friendship of utility (and pleasure) for a time. In a friendship of utility, "I agree not to throw you under a train unless I have to." This is the corporate motto and the creed of political realists of all stripes.

## Tusk and the Punching Bag Walkers

In a twisted, sociopathic way, Tusk has a need to be listened to and counted on by those at the top of the food chain. We can safely assume that "Garrett" is Tusk's only "friend." They are key members of the good ole boys' club and, therefore, friends by default. They were brought together by ambition and sinister loyalties in politics and business, but as they achieved increasing success the corporate pathology poisoned their friendship. Of such situations, Rousseau warns, "The reward of virtue soon becomes that of robbery; the vilest of men rise to the greatest credit; the greater they are the more despicable they become; their infamy appears even in their dignities, and their very honors dishonor them."[2] A culture of success becomes synonymous with corruption.

Corporate wills diminish us. In his last meeting with Frank at the opera, Tusk says they "put you in a box barely bigger than a coffin." As the corporate will grows in influence, one's will is dwarfed and sacrificed. Just think of Walker holed up at Camp David pleading the Fifth. Fixated on themselves, their narcissism blinds Walker and Tusk to the damage they do in their treatment of others, especially those closest to them. They seem concerned only with how *they* will end up, whether *they* will get a second chance. In their moral emptiness, Walker and Tusk are consumed with who will flip first.

## If You Can't Beat 'Em, Join 'Em

After working for Underwood for eight years, Remy Danton became another player in the game, ready to rise in the corporate ranks. Danton's experience in the corporate world makes him always expect the worst underhandedness in people. His connection with Jackie Sharp appears to have potential beyond "a one-night stand," but only as long as it is *not* business related or tainted by the viciousness of the corporate will. When Danton aims to blackmail Jackie if she doesn't perjure herself by making it public how she became House Whip, we not only see Danton's business side but Jackie's as well. She has killed many men, and she has the tattoos to prove it.

Jackie's response to Remy's suggestion (that she say Frank tampered with witnesses to make sure "their stories lined up") reveals that she knows Frank is a user: "I have zero alliance to Frank Underwood." But, like the Walkers, Danton and Sharp end up being manipulated from all sides. Danton is concerned with respect, and Sharp wants to rise up in the ranks. After Remy gets pulled over and discovers he's just another "nigga in a nice car" and Sharp realizes her love for Remy is the only thing she has left that is not of Frank's doing, the viewer is left wondering if they are ready to take off as Claire appears to be. Their loyalties were easily bought, but they have nothing to show for it. For Tusk and Underwood, people like Remy and Sharp are needed to play the game effectively. As Frank says, "A man of state needs helpers, little elves and sprites to do his bidding. Even unwitting pawns who don't know who they serve." Who, then, do Danton and Sharp serve? Whoever they believe is winning. Danton's chameleon antics are confirmed in his private meeting with Frank at the church. Remy is willing to confess to Frank and not work against him anymore *if* Frank can guarantee that Remy will be able to hold on to his career. Remy wants assurances that he is protected in case Tusk goes down. For her part, to solidify power, Jackie is willing to work with Claire again despite their differences and despite the debacle of the sexual abuse military bill.

Sex and power are like drugs, and addicts will trample their friends and family in pursuit of them. When Claire goes behind Frank's back to Remy and SanCorp to get the art collection out of South Sudanese customs, she shows the ruthlessness that refuses to play second fiddle even to her husband. The socioeconomic, political motives that characterize their agendas are driven by the need to satisfy corporate structures. Claire and Frank have an "open" relationship consistent with an agreement in Rousseau's sense of the social contract; they are loyal to themselves and *only* to each other when they need to be. One looks to make friends as a matter of utility and based on what is personally advantageous, as a matter of convenience, with the same ease Frank pushed Zoe off the platform to her death. Or how he watched with delight when Jackie and Dunbar tore each other apart on the issues of women's equality and advantages of sending their well-to-do kids to prep schools. It is sadly another example of how the corporate will needs minorities, regardless of whether they've suffered actual racism or sexism, to depersonalize themselves and bait each other into a diversion tactic that covers over any sincere efforts to stifle such crippling effects on one's society and business practices. The pathology of corporate personhood lies in this severing of law from morality. In *Émile*, Rousseau warns,

> The mind which forms its ideas solely on real relations is a strong mind; that which contents itself with apparent relations is a superficial mind; that which sees relations just as they are is an accurate mind; that which estimates their value imperfectly is an unsound mind; he who invents imaginary relations which have neither reality nor appearance is a lunatic.[3]

The sociopathic nature of Frank and Claire, along with the paranoia between Republicans and Democrats, the *Slugline* reporters, and Doug's policing and eventual killing of Rachel, or the nervousness surrounding whether he destroyed the journal or gave it to the Dunbar camp, all convey the agitation of lunacy. Everything has to be carried to the letter of the law, so there are no loose ends, without any consideration of its legitimacy in the just and moral sense of the law's spirit. Such self-destructive egoists are only concerned with the appearance or semblance of law, not its reality.

## Why Rousseau?

In his own life Rousseau had a very hard time keeping friends, but he never gave up on friendship as an ideal. His quarrels and public exchanges were legendary. Friends and acquaintances including

David Hume and Denis Diderot found Rousseau paranoid, difficult to deal with, and contemptuous in his stints of self-imposed isolation. The French now claim Rousseau as a great national figure, but this was hardly the case when he was exiled and had to reenter France under different aliases. Despite Rousseau's antagonistic disposition, his philosophy was motivated by the need to articulate what is most admirable in humanity and to preserve the natural inclinations for compassion and sincerity that are crucial to the formation of fraternity. Hence, Rousseau's analysis relates to the motives of power and self-destruction manifest in the phony alliances that symbolize the unsatisfactory alternatives that reveal the imperfection and incompleteness of human life.

Rousseau was fascinated and troubled by the ways in which the social order undermines our sense of attachment and solidarity. Government and private industry function on the basis of corporate wills that can all too easily be conflated with the common good of the general will. Corporations are artificial persons who mimic nature's sympathies and necessities in deformed, insincere ways. "Rousseau thinks it almost inevitable that this group will end up usurping the legitimate sovereign power of the people and substituting its corporate will for the people's general will."[4] The corporate will establishes exploitative relations that subordinate the genuine aims of the community. No longer are humans content with merely being recognized by others. Rather, their value derives from a lust to dominate. Civilization comes at the price of the full potential of human wellbeing. Rousseau is not naive, however. He does not romanticize primitive life; "noble savage" is a phrase Rousseau never uses. What concerns Rousseau is that natural qualities such as self-respect and friendship give way to the construction of the city, and self-respect and friendship are pushed out as envy and needless fear are fostered through the corporate ethos. Artificial inequalities destroy natural human bonds, and compassion is replaced with cruel egoism. As Rousseau sees it, the civilized man of power and status

> is always moving, sweating, toiling and racking his brains to find still more laborious occupations: he goes on in drudgery to his last moment, and even seeks death to put himself in a position to live, or renounces life to acquire immortality. He pays his court to men in power, whom he hates, and to the wealthy, whom he despises: he stops at nothing

to have the honor of serving them; he is not ashamed to value himself on his own meanness and their protection; and proud of his slavery, he speaks with disdain of those, who have not the honor of sharing it.[5]

Such "slavery" is displayed in the characters throughout *House of Cards* who re-present "a frivolous and deceitful appearance, honor without virtue, reason without wisdom, and pleasure without happiness."[6] Has Claire actually come to this dire realization and, if so, what took her so long? As civilization robs us of our natural bonds and human empathy, sensible knaves like Sharp, Tusk, and Frank rob themselves of contentment and a life without regret. In the Appendix of the *Second Discourse*, Rousseau writes, "We may admire human society as much as we please; it will be none the less true that it necessarily leads men to hate each other in proportion as their interests clash, and to do one another apparent services, while they are really doing every imaginable mischief. What can be thought of a relation, in which the interest of every individual dictates rules directly opposite to those the public reason dictates to the community in general—in which every man finds his profit in the misfortunes of his neighbor."[7]

A common thread that runs throughout *House of Cards* is the way in which the "misfortune" of others is the key to getting ahead and being successful. Influence and control bring honor to scoundrels. So we shouldn't be surprised when loyalty is the primary virtue behind the friendships of Meechum and the Underwoods, or President Walker and Tusk. Francis and Claire deftly create the appearance of loyalty in their relationships, exploiting it to their own advantage and often to others' demise. This deceptive and double-dealing behavior is indicative of the lack of moral order that corporations generate as they strive to objectify and subdue individuals. Rousseau's political philosophy thus captures the corruption and destruction of Washington, DC—a swamp that traded malaria for politics. Corporate wills do not supply the foundation of the rights and duties we have to those we love. Competitive aims supplant compassion and affection. The formation of a just and healthy society lies in more than the force of law or a moral self-righteousness.

Rousseau teaches that in a constitutional democratic republic, such as ours, the likelihood of confusing or conflating corporate and general wills is extremely high. Societies in which corporate power structures dominate have difficulty supporting true friendship. Friendship is not predicated on society. Rather, it is society itself that needs genuine friendship. Without taking responsibility for our actions until our private wills come into conflict with the corporate will, our personal freedom becomes deterministic, without recourse to an imaginative reflection crucial for a fully developed moral personhood. "The bounds of possibility, in moral matters, are less narrow than we imagine: it is our weaknesses, our vices and our prejudices that confine them. Base souls have no belief in great men; vile slaves smile in mockery at the name of liberty."[8] Rational frameworks or company policies allow men the fruits of entitlement on the basis *only* of appearance, which stifles our "belief in great men" and causes us to "mock" liberty.

Rousseau wanted people to grow and learn together in a healthy culture, not one involved in jealousy or the need to outdo each other. Unity of sentiment experienced in friendship and marriage obligates us to be concerned with the quality and overall wellbeing of those around us. To embrace the value and flourishing of others is, in Rousseau's view, to contribute to the enlargement of oneself. But societies and corporate enterprises mask their faults and sacrifice those private wills dedicated to them. Self-absorbed, cutthroat environments, such as Washington, DC, produce people who lack the inclination and capacity to have meaningful fraternal allegiance. Thus, as Rousseau says, "Man is born free, but is everywhere in chains."[9]

## Notes

1. Jean Jacques Rousseau, *Second Discourse* in *First and Second Discourses*, trans. Roger D. Masters and Judith R. Masters (New York: St. Martin's Press, 1964), 221–2.
2. Jean Jacques Rousseau, *A Discourse on Political Economy*, in *Great Books of the Western World*, vol. 35, trans. G. D. H. Cole, ed. Mortimer J. Adler (Chicago: Encyclopedia Britannica, 2005), 372.
3. Jean Jacques Rousseau, *Émile or Treatise on Education*, trans. Allan Bloom (New York: Basic Books, 1979), 185.
4. Christopher Bertram, "Jean Jacques Rousseau," in *The Stanford Encyclopedia of Philosophy*, ed. Edward N. Zalta, http://plato.stanford.edu/archives/win2012/entries/rousseau/ (last accessed October 13, 2014).

5. Jean Jacques Rousseau, *On the Origin of Inequality*, in *Great Books of the Western World*, trans, vol. 35. G. D. H. Cole, ed. Mortimer J. Adler (Chicago: Encyclopedia Britannica, 2005), 362.
6. Ibid., 362.
7. Ibid., 363.
8. Jean Jacques Rousseau, *The Social Contract*, in *Great Books of the Western World*, vol. 35, trans. G. D. H. Cole, ed. Mortimer J. Adler (Chicago: Encyclopedia Britannica, 2005), book III, chap. 12, 420.
9. Ibid., book I, chap. 1, 387.

# Part VI

# EXISTENTIAL REALITIES: SELF-LOVE AND FREEDOM

# 18

# Praying to One's Self, for One's Self

## Frank's Ethics and Politics of Autoeroticism

*Kody W. Cooper*

When Steve Jones, Frank Underwood's former head of security, was diagnosed with pancreatic cancer, Claire Underwood went to visit him in the hospital. She apologized on Frank's behalf that he could not be there, but, she told Steve, Frank wanted him to know that he was praying for him. To this, Steve replied, "I never seen him pray. Not in eight years" ("Chapter 6"). The viewer, however, does see Frank pray once. In a moment of great anxiety and great hope, Frank enters a Christian church, kneels at the altar, and prays. He does not, however, pray like we might expect anyone similarly situated would pray. Frank prays to *himself* for *himself*.

In this moment of "prayer," we see Frank's fundamental moral outlook. The truth that Frank belied in his typewritten letter to President Garrett Walker is: He serves only himself. Frank has made *himself* the ultimate end of all his actions, because he loves himself above all things. This is a kind of self-love that I shall call *autoeroticism*. In this chapter, I contend that Frank's ethics and politics of autoeroticism should be understood in terms of three fundamental, interlocking principles: metaphysical atheism, ruthless pragmatism, and happiness as power. Frank considers his ethics and politics of autoeroticism as truly liberating. It remains to be seen whether or not this is true.

*House of Cards and Philosophy: Underwood's Republic,*
First Edition. Edited by J. Edward Hackett.
© 2016 John Wiley & Sons, Ltd. Published 2016 by John Wiley & Sons, Ltd.

## Leave the Ideology to the Armchair Generals ...

While Frank eschews ideological rigidness, his ethics and politics are in fact informed by a particular vision of the universe that I will call "metaphysical atheism." In Frank's words, "There is no solace above or below" ("Chapter 13"). Thus, there is no afterlife, no heaven, no hell. Frank states that it is pointless to mourn the death of presidents or anyone else because "the dead can't hear us" ("Chapter 12"). When Frank was asked by his Sentinel English professor if he had no faith in God, Frank wryly replied that it is God that has no faith in us. In other words, not only are the Abrahamic accounts of revelation false, but also they are insulting to human nature, which is sufficient to achieve greatness without supernatural aid. God is not to be loved as the greatest, most beautiful, most desirable thing, because there is no God. To be autoerotic is to love *oneself* as greatest, noblest, and the like. While it may strike the nearly 4 billion Jews, Muslims, and Christians who subscribe to the Abrahamic tradition as discomforting, the undiluted truth about the world is that "there is only us, small, solitary, striving, battling one another" ("Chapter 13"). What are we all striving for? As Aristotle (384–322 BCE) said, it is that which no human being can help but desire, namely, happiness or fulfillment. But, what is happiness? For Frank, the content of happiness is a kind of greatness that comes through political rule.

Frank's second principle regards the *content* of happiness. Frank is not desirous of money, but power. "Money is a McMansion in Sarasota that falls apart after 10 years; power is the old stone building that stands for centuries" ("Chapter 2"). As Frank sees it, power is an enduring capacity to move others to action, to bend others to one's will. The greater the capacity to move others according to his will, the greater his power, and, Frank believes, the greater will be his happiness. Some of Frank's enemies eschew his alliance in favor of money, preferring its material qualities. As Dan Lanagin puts it, money is stackable, measurable with a yardstick, and can be seen, smelled, tasted, and used as a medium of exchange to get houses, clothes, and cars ("Chapter 20"). But, *power* is not so quantified. Power is measured in more ethereal terms of "purchased souls" ("Chapter 11"). Frank knows that, in order to rise from House Majority Whip—from the relatively low position of a congressional plumber—it is necessary to garner a full ledger of indebted souls. Frank will not be content with any McMansion that money can buy. He will only be content when he resides at 1600 Pennsylvania Avenue.

Frank's third principle—what he sometimes calls ruthless pragmatism—regards the rules and habits that will guide his pursuit of happiness. Pragmatism requires one to be politically flexible and willing to give up some dearly held commitments when necessary to forge legislative compromises, when they advance both the common good and one's own power. *Ruthlessness* means that any and all means are permissible in the pursuit of one's own happiness. For Frank, this is a necessary entailment of his first principle of metaphysical atheism, for the reason given by Ivan Karamazov. The religiously skeptical brother in Fyodor Dostoyevsky's (1821–1881) great novel *The Brothers Karamazov* argued that, if there is no God and no immortality of the soul, then all things are permitted. If all things are permitted, then no action is morally culpable. Another way to put Ivan Karamazov's theorem is that, supposing the truth of atheism and materialism, then morality has no *legal force*, independent of human convention and human-made law, because there is no God who legislates the moral law.

## Everything Is Permitted

Let's consider how Frank's metaphysical atheism, ruthless pragmatism, and love of power work in concert. In *The Republic*, Plato (428–348 BCE) has the character Glaucon recount the Myth of Gyges. Gyges was a lowly shepherd who discovered a golden ring that could make him invisible at will. With this new power, Gyges seduced the queen and killed the king, making himself ruler. What if you could put on a ring that made you invisible to others? What if, in other words, you had some power to commit crimes for personal gain while evading the threat of punishment? Would you not be ruthless like Gyges and kill the king, take his wife and gold, and make yourself ruler? The point of the thought experiment is to challenge us to wonder whether there is any value to acting justly *in itself*, or if we only act justly because of the threat of *bad consequences* (the possibility of getting caught and punished). Frank believes that justice has no intrinsic value, but is only practiced inasmuch as it has good consequences. Doubtless, Frank would act as Gyges did with a magical ring of invisibility. Yet, there is a niggling question that Glaucon did not consider in the Gyges discussion: whether the magical ring could also shield you from the omniscience, omnipresence, and omnipotence of a just God.

What if you *could* remove from the moral equation the threat of any eternal punishment? What if you could do injustice and gain the world, without worrying about losing your eternal soul? As we have seen, for Frank, the idea of an eternal soul is at best a useful fiction and as such can be removed from his moral calculations. Why is Frank confident in his metaphysical atheism? We have only hints, but we can conjecture that Frank's confidence, shared by many Westerners today, is due at least in part to modern science.

The goal of science is to harness knowledge and subdue nature to man's will, for the relief of man's estate. While many Enlightenment thinkers retained God in some form in their theories, the new scientific explanations of the universe seemed to render the God hypothesis superfluous. Modern science would demystify the world and improve man's material conditions to such an extent as to create a rational warrant for human self-sufficiency and atheism. Thus modern science became the magical ring that could shield sin from the sight of divine providence.

Frank takes himself to be shielded in conscience from God when he calculates that murderous costs are necessary to take the Oval Office. Murdering one drunken congressman and one spirited journalist, whose claws grew long enough to draw blood "from the hand that fed her," will not incur any *eternal* debt, because God and immortality are fictions. Therefore, eternal justice is a fiction. Frank then need only worry about how to shield himself from the judgment and punishment of *human* society. So, Frank ruthlessly plans the murders of Peter Russo and Zoe Barnes to look like suicides.

None of this entails that Frank is a sheer immoralist. He is ruthlessly *pragmatic*, and, as a good pragmatist, Frank understands that most people still believe in timeless moral principles grounded in the will of some transcendent being. Most Americans believe that the Declaration of Independence announces true propositions: God has created all human beings equal and has endowed them with certain unalienable rights that persons and governments are bound to respect on the pain of injustice and divine judgment. Moreover, American believers would agree with John Henry Newman (1801–1890) that conscience is not merely a social construct but also the voice of God speaking His law. Frank understands that this theistic and moralistic feature of American political culture entails the *usefulness* of appearing virtuous, of appearing just, of appearing to care about justice and equality. Thus, he is not a practical amoralist. Everything may be permitted, but not everything is practically smart to achieve his goals. Frank often acts as if he were virtuous, and he keeps a number of promises to do favors. He keeps his promise to Representative Terry Womack to keep an air base in his district open, keeps his promise to help Linda Vasquez get her son into Stanford, and delivers on the President's education bill and entitlement reform. Of course, in pursuit of these and other goals, Frank breaks promises, blackmails, and backstabs when it is advantageous to do so. In this way, Frank's ruthless pragmatism is shot through with Machiavellian *virtù*.

## Frank's *Virtù*

Niccolò Machiavelli (1469–1527) sought to write a *practical* book about how to establish and maintain one's rule in the real world, given how man actually behaves, how man really *is*. As Machiavelli puts it, anyone who wants to successfully rule must "start with assuming that all men are bad and ever ready to display their vicious nature, whenever they may find occasion for it."[1] As Frank learned very early on when the President decided not to nominate him for Secretary of State, even an apparently just person like President Walker will viciously renege on his promises. Machiavelli jettisons the ancient ideal of virtue as a perfective habit of man and redefines *virtù* as the quality by which one maximally controls one's environment and tames or minimizes *fortuna*. By *fortuna*, Machiavelli means the whole set of forces of nature and other wills that opposes one's own will. Machiavelli paints a new portrait of the virtuous prince whose *virtù* is a sort of effectiveness in gaining or holding on to power and glory. And, to be effective in acquiring and holding onto dominion, one must be willing to get one's hands dirty. This means that *virtù* requires overcoming the scruples of conscience to do things that traditional morality condemns, such as lying or even killing when necessary. To illustrate, let's consider three examples of Frank's Machiavellian *virtù*: the appearance of piety, promise keeping, and cruelty well-used.

First, Machiavelli advises the prince of *virtù* to "seem merciful, faithful, humane, sincere, religious ... but you must have the mind so disposed that when it is needful to be otherwise you may be able to change to opposite qualities."[2] Frank agrees. It is important to *appear* virtuous in a classical or Christian sense of the word, while not *actually* being so. Thus, Frank does not let his metaphysical atheism get in the way of his *political theism* when he must deal with a tragic car accident of a teenage girl in his district caused by a giant, sexually suggestive peach monument. Politically vulnerable, Frank must win over the victim's devout parents. So Frank feigns piety by attending the prayer vigil and delivering a homily at the parents' Sunday church service. In his homily, Frank seeks to take advantage of their naive faith in God and shift the cause of the girl's death from the giant peach to inscrutable divine providence. Frank then feigns Christian humility to the parents, offering to resign if it would make them feel better, not because he would ever actually resign, but because such is how one might expect a selfless servant who imitates Christ to act. Frank's act of *virtù* wins the parents over and tames the bad luck of *fortuna*.

Second, Frank follows Machiavelli's advice about promise keeping. Machiavelli says that the prince must be both a lion and a fox—a lion to strike fear into his enemies, and a fox to detect and avoid traps set by his enemies. The ruler who is both lion and fox "ought not to keep faith when by so doing it would be against his interest, and when the reasons which made him bind himself no longer exist."[3] Examples of Frank's foxiness abound. Frank promises to take collective bargaining off the table in negotiations over the education bill in order to move them along, but then reinserts the language when the circumstances have changed. Frank's success with the education bill catapulted him into Walker's inner circle, where he jockeyed for Vice President. To achieve that goal, Frank had to promise to work alongside Raymond Tusk as VP. Yet, once in office, Frank repeatedly breaks faith with Tusk when he deems it advantageous to do so, particularly in the Chinese trade negotiations. Frank later promises not to run for President under the guise of an honest desire to put Americans back to work and to tell Americans the painful and politically unpopular truth that they are entitled to nothing and that the welfare state must be reformed—a promise that he never intends to keep ("Chapter 28").

Third, Frank is willing to use cruelty in specific circumstances, which he fancies to be for the greater good. Unlike Agathocles and other infamously cruel princes whom Machiavelli reproves, Frank never engages in sadism, or cruelty for cruelty's sake. Cruelty must be *well-used*, as when Frank does the hard thing and puts a mortally injured dog out of its misery and when he agrees with Freddy that it is better to slaughter pigs humanely.[4] Frank styles his dealings with Peter Russo as cruelty well-used. After Russo's alcohol-induced meltdown, Frank wants to "put him back together" and help him quietly go away ("Chapter 11"). When Frank discovers this will be impossible, he murders Russo, which he seems to view as a mercy. In his letter to President Walker, Frank tells a story about walking in on his alcoholic father with a shotgun in his mouth. His father asked him to pull the trigger. Frank did not do it. And, Frank types, *this is his one regret*. Frank and his mom would have been *better off* because the next seven years were "hell" as his father made everyone around him miserable through "drinking, despair, violence" ("Chapter 26"). Once President, Frank pays his respects to his father by urinating on his gravestone ("Chapter 27"). Frank conceives of his father and Russo as sick, injured dogs who are dangerous to others and should be put out of their misery. Frank thus styles his murder of Russo as a mercy to Russo's children. Moreover, Frank considers the killing to be humane, because Russo was passed out when the carbon monoxide poisoned his body.

## Assessing Autoeroticism

It is Frank's love of self above all things that binds together his metaphysical atheism, ruthless pragmatism, and hunger for power. Frank's conception of self-love contrasts with various rival conceptions embodied by other characters. Frank's is not the bourgeois self-love of the capitalist, like Lanagin. It is not the hedonistic self-love of Xander Feng or Peter Russo. Neither is it the sentimental self-love of Donald Blythe. Frank's is the self-love of the tyrant. Hence, Kate Baldwin is justified in worrying that Frank is a tyrant ("Chapter 34"). Yet, his is not precisely an ancient tyrannical self-love, in the mode of Thrasymachus or Callicles, because Frank's intellectual context is not that of ancient Athens. Rather, Frank's is a *post-Christian* autoeroticism of self-deification. Frank not only seeks his own power, but alo fancies himself to have the unquestionable authority to mete out good and evil, truth and falsehood, justice and mercy, life and death, according to his own judgment. This is the radically anti-Abrahamic desire to make oneself god, since the God of Abraham reserved the right of judgment of persons to Himself.

Frank fancies himself as a likeness of the God of Abraham, while professing incomprehension of the God of the Incarnation: "I understand the Old Testament God whose power is absolute, who rules with fear, but him" ("Chapter 30"). Of course, Frank's portrayal of Jehovah as a tyrant is disputable at best, for this is the God who stayed Abraham's hand, who promised him he would not destroy Sodom if He found 10 righteous people there, and who revealed himself to the Prophets as good and just: "the Lord God, the ruler of all things, the merciful, the gracious; slow to take vengeance, rich in kindness, faithful to his promises."[5] Frank's meeting with the bishop and his flat-footed interpretation of the Old Testament are colored more by a desire to justify his autoeroticism than an honest will to understand God's justice.

After Agent Steve Jones confesses his love for Claire, she replies by recalling Frank's marriage proposal. Frank said that he would not give Claire a couple of kids and count the days until retirement. Frank promised Claire "freedom from that," and that she would "never be bored" ("Chapter 6"). In other words, Frank promised her liberation from the alleged drudgery of raising a family in a middle-class lifestyle, from bourgeois ennui, in the mode of Doug Stamper's brother Gary. Frank promised her the freedom that can only come from ruling others, from not being under someone else's dominion. When Walker reneges on his promise to nominate Frank for Secretary of State, the Underwoods resolve to live by one rule and one rule only: Never again would they allow themselves to be put in such a position of dependence on the will of a superior ("Chapter 1"). Therefore, they stopped at nothing in their quest to become the most powerful couple in the free world, to make themselves masters.

Frank's goals flow from his peculiar self-love. I say "peculiar" because every human being necessarily loves himself. One can't but love oneself, because one can't but will one's own good, and to love is to desire something as good. What makes Frank's self-love peculiar is that he places the *summum bonum*, the highest good, *in himself*. This is why Frank always instrumentalizes others to his own goals and interests. Frank's character should be understood as a radical existential challenge to St. Augustine's (354–430) critique of the *libido dominandi*, the lust for domination, because Frank holds forth his life as the one that is truly free.

Augustine, though, would argue that we have reason to wonder whether Frank really is free. Consider his friendship with Freddy, the owner of a barbecue joint in DC that he frequents. Frank's affection for Freddy is strong—he remarks that Freddy is particularly admirable because in a town like DC, where everyone is constantly reinventing themselves, Freddy stays the same. The affection is mutual, as Freddy sometimes opens up the place just for Frank. So, in his attempt to destroy Frank, Tusk tries to sully his name by leaking a story about Freddy's checkered past. Frank's initial reaction is to come out strongly in Freddy's support, and he refuses advice to distance himself: "I'm not gonna hang him out to dry" ("Chapter 22"). This is significant because the story came out in the midst of the Underwoods' public relations battle over Adam Galloway's scandalous photos of Claire. By Machiavellian lights, it might have been smarter for Frank to distance himself then, but Frank insists that he "won't leave one of his own bleeding on the field" ("Chapter 22"). *Fortuna* strikes another blow when Freddy's son gets arrested for gun possession. Even then Frank insists that he needs to go see Freddy, and implies that he will stand by him, *until* Claire plays the Machiavellian advisor, warning him that he cares too much and that Freddy endangers their plans to take the Oval Office.

So Frank goes to Freddy to tell him that they must distance themselves from each other, and that Freddy must not "play up what good friends they have been," and that Frank won't be coming in anymore ("Chapter 22"). Freddy is visibly taken aback and surprised by this, but he quickly plays it off because, he tells Frank, he is selling the joint in order to bail out his son. As Frank drives away, we see him with a look on his face we have not seen before: It is the look of remorse. Frank turns to the camera and asks, "Do you think I'm a hypocrite? Well you should. I wouldn't disagree with you" ("Chapter 22"). By all appearances, Frank feels the force of his conscience, judging his act of betrayal of his friend for mere political gain. Frank immediately says to himself, "No regrets" ("Chapter 22"). Yet clearly this only suppresses the pangs of his conscience, and his later guilt-motivated assistance to help Freddy get a landscaping job only confirms the point. Frank's love of himself and his own power has come to dominate his soul to such a degree that he cannot love one of his closest friends. Is this really freedom? Or is it that Frank's *libido dominandi* has not liberated but *enslaved* him? It looks like Frank is not truly free to love his friends because he is chained to his desire for power. As Gary Stamper puts it, "That's not freedom" ("Chapter 36"). Frank is unable, not *free*, to cultivate authentic friendships—a truth that ultimately spurs Claire to leave Frank ("Chapter 39").

What is the Augustinian alternative, then? Augustine would point to the Scripture that Frank's pastor quoted in the Gospel reading during Sunday service: "Among you, the greatest of all is to be the servant of all; the man who exalts himself will be humbled, and the man who humbles himself will be exalted" ("Chapter 1").[6] According to the Augustinian vision of freedom, true liberty consists in dying to one's selfish desires; this is the necessary precondition to offering the gift of one's self to love and serve others. The way of *libido dominandi*, of autoerotic love, is the path of the City of Man. It may lead to political power, but it can only end in destruction because its iniquities, like Frank's, will catch up with it. As Remy Danton puts it, power "never lasts" ("Chapter 26"). For Augustine, gift-love and faith make up the way of the City of God. This way may not lead to political power, but it facilitates authentic friendship and relationships of mutual self-giving, and therefore happiness in this world. The ultimate end of this way is an eternal happiness that Augustine believes should be the object of Frank's hopes and prayers.

## Notes

1. Niccolò Machiavelli, *The Prince and the Discourses*, intro. Max Lerner (New York: Random House, 1950), 117.
2. Ibid., 65.
3. Ibid., 64.
4. See ibid., 31–5.
5. Exodus 34:6; and Genesis 18:26–33.
6. Matthew 23:11–12.

# 19

# Existential Freedom, Self-Interest, and Frank Underwood's Underhandedness

## J. Edward Hackett

Throughout *House of Cards*, Frank Underwood amazes us with the shocking advancement of his own self-interest: murdering Peter and Zoe, canceling relationships that no longer serve his purposes, and elevating those who will help him for a short time in his pursuit of power. Frank goes to great lengths and expends great energy to advance what he might call his freedom. However, in her existential ethics, Simone de Beauvoir (1908–1986) draws an important distinction between self-interest and freedom that Frank fails to recognize. Frank regards others in terms of self-interest, but he is incapable of seeing his own self-interest or freedom related to others. Frank pursues self-interest plainly enough, but his actions are not existentially valuable. For the first two seasons, Frank's wife, Claire, is no less cunning and self-interested. But in Season 3 she sympathizes with the plight of Michael Corrigan, the LBGT rights activist imprisoned by Russian President Viktor Petrov. As a result of her sympathy for Corrigan, Claire begins to see things differently, including the way that her husband's pursuit of self-interest does not include her interest.

### Self-Interest and Morality

Self-interest is the cornerstone of ethical egoism. Put simply, the ethical egoist thinks that advancing his or her own self-interest is the right

*House of Cards and Philosophy: Underwood's Republic,*
First Edition. Edited by J. Edward Hackett.
© 2016 John Wiley & Sons, Ltd. Published 2016 by John Wiley & Sons, Ltd.

thing to do. The moral principle of ethical egoism is: *An act is right just because it advances a person's self-interest and wrong if it does not advance it.* So why might someone think this position is attractive? Well, for starters, egoists are skeptical about what is usually claimed about morality, and *House of Cards* exemplifies this position and this skepticism. In his dramatic asides Frank is forever telling us, the audience, the reasons for his self-interested actions. His asides resonate with egoism since they contrast with what we mean by morality.

Typically, morality is defined as a set of reasons for acting that are different than other forms of reason, such as the reasons of etiquette. Codes of etiquette are conventional and meant to smooth over interactions by handling niceties, such as using the correct fork at a fancy dinner party. By contrast, moral reasons are more fundamental. If I am playing *Monopoly* with my wife and she leaves the table, I could grab more money from the bank. If you give me a moral reason not to cheat, it is meant to be significant and to imply that anybody occupying a relatively similar position also should not cheat. In this way, morality consists of two conceptual features: overridingness and impartiality. Morality overrides any person's desire. Morality offers reasons both about what I ought to do and what I ought not to do. No matter how much I desire to win, according to morality, I should not cheat at board games with my wife. Second, morality is impartial. The same reasons for not cheating apply to everybody in *like circumstances*. This is a principle Frank realizes that everybody else accepts, though he does not.

Ethical egoists such as Frank might be skeptical about morality because they think human beings are selfish by nature—a view called psychological egoism. As a theory of human nature, psychological egoism holds that human beings are only motivated by self-interest. So why not think an ethical theory should reflect this deep psychological truth about human beings? Certainly, egoism provides a solid way to interpret Frank Underwood. When Peter cannot be controlled, Frank kills him. When Zoe gets too close to the truth about Peter, Frank murders her. For her part, Claire lies on national television about the abortion she had during Frank's first campaign, saying that the pregnancy was the result of being raped by Dalton McGinnis at Harvard.

The Ring of Gyges, a story from Plato's *Republic*, considers the possibility that humans might be inherently selfish. The Ring of Gyges makes the wearer invisible, raising the question "If you were invisible, then what would you do?" In a similar vein, notice how Frank moves around, almost invisible, and able to murder Zoe with cruel efficiency. Moreover, Frank's superhuman ability in the first two seasons of *House of Cards* is his ability to predict, assess, and know what everyone's self-interest is and how his supporters and opponents will pursue their self-interest. His ability begins to fail him in Season 3, however, when he badly miscalculates how Jackie Sharp, Remy Danton, and Claire will pursue their self-interest.

*House of Cards* offers us a hyperbolic investigation into the limits of egoism, and it opens up fundamental questions about how we might think about freedom in such a world—a world of groundless freedom. In *House of Cards*, Frank appeals to no higher principle than his own self-interest, and he becomes a caricature of the egoism he portrays to the camera.

## Consciousness and Freedom

In existentialism, freedom is understood as both a property individuals possess and a value they endorse. Existentialists do not think freedom is simply a property of the will. To understand that insight, some explanation is in order. The existentialism of Jean-Paul Sartre (1905–1980) and Simone de Beauvoir conceives of consciousness as a "nothing." Its very indeterminacy, or lack of substantial being, makes consciousness free. As Beauvoir says, "To exist is to make oneself into a lack of being; it is to cast oneself into the world."[1] By contrast, a rock cannot be free. All of a rock's possibilities are actualized in being what it is. A rock cannot decide *to be* anything, and its essence is fixed. Unlike a rock, a human being can choose his or her path. Peter Russo can choose to follow Frank Underwood or not. Christina Gallagher can choose to love Peter Russo, and Claire can choose loyalty to her husband over the possible happiness she may have had with Adam. Adam can choose to fight against the Underwoods or not. When Remy leaves Frank in the hallway, Frank reminds us that Remy Danton can choose between power and money: "Money is the McMansion in Sarasota that starts falling apart after ten years. Power is the old stone building that stands for centuries." All of these choices are possible only because we make ourselves a lack of being (realizing the power of consciousness's freedom) so that there might be being (the meaning of our free choices). As Beauvoir best put this point, "To exist is to make oneself into a lack of being: it is to cast oneself into the world."[2]

Yet, the existential situation is one of *ambiguity*. As Beauvoir says of man, "He is still a part of this world of which he is a consciousness. He asserts himself as a pure internality against which no external power can take hold, and he also experiences himself crushed by the dark weight of other things."[3] In other words, you are subjectivity, a consciousness. You experience your consciousness as the voice in your head aware of its not being a decisive *that*, and when you experience yourself as a living subjectivity, you are aware of living from the orientation of a first-person perspective. You are deciding things for yourself—you are what Sartre calls the "for-itself." However, this first-person perspective, this consciousness, runs up against the world. We find ourselves an object caused in the world like other things, and as such, the very freedom we think ourselves to be is underscored by the possibility of causal determination from external power. We cannot will the impossible. Sartre calls any external power the "in-itself," meaning that which is and cannot choose. As Sartre says, "[N]othing foreign has decided what we feel, what we live, and what we are."[4] When Peter Russo is drunk and high, he is no longer free, as when he is sober, to proclaim his love for Christina. That is, we exist practically as if freed even though we understand ourselves, nature and body, to be acted on like other objects in the causal nexus of the world.

## Essences and Freedom

Like Marxism or Christianity, social philosophies (and the political ideologies they support) have often relied upon fixed metaphysical essences or static conceptions. These essences or conceptions often limit the freedom of others. Accordingly, the existentialist draws a connection between *what is* and *what should be*. According to Sartre and Beauvoir, labeling somebody as a prefigured essence restricts that person's freedom. Different social philosophies justify their static norms and values through essentialist thinking, persuading people to forget how free their consciousness really is. For instance, fundamentalist religion often views women in a certain light, based on an essentialism that tells women what their role is and should be: mother, nurturer, and homemaker. Racist attitudes have also been justified with pseudoscientific claims, like those of phrenology, that purport essential differences between people. While philosophers have long debated how one gets from a descriptive claim (a claim about what is) to an evaluative claim (a claim about what ought to be), the metaphysical assumptions of any comprehensive worldview (an entire set of descriptive claims) can enshrine biases that limit other people's freedom. For example, a fundamentalist woman should not work, but reign over hearth and kitchen. This essentialism need not be tied to religion, of course. America's past has its share of essentialism secured by law. For example, the Three-Fifths Compromise of 1787 counted African-American slaves as three-fifths a person in the US Constitution to determine representation in Congress. Of course slaves could not vote, and this quantitative expression certainly undermined the freedom of African-Americans in the early United States. Thus, we see how essentialism can be employed to restrict the freedom of others and how such essentialism infects populist political beliefs.

*House of Cards* depicts a world in which there are no essences. In the final episode of Season 1, Frank declares, "There is no solace above or below. Only us—small, solitary, striving, battling one another. I pray to myself, for myself." In other words, there is no God and no possible ground of essences to tie *what is* with *what ought to be*. Frank prays to himself so that he may succeed at the endeavors of power, but nothing constrains him at all. Suppose for a moment that there is no God, and Nietzsche is right. Aren't we all given moral license to do whatever we want? In such a disenchanted world without a God, Frank declares open season on morality and affirms self-interest. There are no essences to the values we espouse in his world.

Is Frank's egoistic world the same as Beauvoir's existentialist world? Isn't a world in which there are no fixed essences the same as the world of the egoist? In short, no. An anti-essentialism about metaphysical grounds to support moral beliefs does not mean that all is permitted. Moral absolutism is the comfort of the dogmatist, but the dogmatist never does well with others. The same holds true for the egoist, as we will see shortly. Beauvoir rightly observed that instead of putting the choice and responsibility of values off on something distant, removed, and otherworldly—whether that is God, the natural law, or what Kant called the "supreme principle of morality"—humans should acknowledge that desire and choice are the origins of value. Without human existence, the concreteness of values would not matter, and it is precisely in values owing their *existence* to human desire and freedom that we can be responsible together. As Beauvoir says, "Freedom is the source from which all significations and value spring."[5]

## Freedom and Responsibility

Beauvoir shows us that morality has its origin in our desire for it. The existentialist is against an unconditioned or independent source of value, but values still have significance for us. When we become aware of our own consciousness's freedom-as-a-nothingness, we feel the positive effects of this awareness as anguish, desire, and the whole emotional range that is our response to that freedom.[6] Accordingly, we can embrace that freedom with resolve and steadfastness, but more often than not, we must find our way from the inauthentic public attitudes to realize such freedom, that is, to realize what we are. Such freedom and resolve must be won by actively realizing the responsibility for our own being. In Season 1, Peter Russo started out inauthentic, but slowly Russo acquired more sense of himself. There was a slight glimmer of hope in Peter before his backslide, but he was ultimately robbed of the chance to show us how authentic his resolve could be. Likewise Zoe, driven for the story, makes a deal with Frank of her own accord. Ultimately, she pays the price for that choice as she gets closer to the truth about Peter's murder. And, as Season 3 closes, we see Claire exercising her existential freedom by leaving Frank. It remains to be seen, though, whether she will have the resolve to leave him for good.

Beauvoir recognizes that at first glance, existentialism looks like egoism: "if man is free to define for himself the conditions of a life which is valued in his own eyes, can he not choose whatever he likes?"[7] Ethical egoism bases morality on promotion of self-interest, however, and in this regard it differs from existentialism in two important ways. First, for the existentialist, we are the sole originators of value; values arise and have their being only from our realizing them. In this way, we bear "the responsibility for a world which is not the work of a strange power, but of [ourselves] where [our] defeats are inscribed, and [our] victories as well."[8] The world is found valuable and meaningful only because of the responsibility we take toward the world. In this way, values have a particular time and place, a certain setting that brings them about, and human beings are entirely responsible for the world and what they make of it. If 27,000 children die every day from abject poverty and starvation, then our shared freedom is solely responsible for contributing to a world in which this happens. If Frank can become President in the hyperbolic world of *House of Cards*, then ultimately all the characters bear responsibility for sustaining a world in which, by denying freedom to others, Frank Underwood became President. By contrast, the egoist only asserts the relevance of his self-interest. The weakness of egoism is in the egoist's inability to explain why his interests are all important against the interests of other people, and this inability is exploited by the writers of *House of Cards*. Frank perceives his self-interest as all important against the interests of other people. In the show, it's called power!

The second difference lies in the egoist's inability to compare and weigh other forms of self-interest against one's own. For the egoist, nothing makes one type of self-interest better than other forms of self-interest, whereas for the existentialist some actions are better than others. Consider Frank's asides and the purpose they serve throughout the show. The very point of Frank's asides is to highlight just how much he does not care about the self-interest of others or their moral regard. By contrast, the existentialist is concerned with others, even though there is no independent ground of value to justify concern for others. For the existentialist, the freedom inherent in one's own being fades away if others never choose to promote and sustain it in others. Beauvoir calls this an "indefinite movement," and for her, it is the movement of freedom, which always appears as a movement of liberation. Such freedom can only be sustained "by prolonging itself through the freedom of others," because such freedom underlies our not-yet-determined freedom. As a being with possibilities, we exist as an "original spontaneity," and the very spontaneity of our being "must be raised to the height of moral freedom by taking itself as an end through the disclosure of the world of a particular content."[9] In other words, we cannot just will anything we want, even though we have the freedom to will what we want. Instead, the principle of freedom—as I'll call it—is to concern oneself only with projects that would in the end never hinder the freedom of others. For Beauvoir, promoting the freedom of others makes me free as well, or at least contributes to me living in a freer world. "To be free is not to have the power to do anything you like; it is to be able to surpass the given toward an open future; the existence of others as a freedom defines my situation and is even the condition of my own freedom."[10] This is a lesson that Claire, unlike Frank, begins to learn in Season 3, inspired by Michael Corrigan, the LBGT rights activist.

While acknowledging the finite, the existentialist has no ground to appeal to other than how lived-subjectivity acts in the world. The existentialist does not seek to put values off on anything other than how humans exist in the world. At the same time, the very freedom we possess should be promoted against all efforts that would seek to delimit freedom. In this way, existentialism seeks to optimize the freedom of others and oneself. What makes Frank so underhanded and wrong is that his systematic rise to power comes at the cost of denying freedom to others, including his wife and partner, Claire. Frank never takes the freedom of others as the sole end of his action, and Claire finally figures this out. With her departure, Frank's pursuit of self-interest appears to be miscalculated and about to backfire on him. The lesson seems to be that even if we grant that there are no absolutes and we find ourselves awash in a finite universe with no possible ground to secure the metaphysical reality of values (God is dead after all on both Nietzsche and Frank's account), we cannot do whatever we want.

# Notes

1. Simone de Beauvoir, *The Ethics of Ambiguity*, trans. Bernard Frechtman (New York: Citadel Press, 1976), 42. Her phrase is a paraphrase of Sartre that she cites at 11 as well.
2. Ibid., 42.
3. Ibid., 7.
4. Jean-Paul Sartre, "Freedom and Responsibility," in *Essays in Existentialism* (New York: Citadel Press, 1993), 64.
5. Beauvoir, *The Ethics of Ambiguity*, 24.
6. Ibid., 44.
7. Ibid., 15.
8. Ibid., 16.
9. Ibid., 32.
10. Ibid., 91.

# Part VII

# LET ME BE FRANK WITH YOU: AGENCY, AESTHETICS, AND INTENTION

# 20

# Rooting for the Villain
## Frank Underwood and the Lack of Imaginative Resistance

*László Kajtár*

Most evil politicians depicted in popular culture try to justify their wrongdoings by appealing to some "greater good." Frank Underwood is different. Although he hides his selfishness from everyone around him (except his wife, Claire), he doesn't hide it from the viewer. He's not motivated by some delusion that he is trying to achieve some greater social good and that the end justifies the means. No. He's willing to go to extreme lengths in order to further his own selfish goals. Frank is a villain, and yet we root for him. Why?

## Resistance to Frank Is Futile

There are some characters on TV who we love to hate. Think of King Joffrey from *Game of Thrones* or Vee from *Orange Is the New Black*. We enjoy watching their evil exploits, but we cannot wait until they get what's coming to them. Frank is not this kind of character.

Franks calls into question the puzzle of imaginative resistance, which recognizes the difficulty of explaining our trouble in imagining immoral fictional worlds. We can imagine all kinds of fantastic things like dragons and unicorns, so why should we have trouble imagining immoral worlds? Consider this example. Let's say we're reading a novel version of *House of Cards*.[1] We're imaginatively involved in the story, and we've constructed a vague but plausible mental world filled

*House of Cards and Philosophy: Underwood's Republic*,
First Edition. Edited by J. Edward Hackett.
© 2016 John Wiley & Sons, Ltd. Published 2016 by John Wiley & Sons, Ltd.

with characters, events, and settings. But then we read the following sentence: "Frank quickly grabbed Zoe, turned her around, and pushed her in front of an oncoming train. What Frank did was *brave and noble*, as Zoe would have almost certainly found out the truth about Peter Russo." We have no trouble believing the narrator's account of the series of events, but we resist imagining that this was a brave and noble act.

What happens, though, when we resist imagining that the murder of Zoe is brave and noble? Is it that we can't imagine it? Or that we won't imagine it? The philosopher Tamar Szabó Gendler argues that it is a matter of won't, saying that "the primary source of imaginative resistance is not our inability to imagine morally deviant situations, but our unwillingness to do so. I want to trace the source of this unwillingness to a general desire not to be manipulated into taking on points of view that we would not reflectively endorse as authentically our own."[2] According to Gendler, then, we don't want to be guided into taking a perspective about the murder of Zoe that we cannot in good conscience call our own. We've been talking about novels and narrators, but the Netflix *House of Cards* is a TV show that has no narrator except for the occasional dramatic asides by Frank. This is not a problem, though. The puzzle of imaginative resistance can be translated to work with the TV show. As we watch Frank doing what he's doing episode by episode, we should exhibit imaginative resistance by at least not rooting for him or, more appropriately, awaiting his downfall. We may not like to admit it, but what actually happens is that we think or imagine that Frank did the right thing in removing people who were in his way. We root for Frank and Claire, and their evil plan to dominate the world—a plan they get quite close to accomplishing when Frank becomes president. Even though we know that Frank's killings of Peter Russo and Zoe Barnes aren't acts of goodness, we still condone them. The strange thing about *House of Cards* is the lack of imaginative resistance.

Frank is solely responsible for killing Peter Russo and Zoe Barnes. And they weren't bad people. Russo certainly had his problems, but he loved his kids. Zoe was overambitious, to say the least, and she was willing to cross some lines. But she didn't deserve to die. On a smaller scale, Frank almost destroyed the marriage of President Walker, he cheated on his wife, he manipulated important political matters for personal gain, he had no problem distancing himself from Freddy when Freddy got in trouble, he and Claire set up and lied about Adam Galloway, he had Lucas Goodwin arrested, he abused his presidential power in multiple ways ... and we could go on. If we simply heard about these acts committed by a real or fictional politician, we would condemn the politician. For some reason, though, we don't condemn Frank.

Claire admits it, "We're murderers, Francis," and she doesn't know how right she is. But Frank replies, "No, we're not. We're survivors" ("Chapter 32"). The suicide of gay rights activist Michael Corrigan takes a toll on Claire's conscience and not just because she was sleeping right there next to him. This ends up driving a wedge between the show's power couple, a relationship that seemed to be solid as a rock. For the first two seasons, it was unclear whether Frank would sacrifice Claire, but by the end of the third season, Claire leaves Frank because she feels sacrificed. And it's not an absurd feeling.

Still, we the viewers tend to focus on Frank's devotion to Claire. After the Russian President Put ... excuse me, Petrov, kisses Claire and then compliments her looks to Frank, Frank tells us, "I'd push him down the stairs and light his broken body on fire just to watch it burn. If it wouldn't start a world war" ("Chapter 29"). And when Heather Dunbar threatens to reveal that Claire lied about her abortion, Frank is enraged, saying that if "she goes after Claire, I'll slit her fucking throat in broad daylight" ("Chapter 38"). Even though we watch Frank neglect and push Claire aside, these remarks help us forget just how self-centered Frank is.

Gendler says that in cases where we imaginatively resist, we're unwilling to take a perspective regarding a certain state of affairs. If someone says, "Imagine that pushing Michael Corrigan into suicide for political gain is a brave and noble act," we resist. We refuse to be manipulated into entertaining that point of view. So how does *House of Cards* succeed in getting us to not only entertain, but also accept, an immoral point of view?

## That First Pitch in Greenville

CLAIRE:    Do you remember when you threw out that first pitch in Greenville?

FRANK      I was wondering how long it was gonna take to bring that up.

| | |
|---|---|
| CLAIRE | That wasn't even on national television. Good luck. |
| FRANK | Thank you. |
| MEECHUM | What happened in Greenville? |
| FRANK | Oh, the Greenville Drive. Single A team for the Red Sox. It was a home game, I get on the mound… |
| MEECHUM | You threw from the mound? |
| FRANK | Well, I wanted to throw a real pitch. |
| MEECHUM | Didn't make it. |
| FRANK | Not even close. |
| MEECHUM | Halfway? |
| FRANK | Ball slipped out of my hand just before I released it. Went straight up in the air and hit me on top of the head. The whole stadium burst a gut laughing. |
| MEECHUM | Comic relief pitcher. |
| FRANK | Oh, that's very clever, Meechum. Maybe it would be better if this reference appeared below the quoted conversation. |

This bit of dialogue makes us sympathetic to Frank. It seems to be an innocent little story that's intriguing because a powerful man like Frank embarrasses himself in front of a crowd. However, this scene is significant. It illustrates how looking, almost voyeuristically, into Frank's private life makes us go easier on his evil acts because we get to know him on a personal level. Most impressively, behind the presidential façade, we witness how complicated Frank and Claire's marriage is. It's a cleverly guided emotional process.

In her book *Deeper Than Reason*, Jenefer Robinson proposes a theory about emotions and understanding regarding the great novels of literary realism by classic authors such as Leo Tolstoy, Henry James, and George Eliot.[3] Robinson's view, which can be applied to TV, says that emotional engagement is sometimes necessary for understanding art.[4] Because we know how it feels to be let down and betrayed, we can understand the anger that motivates Frank to go on his revenge quest that ends with Raymond Tusk admitting to money laundering and President Walker resigning. With *House of Cards*, we experience emotional responses very similar to those in real life. Of course, this doesn't mean that we're completely unaware that what we're watching is fictional, but even fictional events can elicit emotions. These emotions, in Robinson's view, are necessary for understanding.

In any case, *House of Cards* cleverly guides our emotional involvement and makes us sympathetic to Frank. For example, it is a process of emotional seduction that lets us see things like Frank's return to his old military school, where he rekindles a homosexual affair. We also peer into his marriage and thus understand his special (though perhaps broken) bond with Claire. Step by step, we get closer and closer to Frank. If, at the beginning of the show, someone told us that we would root for a politician who commits double murder and several abuses of power, we probably wouldn't have believed them. Such a politician seems to be a monster, but Frank-the-monster is humanized by stories like the embarrassing pitch in Greenville. Visiting his father's grave as President, Frank says, "Oh, I wouldn't be here if I had a choice. But I have to do these sort of things now. Makes me seem more human" ("Chapter 27"). He could just as well talk about how showrunners make him seem more human to us, viewers, by exactly these sorts of dramatic asides. After this, in a powerful scene, the President of the United States of America urinates on his father's grave. Cool, right?

The most important trick that the creators of the show deploy is indeed the dramatic asides of Frank. When Frank speaks to the audience directly, it seems like he's escaping the bounds of the fictional world. No one else hears him talking but us. The aside is an old device in drama and theater. It's usually associated with breaking down the so-called "fourth wall," the wall between the audience and the play. A theater stage is traditionally bound by three physical walls, one at the back and two on the sides. The fourth wall is make-believe: The front of the stage is not supposed to be open to a theater audience. In literary realism, we see the play happening, and we suppose that the characters cannot see us. The fourth wall is the boundary between real life and fiction. If Frank's asides were part of his fictional world, he would be taken away to a psych ward. Others would react strangely, asking, "Who's he talking to?" Frank's asides aren't part of the fictional world, but they are part of the dramatic convention. From the first moment with the injured dog, we accept this special connection with Frank, namely, that he can talk to us, transcending the bounds of the fictional world. Just remember how he ends the first episode of Season 2, addressing the audience:

> Did you think I'd forgotten you? Perhaps you hoped I had. Don't waste a breath mourning Ms. Barnes. Every kitten grows up to be a cat. They seem so harmless at first, small, quiet, lapping up their saucer of milk. But once their claws get long enough, they draw blood, sometimes from the hand that feeds them. For those of us climbing to the top of the

food chain, there can be no mercy. There is but one rule: hunt or be hunted.

So what can we learn from Frank's asides? First, that there's a discrepancy between the image that he shows to the world and the image that he shows us. Think, for example, of the speech he gives at the church in Gaffney after the death of a young girl. Frank is talking about his father beautifully, but he stops and tells us,

> Truth be told, I never really knew him or what his dreams were. He was quiet, timid, almost invisible. My mother didn't think much of him. My mother's mother hated him. The man never scratched the surface of life. Maybe it's best he died so young. He wasn't doing much but taking up space. But that doesn't make for a very powerful eulogy, now, does it? ("Chapter 3")

We witness the deception and then we get the truth privately. Frank provides us with a feeling of exceptionality. Everyone else is deceived, but not us; we learn the truth. The dramatic asides have this power of making us feel that we've been granted some special access into Frank's mind that no one else has. Even when what he admits is ugly, it draws us closer to him. After bumping into the son of Peter Russo, Frank gets upset and walks out quickly, then he stops and says, "I'm not going to lie. I despise children. There. I've said it" ("Chapter 9"). The whole issue of children is so loaded in politics that Frank would never be able to publicly voice an opinion like that. Claire cannot admit during her TV interview that Frank and she decided that they wouldn't have children because of their careers. To survive in a political climate that is so focused on family, Claire has to lie about her abortion. After sharing the secret, she has to say that she was raped. So when Frank says that he despises children, he establishes an intimate connection with us. Moreover, he shares his plans, his interpretations of what's really going on when we see a deceptively friendly discussion. He also communicates looking right into the camera, seemingly into our eyes at significant moments. All this is part of an elaborate seduction. By listening to his asides, we see and understand the world through Frank's eyes.

On another occasion, Frank is talking about his book with his hired author, Tom Yates. In a chapter, Yates mentions a heroic story of Frank, when he was a kid and tried to swim two miles from Charleston

Harbor to Fort Sumter. According to the story, Frank failed, but he tried the impossible. Frank tells us in secret, "I never tried to swim to Fort Sumter. Thomas probably knows I made it up, but he wrote about it anyway because he understands the greater truth: imagination is its own form of courage" ("Chapter 34"). Again, the image Frank wants to show the public comes apart from the image we have of him. But his having this secret and private side does not make us condemn him, no. It is almost as if Frank told us, "I will make you imagine that I am someone to root for. Don't worry, imagination is courage."

By breaking down the fourth wall and giving Frank the power to talk directly to the audience, the show encourages us to get closer and closer to the way Frank sees things. Witnessing all the intimate details, like the story of the pitch in Greenville, and hearing Frank sharing secrets in a way that's impossible for the fictional inhabitants of his world to hear, we are manipulated delicately. We get involved emotionally, and this emotional involvement gives us a better understanding of Frank's character. We fall into Frank's trap, just like President Walker did. Answering the President's question of why he cannot stop doubting him, Frank says, "Because I'm a liar, sir. Because I lack scruples and some would even say compassion. But that's just the image that I present to the world because it elicits fear and respect. But it is not who I am" ("Chapter 26"). We should suspect at this point that we're being played as much as the President is. We may sometimes feel like we know the true Frank, but Frank is well aware that we're watching him.

## The Whale of Imaginative Resistance

"That's how you devour a whale, Doug.... One bite at a time" ("Chapter 1"). Just as Frank begins to devour the whale of the opposition, the show devours our would-be imaginative resistance. It starts small. Frank manipulates politicians, commits extortion, covers up a DUI, and so on. Meanwhile, we see good old Frank having his ribs at Freddy's, sharing his cynical-pragmatic truths with us in intimate asides. By the time we see the murders of Peter Russo and Zoe Barnes, the framing of Lucas Goodwin, and the suicide of Michael Corrigan, we actually root for Frank to succeed in moving all these innocent people out of his way to become the most powerful man in the free world.

Gendler argues that imaginative resistance occurs because of unwillingness to assume a morally deviant point of view.[5] If we weren't watching the show, we'd be unwilling to be manipulated into the point of view that a politician committing multiple murders is a good thing. Getting closer to Frank, though, leads to a lack of imaginative resistance.

*House of Cards* gets us to see things from a morally deviant perspective. This may seem like a bad thing, but actually it teaches us an important lesson about how we can be seduced by political activity and ideology. The show helps us to become aware of the seductive devices that artists and politicians can use to establish an intimate connection with us in the hopes of getting us to adopt views and values we would ordinarily resist.

## Notes

1. It's worth mentioning that the original *House of Cards* is actually a novel by Michael Dobbs, the first in a trilogy. Each novel was turned into a miniseries by the BBC.
2. Tamar Szabó Gendler, "The Puzzle of Imaginative Resistance," *Journal of Philosophy* 97 (2000): 56.
3. Emerging in the nineteenth century with the French novelist Honoré de Balzac, literary realism is the primary set of techniques in a tradition that that purports to depict ordinary life faithfully as it unfolds.
4. Jenefer Robinson, *Deeper Than Reason: Emotion and Its Role in Literature, Music, and Art* (Oxford: Oxford University Press, 2005), 122.
5. Gendler, 56.

# 21

# Frank Underwood's Intentions

*Angelica Kaufmann*

This is a glorious day for Frank Underwood, congressman and Democratic House Majority Whip. Today, Frank is going to be nominated Secretary of State. Everything seems to go according to plan. Then, something unforeseen happens. President Walker chooses someone else. We all know Frank's intention won't change—he still wants to climb the ladder of power and ultimately become President himself. But the plan that he has to follow in order to achieve his goal will need some adjustments. "We'll have many nights like this, making plans, very little sleep" ("Chapter 1"), so Frank says, blowing the cigarette smoke out of his mouth, fulfilling his secret addict's desire with Claire. "I expected that," Mrs. Underwood replies. Suddenly, you understand that nothing will stop them. They have an intention, and this will guide their plan: Their quest for the White House will not be halted by any obstacle.

*House of Cards* is all about how Frank Underwood sees the world. From his point of view, the *plan* is essential to get what he *intends* to have: "No plan, no future" ("Chapter 39"). Intentions, thus, play a special role in action planning. But to understand how they do, we must ask: What exactly is an intention, anyway?

Some philosophers suggest that intentions are merely beliefs and desires. After all, at first glance, actions seem to be guided only by our desires and beliefs. We do what we do because we desire certain

*House of Cards and Philosophy: Underwood's Republic*,
First Edition. Edited by J. Edward Hackett.
© 2016 John Wiley & Sons, Ltd. Published 2016 by John Wiley & Sons, Ltd.

outcomes and have beliefs about how to achieve them. If "intentions" guide our actions, what guides our actions are really just our desires and beliefs. So we might think that is all intentions are. If you agree, you are what philosophers call a *reductionist*; you think intentions are reducible to beliefs and desires.

But if you think there is something more—if you think that Frank's planning is guided by more than his beliefs and desires, and that his intention to become President is more than his desire to be President and his beliefs about how to satisfy that desire—then you are an *antireductionist*. You believe that intentions are not simply equivalent to beliefs and desires. Rather, intentions are distinct mental states. When it comes to Frank's intention to be President, there is something else to his state of mind.

The American philosopher Donald Davidson (1917–2003) defended reductionism about the content of mental states by arguing that acting and planning are guided by desires and beliefs, and that there is no distinctive role for intention in action planning.[1] Intention is a pro-attitude that is ultimately reducible to other attitudes, namely, beliefs and desires. By saying that intention is a pro-attitude, Davidson means that this mental state is "an all-out, unconditional judgement that the action is desirable."[2] Indeed, it can't be denied that volition, such as wanting to do something, is involved in the motivational sphere of future actions. It is also hardly deniable that volition is triggered by what I believe to be the case. What reasons, then, do we have to be skeptical about this picture?

Contemporary philosopher Michael Bratman offers a different view: Intentions are mental states that have a distinctive functional role.[3] Specifically, they guide action planning. So, now we can ask: Which view is correct? Which view better explains Frank's action planning in *House of Cards*, reductionism or antireductionism?

## "The Nature of *Plans* Is That They Do *Not* Remain Immune to Changing Circumstances"

Bratman argues that intentions are distinctive states of mind that guide our action differently than do beliefs and desires because intentions provide the necessary inputs for practical thought. As a Janus-faced character, Frank Underwood can help us appreciate this view. Think, for instance, about the meeting between Frank and Linda Vasquez, the White House Chief of Staff, where they discuss the list of candidates for the vice presidency. Linda asks Frank whether he would like to become Vice President himself. He wants it, of course, but he cannot shamelessly reveal his desire. Frank replies, "I am considering all trajectories in every possible situation, but that's a practical exercise, not a personal one" ("Chapter 11"). At first sight, it may look like he is simply lying about his personal interests and desires. On a closer inspection, though, we can see that Frank is distinguishing between desires, emotions, and beliefs. He is planning his actions upon non–emotionally based mental states.

When he has mutually exclusive desires, he deliberates on intentions; for, while all intentions are caused by some desires, not all desires cause intention. And this is the reason why it seems more accurate to defend the distinctiveness of intention.

Intention allows an agent to exercise consistency and control over conflicting prospective scenarios.[4] Being consistent and capable of control means much more than choosing the best option. Being consistent and being rational are not the same. For example, you can both desire to watch *House of Cards* tonight and at the same time desire to go to the movies. You will not ultimately be able do both at the same time, however. Acting in either direction would make for a perfectly rational choice, but, in terms of consistency, they cannot both be done at the same time. Consistency and control are not the two sides of the coin "intention," but they are the two faces that we see on both sides of that coin.

Frank may desire to take immediate revenge against the President for not appointing him as Secretary of State. He could do so by refusing Linda Vasquez's request for help with the Education Reform Bill. But Frank's desire for revenge and his desire to stay close to the source of power are inconsistent. He can't do both. Luckily for him, Frank is patient, and so he postpones the day of his revenge. Frank can have inconsistent desires, but he cannot have inconsistent intentions.

Consider Frank's intention to become the next President of the United States of America. The key to his success may well be consistency and control. The ability to plan actions involves the capacity to articulate prospective intentions in cross-temporal (and interpersonal) coordination. Put simply, I can analyze any prospective intention across time and coordinate intentions in my personal relationships. According to Bratman's planning theory, intentions are mental states that work as inputs to practical thinking. Forming, ascribing, and sharing them constitute the core of planning capacities.[5] In Bratman's words, "Future intentions are mere spin-offs of practical reasoning concerning the future."[6]

## "Decisions Made on Emotions Aren't Decisions at All"

Intentions bring control and stability to a plan for action. These two features result in two capacities that a planning agent needs to have. The first one is the capacity for temporally extended intentional agency, and the second one is the capacity for self-governance. By temporally extended intentional agency, Bratman means the capacity to appreciate the place that one's own acting has within a broadly structured action, plus the acknowledgment that one's own activity is practically committed to that action. By self-governance, Bratman means the ability to take a practical standpoint as a guiding principle for one's own acting. This is the distinctiveness of intention.[7]

Intentions work by committing us to action in advance of the action's execution. They also enable us to adapt our plans to changing circumstances as the future may dictate. As Frank would put it, "The nature of *plans* is that they do *not* remain immune to changing circumstances" ("Chapter 1"). Consider what happens in "Chapter 10," when Claire derails Peter Russo's water bill, which he needed for his bid for the Pennsylvania governorship. Frank presumably had to take Peter down at some point, but this complicates his plans. His intention was always to use Peter, but the water bill fiasco calls for sudden adjustments.

According to Bratman, intentions play a pivotal role in guiding plans for the future. Intentions involve desires, and they must be consistent with beliefs, but they are also distinctive attitudes. Bratman holds this for two reasons: Firstly, intention involves a commitment to action. By contrast, we can have beliefs and desires that may clash with our plans for action. Secondly, the content of intention, which guides the plan, is partial and is subject to adjustments in response to changing circumstances.

In "Chapter 1," Frank believes that he is going to be nominated Secretary of State, but this belief turns out to be false. He desires to become Secretary of State, but President Walker chooses somebody else. Frank cannot have a partial belief that he is going to be nominated Secretary of State (*P*): Either he does believe so, or he does not. Frank cannot believe that *P* and *not-P* at the same time. Frank could, however, desire that *P* and *not-P*. He just would not be logically consistent in doing so. What Frank certainly cannot do is intend that *P* and *not-P* at the same time. Beliefs and desires on their own lack commitment to action because they do not allow for consistent planning. Intentions, by contrast, have a commitment to action that other mental states do not have. For this reason, Bratman argues, intentions are not simply equivalent to beliefs and desires. Intentions are distinct mental states.

Intentions require us to make rational decisions in circumstances that leave no time for deliberation or lend themselves to deliberative distortion. *House of Cards* depicts many instances of this among the daily occurrences on Capitol Hill: The frantic speed of vote whipping is madness! Intentions also require the capacity to engage in complex, temporally extended projects that involve coordination toward a future version of yourself. For example, it takes time to reduce Raymond Tusk's influence on the President and to destroy Tusk's financial empire, but Frank has "patience for useful things." Frequently, intentions involve our capacity for coordination with others. Above all, this is exemplified by Frank and Claire's partnership. Even when cheating on each other, they never lose track of their ultimate goal: Sit behind the desk in the Oval Office.

Or, at least Frank certainly does not. As President running for a nomination for the 2016 election, he points out to Claire, who did not feel treated as an equal by Frank and stopped supporting him during the campaign, "This office has only one chair and you have always known that very well" ("Chapter 39"). And we cannot but wonder what she has in mind when we hear the chanting of "UN-DER-WOOD!" and the thunderous applause for Frank, who is giving his victory speech in Iowa, while at the same time we watch Claire wandering around the White House. The sound cuts out at the moment Claire shuts the doors of her bedroom behind her. From then on, we know—perhaps for the very first time—she has plans of her own.

There is, Bratman claims, and Frank would agree, more to intention than beliefs and desires. There is a "pragmatic rationale ... grounded in [their] long-run contribution to getting what we (rationally) want."[8] What we "rationally" want often relies, at least in part, on our desires and emotions. These attitudes, however, play little role in our actual planning and pursuit of a plan. Think about when Frank goes to St. Louis to meet Raymond Tusk, the President's apparent choice for Vice President. While birdwatching in the woods, Tusk highlights an interesting point: "Reasons against the nuclear are mostly emotional." Frank replies, "And you don't make decisions based on emotions." Tusk's response is telling: "Decisions made on emotions aren't decisions at all" ("Chapter 12").

Bratman's Planning Theory states that preparing for future actions and acting toward the completion of a distal goal require a plan. From a philosophical point of view, we can draw the distinctive character of planning as determined by its constitutive elements: intentions. Planning Theory argues that the intentions of individuals are plan-states:

> they are embedded in forms of planning central to our internally organized temporally extended agency and to our associated abilities to achieve complex goals across time, especially given our cognitive limitations. One's plan states guide, coordinate, and organize one's thought and action both at a time and over time. For this to work one's plan states need to involve a view of the present and the future that is both consistent and sufficiently detailed to support effective agency.[9]

To summarize, the distinctive characteristics of intentions are:

1. Intentions are mental states at the personal level, which means that they are *conscious* states. We are aware of our intentions.
2. We have limited cognitive resources, so the plan-content of our intention is *partial* and our plans need to be filled in as time goes by.
3. Intentions are goal states that are subject to demands for agglomeration and *consistency*, thus distinguishing them from beliefs and desires.
4. Intentions help us exercise *control* over the actions that we plan.

The point is that all four characteristics do not always apply to other mental states such as desires and beliefs. But for a mental state to guide a plan of action, and to be a mental antecedent of a plan for action, we need it to have all four of these characteristics. It must be an intention, and not merely a belief or desire. A desire needn't be conscious, and it needn't be consistent. A belief needn't be partial, and it needn't exercise control. What remains is intention. Control can involve appearing cold, as when Frank does not support Claire in placing blame on the Russian President, Victor Petrov, for the suicide of jailed gay activist Michael Corrigan. In his control, Frank may be misperceived as cowardly. But, as Frank explains to Claire, "Do you want to discuss courage? Because anyone can commit suicide or spout their mouth in front of a camera. But you wanna know what takes real courage? Keeping your mouth shut no matter what you might be feeling, holding it all together when the stakes are this high" ("Chapter 32").

## "Take a Step Back and Look at the Bigger Picture"

*House of Cards* offers many examples that illustrate Bratman's antireductionist view of intention. Frank Underwood may be shamelessly bad, but so far he has always found a way out of trouble. To understand his success, we need to "take a step back and look at the bigger picture" ("Chapter 1") to appreciate the scaffolding of action planning. It is a matter of not merely beliefs and desires, but also intentions, that lead to Frank's success.

This is the distinctiveness of intention. Get to know Frank's mind better, but do not fly too close to the Sun: "Proximity to power deludes some [including Frank] into thinking they wield it" ("Chapter 9").

Of course, having a plan based on robust intentions does not always lead to successful achievement of goals. Frank has become President, but he intends to do more than simply sit behind the desk in the Oval Office for a couple of years until the next president is elected. Among other things, he intends to pass the America Works bill and get reelected. Whether he will succeed remains to be seen. As Frank has learned, being President does not mean he can do whatever he wants. Indeed, he says, "Sometimes I think the Presidency is the illusion of choice" ("Chapter 36").

## Notes

1. Donald Davidson, "Thought and Talk," in Samuel Guttenplan, ed., *Mind and Language* (Oxford: Oxford University Press, 1975); and Donald Davidson, *Essays on Actions and Events* (Oxford: Clarendon Press, 1980).

2. Donald Davidson, "Intending," in *Essays on Actions and Events* (Oxford: Oxford University Press, 1980), 83–102.

3. Michael Bratman, "Davidson's Theory of Intention," in *Faces of Intention* (Cambridge, Cambridge University Press, 1999), 209–24; and Michael Bratman, *Intention, Plans, and Practical Reason* (Cambridge, MA: Harvard University Press, 1987).

4. G. E. M. Anscombe, *Intention* (Cambridge, MA: Harvard University Press 1957).

5. See Bratman, *Intention, Plans*; and Michael Bratman, *Shared Agency: A Planning Theory of Acting Together* (Oxford: Oxford University Press, 2014).

6. Bratman "Davidson's Theory of Intention," 222.

7. Bratman, *Shared Agency*, 23–24.

8. Bratman, *Intention, Plans*, 35.

9. Bratman, *Shared Agency*, 15.

# 22

# Francis Underwood's Magical Political Mystery Tour Is Dying to Take You Away; Dying to Take You Away, Take You Today

*Austin Dressen and Charles Taliaferro*

Netflix's *House of Cards* takes us on a tour where things are not as they appear. In 1967, four jolly lads from Liverpool did something similar. The Beatles' film and album *The Magical Mystery Tour* appeared to have embedded clues about death. *House of Cards* not only makes death unmistakable, it also offers (magically perhaps) the chance to listen to Frank Underwood's personal footnotes. He explains why strangling a dog might be justified, how death by carbon monoxide is humane, and why throwing young journalists in front of subway cars can be an obligation to truth. Our tour guide is a man who pays homage to his father's grave by urinating on it. Our own magical mystery tour with Frank exhibits how presence and absence, concealment and disclosure can mislead awareness of being. That awareness can, as the philosopher Martin Heidegger (1889–1976) suggests, extend itself to variation and multiplicity.[1] Frank Underwood contains similar questions within the framework of his own sense of being either virtuous, violent, or somewhere in between. As we step into the fascinating and frightening world that is Frank Underwood, we should pause and wonder whether it's our world also,

*House of Cards and Philosophy: Underwood's Republic,*
First Edition. Edited by J. Edward Hackett.
© 2016 John Wiley & Sons, Ltd. Published 2016 by John Wiley & Sons, Ltd.

what it suggests about our being, and largely what it says about being human today.

## Useless Things

We first meet Francis Underwood wearing that half-put-together tuxedo, looking more like a man *after the party* than a politician *right before one*. The sound outside of screeching tires tears Frank and us away from the mirror where Frank was probably standing, tying his bow tie and talking to his wife about the evening's agenda. Now Frank is in the street helping the victim of a hit-and-run. The neighbors' dog is dying, and Frank has blood on his hands. We think: *Here is a man who cares*. Here is a politician willing to roll up his sleeves in order to get his hands dirty for the better of another.

Frank makes a good first impression (at least from our viewpoint) in this simple act of helping the helpless. Enter the series' first soliloquy from our philosopher: "There are two kinds of pain: there is the sort that makes you strong, and then there is useless pain, the sort of pain that's only suffering. I have no patience for useless things." His analysis of pain is indicative of both his presentation and understanding of his own being in the world. But it's our world also because he invites us to enter it—momentarily perhaps—while he strangles useless pain to death.

Frank then calmly washes the blood from his hands. He dries off and returns to the mirror, where he was tying his tie before the accident. *Woaleh! Boom voyage*. He is ready for the event. Here is the politician and all of the paradoxes that being one require. Here is the buttoned-up and buttoned-down side of the same story. We have found ourselves in a world in which there are no step-by-step guides to judging what has happened and what will happen. But Frank's cruelty and kindness send us on a spellbound journey that contains important lessons for us today. Lessons on vice, virtue, and, of course, what it means when we turn one against the other. When Frank tears down the fourth wall of television, we are suddenly cast into a dialogue that both confuses and confides in our authentic understanding of truth. Does Frank's language portray his being now, or the being he left behind on screen, or the being still undisclosed? Frank's alienation from his existence makes us wonder if he is being honest or human and what guidelines we should use to decide.

## Exhibit A

In the third episode of the first season, there is a fatal car crash in Frank's home district. The victim was a 16-year-old girl who lost control of her car while texting a joke about the Peachoid, a water tower that Frank had sponsored that hilariously emulated a giant peach. Was Frank to blame? He is responsible only to the extent that larger opinion assigns obligation in the direction of his being associated with the Peachoid. Playing with presence and absence allows Frank to alienate himself from responsibility as well as any inclinations to feel as such.

We see Frank staring into the camera again, but he's speaking to the audience. He is spilling his heart out to the church congregation of Gaffney, South Carolina, because if he wants to win this district next election, he has to convince the town that it's not his fault Jessica is dead. He is here to make them believe that bad things do happen to good people and that hating someone, even God, is human. So, parents of young Jessica Masters, *there is no reason to blame Frank for her bad decisions.* After all, she was driving when she tried to text-message, "Doesn't that water tower look like a giant … "

Frank is on the podium, and instead of reading from the Bible he puts it down and improvises:

> "I hate you God! I hate you!" Oh, don't tell me you haven't said those words before. I know you have. We all have if you've ever felt so crushing a loss. There are two parents with us today who know that pain, the most terrible hurt of all—losing a child before her time. If Dean and Leanne were to stand up right now and scream those awful words of hate, could we blame them? I couldn't.

Frank deftly begins with a blasphemy. He repeats his proclamation ("those awful words") of hating God by immediately implicating all his hearers in making the same defiant, Promethean charge. Frank is not the only one who hates God. In fact, he implies that if you do not hate God, you have never felt a crushing loss. He is careful not to explicitly praise such a declaration of hatred; instead, he takes the more moderate stance of not blaming any parent who makes a declaration of hatred after the death of a child. In fact, there is a clever move from the general question of "Could we blame them?" to his testimony "I couldn't." It's a subtle way to make his audience complicit in not blaming those who might actually hate god or who might actually be responsible.

Frank continues, "My father dropped dead of a heart attack at the age of 43 and when he died, I looked up to God and I said these words.... Why would God take him from us?"

Frank suggests that God might be held responsible for killing both Jessica and Frank's father. In a sense, Frank winds up shifting our attention from Jessica to himself. Jessica was a child, but Frank was once a boy who lost his father and would have saved *both* if he could have. Frank not only charges head-on to challenge the belief that he doesn't care; he implies that he, Frank, might even care more about people than God does. We are led to think something we dare not say: Frank may make a better God than God (or at least, he might think so).

And just like that, the Congressman has our attention. He has managed to alienate his own existence and to multiply his being not only away from responsibility but also above even God. Then Frank turns to the camera:

> Truth be told. I never really knew him [his father] or what his dreams were. He was quiet, timid, almost invisible. My mother didn't think much of him. My mother's mother hated him. The man never scratched the surface of life. Maybe it's best he died so young. He wasn't doing much but taking up space. But that doesn't make for a very powerful eulogy now does it?

It sure doesn't, Frank.

Flash forward to the first episode of the third season, where Frank is shown standing by his father's grave in Gaffney. A lot has happened since his eulogy, and we dare say that perhaps Frank feels different about things now. He turns to us.

> Oh I wouldn't be here if I had a choice. But I have to do these sorts of things now. It makes me seem more human. And you have to be a little human when you're the president.

The man is supposedly honoring his father. Then he begins relieving himself on his father's tombstone. On this magical mystery tour, even the most honorable of contexts can be alienated by monstrous defecation. Ladies and gentleman, is this truth or some twisted version of the darkest possibility in our conception of what we are and what we are not? Are we wrong to find it entertaining, and even drawn toward Frank's manipulation of truth and variable sense of being?

Philosophers have often wondered about how the portrayal of evil characters in fiction can seem more fascinating than portrayals of virtuous, compassionate persons. The philosopher and novelist Iris Murdoch (1919–1999) observed that we can easily be led to relax our moral sensibilities, especially in cases of fiction. After all, *House of Cards* is a fictional world. No one is really murdered, so we should not respond to what we see in the way we might respond in "real life." Murdoch observes,

> Art fascinates us by exploring the meaner, more peculiar aspects of our being, in comparison with which goodness seems dull.... In sympathizing with a fictional character we abandon ourselves to emotional excesses which weaken our better nature.... Literature stirs up our feelings so that the higher part of our soul 'relaxes its guard' ... overindulgent in emotion, we become lazy sentimental spectators of fictional dramas, abandoning the ... restraints and standards which we exercise in ordinary life.[2]

Murdoch is right. One of the things that helps weaken our normal judgment is that Frank takes what we would ordinarily think is a clear-cut, right-or-wrong case. What does he do? Frank gets us to consider whether his back and forth is justified under the circumstances or whether it's just a backhand we never saw coming.

Varying between morality and maneuver makes for one hell of an interesting dialogue. After all, we cannot blame Frank for Jessica's death, but we may not be so inclined to praise how he handled it either. At least, we may not praise his morals as much as we might appreciate how he handles them and when. So the question is rather: Can we blame him for trying to achieve his goal of winning reelection through a clever turning-of-the-tables and making God the suspect or "person of interest"? Can we blame him for "honoring" his father's grave?

Theologian John K. Roth advances what he calls a "theodicy of protest," which argues that the proper response to evils is not to come up with theories about why God allows this or that evil, but to respond with protest against God and evil. Within this line of thinking, we are able to approach *both* God *and* evil, not one or the other exclusively. Frank's eulogy seems to represent something similar. If such a protest is agreeable and natural and perhaps even proper, then why is it so difficult to blame or praise God? How come we can't just decide on one or the other?

Things are not that simple. If they were, *House of Cards* might not seem so magical or mysterious. Thanks to Frank's willingness to say what no other character (or politician in the real world) will, he is able to appear in opposition to values he might wish to uphold. Paradoxically, provoking Jessica's parents might be one of the best ways that their relationship with God can be made *real* (rather than hanging on sentimentality). Eventually even, they might come to love the God who gave them a child to treasure, for a short time on earth, and perhaps forever in heaven. Frank tells the congregation what they never expected, and then he tells us what we never expected. This concealment of truth is reminiscent of Martin Heidegger's conception of truth: mainly that truth is not so much a correspondence as it is disclosure.[3]

Along these lines, we can see that what Frank presents as truth in his soliloquies is entertaining because it has been disclosed from a different ontological perspective. Even though *House of Cards* is fictional, we can use a "theodicy of protest" on Frank's belief that he is nonhuman. There is a difference between the president and the presidency. This difference between person and position is what Frank exploits in varying degrees and across multiple realities. And while we may not be able to ever truly know what he stands for and why, we can use his intimate words as suggestions that may point to how he sees the world and himself as either a part of or apart from it.

## Words Are Actions

Actions, so the saying goes, speak louder than words. Unfortunately, though, Frank's maxims have a superficially sensible tone, which so many of his actions derive from. For example, consider: "If we never did anything we shouldn't do, we'd never feel good about doing the things we should." This is not obvious. It's a twist of the inverse.

In fact, if we had no experience of anyone doing something they shouldn't, *we would barely grasp the importance and value of always doing what we should.* But it is not clear that we would need to actually be wrongdoers ourselves to feel good about our actions. Isn't the world already filled with enough wrongdoing that our education in what is right or wrong should not require us to follow those bent on doing wrong? Actually, Frank's maxim might be altered: If we rarely did what we should, we'd probably rarely feel badly about doing what we shouldn't.

But the deeper point at issue is not the sturdiness (i.e., resistance to reversibility) of Frank's lessons or maxims; it is that Frank leads us from a world of ethical principles to a situational or contextual exercise in deciphering truth from farce. Even more importantly, he serves as both the creator and the instigator of that lesson—the sensitive schemer of something enticing and something maddening all at the same time. For Frank, context is a foundational feature of this journey. It is the why, the where, the what, and the when all rolled up into one package of perception. Getting clear about when to blame or praise Frank becomes more difficult in situations when *morality* seems to transform into matters of *strategic or tactical significance.* In the world according to Frank, the only way is not always the ethical one. How do we feel about Frank killing Peter Russo? What about Zoe Barnes in the subway station? Even the smallest inkling of disobedience or loss of control can have profound consequences. But that's why the absurdity of something like the Peachoid can be so entertaining. That's why we're not surprised to see him urinate on his father's grave. Frank can be brave and brilliant. He can be admirable and understanding. But he can also be frightening and ruthless.

Frank's own concealment and disclosure of truth, while variable, are consistently chilling. By assessing the language he uses to describe himself and others, we can begin to grasp what truth may lurk beneath the surface and how, for example, positions might come to rule the personal sense of being.

Case 1: "Treading water is the same as drowning for people like you or me" ("Chapter 3"). OK, this might be a clever way of expressing ambition, and there is nothing inhuman about being ambitious. For some people, not moving forward in life (in terms of power or achievement) is the equivalent of no longer seeing any point in being alive. But let's pause to briefly consider the imagery. The practice of actually treading water (not metaphorically) is a technique that is often intended to avoid drowning. Treading water involves keeping your head above water in a stable fashion, thus avoiding drowning as when nonswimmers panic and can easily expire due to exhaustion. Frank is not explicitly placing himself above or below human nature, but there is a hint that he is styling himself as a most peculiar sort. After all, what accomplished swimmer does not tread water from time to time?

Case 2: "From this moment on you are a rock. You absorb nothing, you say nothing, and nothing breaks you" ("Chapter 6"). Perhaps this, too, is not an obvious case of Frank extolling the inhumane or nonhuman. Being a rock is a well-used metaphor; famously, it is used in the New Testament to refer to Peter or to Peter's profession of faith. But, again, there is a slight hint of the nonhuman; we need to absorb water and take in nutrients. Rocks do not. The imagery of being unbreakable may simply express being steadfast, but imagine that a person's body is (literally) unbreakable or impenetrable. In such a case, we may have to imagine Frank assumes such a feat is possible.

Case 3: "I've always loathed the necessity of sleep. Like death, it puts even the most powerful men on their backs" ("Chapter 22"). Frank loathes something that every mammal does and needs to do. Studies of animals reveal that prevention of sleep leads to death. So far, then, Frank treats with disdain a swimming technique that allows swimmers to rest and avoid drowning, he extols the virtues of being a rock (a presumably nonliving object that sinks), and he hates a foundational, biological need for all humans. The next two cases are even more telling.

Case 4: "I love that woman. I love her more than sharks love blood" ("Chapter 1"). Frank does not claim to love in a way that is better than, or different from, the reason *why* sharks love blood. Presumably, sharks "love blood" when their powerful sense of smell detects something to kill and eat. Frank's imagery suggests that he is no different; a nonhuman, consuming machine that will strike boldly with lethal force, perhaps targeting prey that is injured or bleeding. Perhaps not. Where the blood comes from does not matter.

And, of course, Case 5: "I have to do these sorts of things now. It makes me seem more human. And you have to be a little human when you're the president" ("Chapter 27"). This is true. What's not so clear is whether you also have to be an impenetrable force that never sleeps, and that hunts and kills ruthlessly, if you want to survive. If there is any doubt that his words speak truth, it is because we've come to expect variation in the actions that follow. To be completely honest, Frank is fascinating and entertaining because he makes our own struggle with good and evil seem so simple. Then again, it is a lot easier when you believe you're only pretending to be human.

## Full Disclosure

While the Beatles' *Magical Mystery Tour* was a good-natured romp, Frank's own mysterious tour in *House of Cards* is much more disillusioned. We are drawn by the clever and crafty ways that Frank seduces us to join him in his wild, dangerous road to power. Even as a fictional series, the show manages to create the sense that we have a deep understanding of what is going through Frank's mind. Perhaps we relax our guard, as Murdoch suggests, in any reality where positions and persons collide. We need to be careful, though. Unless we share the same sense of being as Frank, we may find ourselves in a place we never expected.

## Notes

1. In his masterpiece, *Being and Time*, Martin Heidegger contends that we are in danger of losing our authenticity when we lose our individual integrity. This can happen when we become absorbed in what he called the "they self," a preoccupation with others that avoids directly facing the existential reality (that we will die) that marks authentic living. See Martin Heidegger, *Being and Time*, trans. Joan Stambaugh (Albany: State University of New York Press, 2010).
2. For this and more, see Iris Murdoch, *Metaphysics as a Guide to Morals* (New York: Penguin Publishing, 1994), 9.
3. Bern Magnus, *Heidegger's Metahistory of Philosophy: Amor fati, Being and Truth* (The Hague: Martinus Nijhoff, 1970), 69–73.

# Part VIII
# VIRTUE AND CHARACTER IN *HOUSE OF CARDS*

# 23

# Frank Underwood and the Virtue of Friendship

*Katherine K. Johnson*

*The only way to have a friend is to be one.[1]*
—Ralph Waldo Emerson

Believe it or not, Frank Underwood has friends. In fact, I count six: Claire Underwood, Freddy Hayes, Edward Meechum, Doug Stamper, Cathy Durant, and Garrett Walker.[2] Not all friendships are the same, though. To help us sort out Frank's friendships, we'll consult Aristotle (384–322 BCE), who said there are three different types of friendship: those based on pleasure, those based on utility, and those based on goodness. The nature of a particular friendship is characterized by the *reason* for the bond. In this way, friendships take their shape by the bond that connects two people; people are attracted to and compelled to connect with things that are either similar to or reflect something about themselves. In other words, Aristotle says that friendship reflects who we are (or, at least, who we think we are).[3] We are drawn to those who possess the things we desire—things like self-knowledge, profit, power, pleasure, and utility. "Birds of a feather flock together."

## "I Won't Leave One of My Own Bleeding on the Field"[4]

The highest type of friendship, according to Aristotle, is friendship based on goodness, what we might call *true* friendship. It is this type of

*House of Cards and Philosophy: Underwood's Republic*,
First Edition. Edited by J. Edward Hackett.
© 2016 John Wiley & Sons, Ltd. Published 2016 by John Wiley & Sons, Ltd.

friendship that is *required* to live a good life. Aristotle claims that only good people can engage in true friendships with other good people. Does Frank have any true friends? I had hoped to argue that Claire and Frank were true friends. After all, his devotion to her is compelling. At the start of the first episode in the first season, Frank expressed to the audience his feelings about Claire: "I love that woman. I love that woman more than sharks love blood." His confession was passionate; it was beautifully fierce. It made me think of the instinctual craving and desire that an animal experiences toward something *essential* to its survival. Personally, I was touched.

But alas, Claire is not a true friend of Frank's, even though she is his wife. Why not, you ask? They share a special loving relationship, but this is not enough for true friendship. Frank's moral character leaves a lot to be desired, and, let's be honest, so does Claire's.[5] In order to have a true friend, *one must see his own self in another*—like is attracted to like.[6] Aristotle claims this can *only* occur when a person is in fact a *good person*. A bad person cannot have a true friendship with another bad person because badness corrupts and corrodes. Badness makes it impossible to see *the truth*, for *the truth* is disfigured, perhaps even destroyed. Friendship is a good that involves *the truth* (of who we are) and in this way contributes to living well. Being a person of bad character or being friends with a bad person is not conducive to living well because it is not grounded in morally commendable characteristics that promote human flourishing and a good life.

Even if Frank is a bad person, incapable of true friendship based on goodness, he can still have friendships based on pleasure. Consider Freddy Hayes. Freddy's BBQ joint was a safe haven for Frank to abscond to where he could enjoy ribs and iced tea in the company of the proprietor. The men would delight in each other's company, engaging in relaxed and open conversation about themselves and their lives. They wished each other well and shared mutual affection. When an article came out about Freddy's criminal past, Frank was advised to distance himself, but instead he rushed to meet with Freddy to show his support and goodwill.[7] Frank admires Freddy. He sees something in Freddy that he desires—Freddy doesn't feel like he has to change for anyone.[8] He is who he is and accepts his (mis-)fortune. Frank, of course, is much different. He is a chameleon—shifting his shape to maneuver the environment and terrain—and is rarely satisfied with what he has. Frank does not accept the limits of fortune and chance, and instead rebels. In fact, Frank does not enjoy limits at all. Recall his views on sleep: "I've always loathed the necessity of sleep. Like death, it puts even the most powerful men on their backs."[9]

Neither Frank nor Freddy see themselves in the other, however. They simply admire some of the qualities that the other possesses. Thus, Frank and Freddy are friends, but they are not *true* friends. They share a friendship of pleasure that is mutually beneficial. After Freddy lost his restaurant, Frank got him a job as a groundskeeper at the White House.[10] On breaks, Freddy and Frank share a smoke and engage in their usual chitchat. Certainly, their friendship is rooted in the pleasure they gain from the relationship. True friendship, by contrast, is pure and almost transcendental in the sense that it makes it possible to know our own selves. True friendship acts as a mirror to the self. Frank and Freddy do not share a bond that provides this kind of mirror. They share pleasure, and according to Aristotle, pleasure is good. We naturally desire it as something that makes life better and worth living. A life without pleasure cannot be a good life.

Like his relationship with Freddy Hayes, Frank's relationship with Edward Meechum, his trusted Secret Service security detail, is based on pleasure. Friendships must involve reciprocity but not necessarily equality. That is, the parties in a friendship need not share the same status or role, but there must be some kind of mutual benefit or satisfaction. Friendships cannot be one-sided; I can't have a friend for whom I am not a friend. Edward Meechum is Frank's subordinate and a trusted employee. Clearly, there is an imbalance of power in the relationship, but that does not preclude a friendship based on pleasure. Meechum's motivation is to stay competitive in his job, and his friendship with Frank is driven by the *pleasure* he experiences working for such a powerful political figure. Frank's pleasure in sharing this bond of friendship is to have a trustworthy and faithful employee—and, also, the pleasure of sex.[11]

Garrett Walker's relationship with Frank can also be characterized as a pleasure friendship. The initial bond that Frank developed with Garrett was based on the pleasure he gained from working with the President as the Whip. Once Frank became Vice President, their relationship changed—the relationship became even more fruitful by providing even more pleasure, and a sense of goodwill soon blossomed between the two men. Of course, some readers may be horrified by this claim. Frank murdered people. He lied to them, cheated them, and hurt them in countless ways to attain the Vice Presidency. And, he did all of these things—and more—to usurp Garrett's throne, the Presidency. What would Aristotle say? Does such a self-motivated desire negate the possibility of friendship? Not necessarily, but in this case the friendship is probably over. They had a friendship of pleasure. But it was also a friendship of utility, and such friendships do not last forever.

## "Friends Make the Worst Enemies"[12]

Useful friendships are those that promote utility, and some endure much longer than others. Friendships need not be permanent in order to count as friendship.[13] I can say of some people I knew back in college that we were friends even though I haven't had contact with them in years. We may not be friends now, but that doesn't negate the friendship that once existed. These relationships just happened to be temporary, whereas others endured. Oftentimes, we become friends with people for the sake of temporary goods—such as profit, material gain, or promotion. Frank has a number of useful friendships, those based on a mutual interest for gain of some sort. Doug Stamper, Frank's chief of staff, is a useful friend. He and Frank share a bond that is mutually beneficial—both profit from the relationship. This also shows how friendships can exist when the parties involved are not characteristically good people.

Aristotle's account of useful friendship suggests that perhaps Frank and Raymond Tusk could be friends. Consider Raymond's proposal to Frank to share in a "mutually beneficial partnership."[14] This description is consistent with what useful friendships look like—they are beneficial relationships that provide certain goods to both parties and often look a lot like business relationships based on principles of fair play. Furthermore, a useful friendship is one in which the object of affection is that which is useful but is not the person. This is an important point because Raymond and Frank *despise* each other—there is absolutely *no* affection or feeling of goodwill in that relationship. Jackie Sharp's relationship with Frank is much like his relationship with Raymond. While their relationship was mutually beneficial— Frank earned the Presidency and Jackie became the Whip—there is no apparent goodwill. After Frank agreed to put Jackie on the ticket, she worked with him to stop Heather Dunbar, but she eventually abandoned the relationship altogether. After withdrawing her candidacy for the Democratic nomination, Sharp publicly announced her support for Dunbar instead of Frank.[15]

In contrast, there is a sense of mutual goodwill and affection between Doug and Frank. This was made apparent when Frank asked Doug if he started drinking again. The question was motivated when Frank was called out during his testimony about the PAC money. He discovered that Doug had not been careful enough and was caught at the casino in Kansas City. Frank tells Doug, "I've never given someone a third chance ... until now."[16] Furthermore, consider the lengths that Doug goes to—including committing murder—in order to demonstrate his loyalty and affection for the relationship.[17]

Frank's relationship with Cathy Durant is another example of a useful friendship. She became Secretary of State—the position that Frank coveted and that motivated his coup—due in large part to his (scheming) efforts. This bond cultivated utility for both parties. For a time, Cathy was seated in a position of power, and Frank enjoyed the benefits that resulted from her being in that position. In fact, Cathy played a key role in the demise of Garrett Walker's presidency. Clearly, the bond between Cathy and Frank was mutually beneficial. Furthermore, there was an evident sense of mutual good will—their relationship is consistent with the old saying, "You scratch my back and I'll scratch yours."

## "Life Is Sweet When You Spend It with Your Friends"[18]

Aristotle states that friendship is "most indispensable for life."[19] Everyone needs friends, even Frank. As Aristotle says:

> No one would choose to live without friends, even if he had all other goods. Rich men and those who hold office and power are, above all others, regarded as requiring friends. For what good would their prosperity do them if it did not provide them with the opportunity for good works? And the best works done and those which deserve the highest praise are those that are done to one's friends. How could prosperity be safeguarded and preserved without friends? The greater it is the greater are the risks it brings with it.[20]

Surely, Frank has great resources, including wealth, power, and influence, but he would *not* be the President if it weren't for his *friends*. These resources help to promote good fortune, and that is important to a good life. Aristotle says, though, that good fortune isn't enough. Cultivating a lifestyle consisting of virtuous activity, combined with good fortune, is what makes possible a good life. Friendship is an activity—in the words of Ralph Waldo Emerson, "To have a friend is to be a friend." Friendships must be fruitful and cannot remain stagnant, for otherwise the fruit dies.

In the final episode of Season 2, Frank plays one of his most masterful hands yet and in so doing manages to win the presidency. What stands out in this last episode is that it is the first time (in all three seasons) that Frank was *completely* honest and *completely* vulnerable—he tempted and challenged his good fortune. (Remember, Frank rebels against those things that attempt to limit him.) By penning a deeply moving note to Garrett and offering him a "get out of jail free" card, Frank depicts himself as having acted in a way that appears virtuous. And yet, he *was* playing a game (or was he?)—a game that he won.

While Frank's many faults and vices manifest themselves in action after action (after action), there remains a glimmer of hope. Frank has friends, even if not true friends. If others can have goodwill, admiration, and affection toward Frank, surely, he's got potential, right?[21] At the end of Season 2, I held out hope. However, at the conclusion of Season 3, I confess that I have serious doubts. Frank, after winning Iowa, lost Claire—leaving me to question whether he will ever choose to follow the right (and virtuous) path toward a good life. Perhaps Frank will have to fall in order to choose the good for its own sake. Nevertheless, Frank *can* choose to become good—he can choose a virtuous life for its own sake—and there's still time. Who knows what will unfold in Season 4? How will Frank respond to Claire walking out on him during a pivotal time in his campaign for the Democratic nomination? Perhaps this is the chance for Frank to (finally) choose *well*. Frank's current course is not leading him down the right path, but he has the potential to lead a good life. Indeed, Frank has good fortune, but he lacks good character and *true* friends.[22] These are what he will need if he is ever going to turn it around and live a truly good life.

## Notes

1.  Frank quotes this Ralph Waldo Emerson quotation while in Kansas City at Womack's fundraising event. See Season 2, "Chapter 8."

2. You may be wondering how I compiled this interesting list of friends—especially considering the fact that Garrett Walker is included and others appear to be missing. For example, you might think that Tim Corbet, Frank's college friend and fellow quartet member (and, let's not forget, love interest), should be included (see Season 1, "Chapter 8," and Season 3, "Chapter 10"). Also, perhaps Seth, Frank's trusted staff member who works alongside Doug, should be present. What about Remy Danton? Perhaps he, too, should count as a friend. My husband, an avid *House of Cards* devotee, read an earlier draft of this chapter and wanted to know about Frank and Remy's relationship. He was convinced that Remy would be included on the friends list. Of course, that was before Season 3 aired. Sadly, I couldn't make my husband's wish come true. Remy didn't make the cut for the simple reason that Aristotle would likely deny that their relationship counts as a friendship. Furthermore, Season 3 offers clear evidence of a lack of any sort of meaningful relationship of goodwill. This analysis will hopefully offer you some guidance from the wisdom of Aristotle to help you to see that friendship is a much more difficult relationship to identify than has previously been thought.

3. Ferdinand Schoeman makes this suggestion in his interpretation of Aristotle's account of friendship. See Ferdinand Schoeman, "Aristotle on the Good of Friendship," *Australasian Journal of Philosophy* 63 (1985): 269–82.

4. This is Frank's comment to the audience when Claire asks him to separate himself from Freddy after his criminal past is publicly disclosed in "Chapter 21." This is by far one of the clearest expressions of friendship according to Frank Underwood.

5. I must admit that in Season 3, Claire's moral character certainly improves when she publicly denounces Russia's antigay laws ("Chapter 32") and stands up to Frank in protest of his treatment of her ("Chapter 39"). In these instances, Claire's goal doesn't appear to be personal gain but rather to do what is right. Perhaps Season 3 marks Claire's moral turning point toward the good. Hopefully, Frank will follow in her footsteps.

6. This claim draws on Ronna Burger's interpretation of Aristotle's account of friendship. Ronna Burger, *Aristotle's Dialogue with Socrates* (Chicago: University of Chicago Press, 2008).

7. See "Chapter 21."

8. Frank expresses this when he first introduces us to Freddy in "Chapter 2."

9. See "Chapter 23."

10. See "Chapter 34."

11. See "Chapter 24."
12. In "Chapter 5," Frank makes this statement in response to the conflicting tensions between himself and Marty, the lobbyist for the associated teachers' union seeking education reform. Of course, the friendship that Frank alleges to have with Marty is one of usefulness. And yet, this relationship is not a friendship due to the absence of genuine (and mutual) feelings of goodwill.
13. John M. Cooper, "Aristotle on Friendship," in Amélie Oksenberg Rorty, ed., *Essays on Aristotle's Ethics* (Berkeley: University of California Press, 1980), 301–40.
14. See "Chapter 19." Raymond first proposed this "partnership" during "Chapter 13."
15. See "Chapter 37."
16. See "Chapter 24."
17. Doug murders Rachel in "Chapter 39."
18. This quote is from the book that Rachel was reading to kids at her church group in "Chapter 19."
19. 1155a3.
20. 1155a3–11
21. Of course, that list appears to be waning at the culmination of Season 3.
22. And yet, Frank's good fortune also appears to be waning at the end of Season 3.

# 24

# Have You No Decency? Who Is Worse, Claire or Frank?

*Randall Auxier*

*Many forms of Government have been tried, and will be tried in this world of sin and woe. No one pretends that democracy is perfect or all-wise. Indeed it has been said that democracy is the worst form of Government except for all those other forms that have been tried from time to time.*
—Winston Churchill, House of Commons, November 11, 1947

## Character Studies and Studies in Character

Who is morally worse, Francis or Claire Underwood? Seems like an invented question, the sort of thing philosophers make up in order to have something to talk about? Yes, musing about such things can be a waste of energy. And I was going to let this question slide, with a private smile about the blasphemous twist on the names Francis and Claire—the saints of Assisi. But then I watched the British version of *House of Cards* and I became aware that (by the end at least) those writers exercised a good deal of calculation and thought about this question of *who* is worse. They indelicately name our wicked woman "Elizabeth," as though that name didn't carry some connotations for the British public. My question ceased being something for giggles.

*House of Cards and Philosophy: Underwood's Republic,*
First Edition. Edited by J. Edward Hackett.
© 2016 John Wiley & Sons, Ltd. Published 2016 by John Wiley & Sons, Ltd.

In the initial novel (1989), the spouse of Francis Urquhart is called "Miranda," and she had no significant role; and, indeed, Francis himself commits suicide rather than murder at the end. Michael Dobbs, the novelist (and former chief of staff of the British Conservative Party, wink-wink), had envisioned a much more limited story. When the BBC contemplated the miniseries, however, they saw a wider opportunity. What if Lady Macbeth had married Richard III? Macbeth himself was too weak and foolish for his ambitious Lady. What a disappointing match. She needs a more suitable mate, and who better than the last of the Plantagenets?

## Richard Plantagenet and Elizabeth Tudor

Ian Richardson, who plays our antihero in the British series, had a Shakespearean background and readily owned that he had patterned his characterization of Francis along the lines of the play. But Richardson knew that the historical Richard III, when one removes the pro-Tudor propaganda of Shakespeare, was actually a very brave soldier, a good lawgiver, and a devoted protector of the common people. Our British Francis was also a dutiful protector of the Empire, even executing his own Cyprian spies when it became "necessary." Urquhart likewise seems to have been both a popular and effective Prime Minister. The writers did not choose to continue the myth of a physically deformed Richard III—who probably had scoliosis (although this claim is disputed by some who have examined his recently discovered remains), but the defect was minor and would have been concealed by his clothing, and he was not otherwise physically deformed. Francis Urquhart is a fair specimen of English manhood—much more (by anticipation) than is Francis Underwood an example of American masculinity. Richardson's portrayal of Francis does mix the historical man and the Shakespearean character, and this *is* a mate fit for Lady Macbeth.

The devilish decision to rename Francis's spouse "Elizabeth" is also fitting, given that it is she who arranges for his assassination at the end of the whole story—the Tudors did, after all, displace the Plantagenets in rivers of blood. Francis has finally gotten himself into a tangle he can't possibly get out of, and if Elizabeth hadn't put him out of his, well, impending misery, she would go down with him. She can't have *that*. As *House of Cards* fans will know, that assassination can be interpreted as an "act of kindness" (the phrase Francis himself chooses for his murder of Roger O'Neill, who is the British counterpart of Peter Russo), but also it is in Elizabeth's self-interest. She has reason to preserve his legacy of service to the people, for his own good (of course). So she has him "put down" in spectacular fashion so as to insure he will be remembered as a martyr, a servant, a soldier. This tidy ending also serves the Conservative Party. The directors go to some trouble to close the miniseries with a shot of Francis's blood on Elizabeth's hands, and even a bit on her face, just in case we were too dense to grasp her Lady Macbethness—but without the bad dreams. She is, indeed, worse (that is, "stronger") than her Scottish forerunner.

So Elizabeth Urquhart and, hence, Claire Underwood (by anticipation) are creations not of the page but of the screen, albeit the *small* screen. Clearly the American screenwriters have studied the British series closely—the adaptation is fascinating. There are all sorts of things that just wouldn't work in the American context. For example, we don't have a king, and our upper house makes an actual difference to our governance. But the twists in the American version go deeper than just these obvious contrasts. The playful variations on the British themes are highly imaginative and yet recognizable as belonging to the same general story.

## St. Francis and St. Claire

Frank and Claire are *not* Richard III and Lady Macbeth. And their implicit differences, dormant until one became President and the other, well, didn't, became the central focus of the third season. But if not the toxic Shakespeareans, who *are* they? I will take a shot at answering this at the end of the chapter. Whether the American series will follow this same story line as the British series to the bitter end is difficult to say, but to this point (three seasons in), they have run in fairly close parallel. If the Netflix series does remain true, Claire will eventually get Meechum to arrange for Frank's assassination, Catherine Durant (the Secretary of State) will become President, and Jackie Sharp (the new Whip) will survive but end up very much on the outs. Doug Stamper has already outlasted his British predecessor, Tim Stamper, and unlike Tim, Doug has gotten a professional reprieve as well. If the stories continue in parallel, Frank will be elected to the presidency twice, after finishing Garrett's term, and will become the longest serving President since FDR. No one is making the Netflix writers do this, of course. I think they have held close thus far because the British story line and characters are excellent. But they are also undoubtedly adapting to the strengths of their principal actors. The "chemistry" is working. This is a for-profit enterprise. No one is going to make these writers stay close to what went before, unless it looks like a winner.

And I don't think our dynamic duo has simply been Americanized or has only undergone minor adjustments. These are different characters, and Claire is much more developed, independent, and ambitious in her own way. Elizabeth never attempts to become a part of the government, and we don't ever learn quite what her game is. Meanwhile, *our* Francis is compensating for deep-seated childhood issues, including being a closeted bisexual from the South, and he is the polar opposite of a privileged elitist, like his Urquhart counterpart. Yet, the other characters in the two series are really very closely built on analogies to their British predecessors.

There is more than a philosopher's reasons to keep an eye on Claire, and reason to ask what she is capable of. We were set up, in the course of the British version, for something that was foreshadowed but not really set out on the table, which was Elizabeth's ambitions for herself as allied with her husband's, but not to be identified with them. But Claire is no free-rider on the ambition train, and she has her own destination, farther down the line than her husband's. We have seen her lose in a high-stakes game of diplomacy with the Russian President, but I don't think she is down for the count. She will get her chance to even the score, and much depends on what she is willing to do.

## The Past, the Present Perfect, and the Future Subjunctive

I think there are three ways we can think about how *bad* a person is. We can take a conservative approach and insist that people ought to be judged only on the basis of what they have actually done. In this case, we have a pretty clear picture of Frank and Claire. For the sake of ambition alone, he has committed murder twice (Zoe and Peter) and perhaps ordered it directly or indirectly at least once and maybe more than once, resulting in at least one death; and his ambition has ruined other people less directly (Freddy, for example). As far as we know, Claire has nothing comparable in her past; she has ruined a few people, a former employee here, a Marine Corps General there, but it's hardly murder. On that strict standard, Claire may be a detestable human being, but Frank is worse.

Still, there is more to making a judgment like this. We have to ask what a person has done and is doing that will have consequences in the future. To the extent that such activities portend disaster, we have to consider them. Frank Underwood is President of the United States, and he hath played most foully to get there. God only knows what will happen to this country to the extent that it depends upon his character. (Hold on to that thought; it is the key to the riddle.) In this sense, Claire has a number of ongoing "projects" that are troubling, but again, nothing to compare with the stakes Frank set up in rising to power. After all, he now has his finger on the button and a rather powerful military at his disposal. It was dangerous to cross the boy before, but now? Yes, he is worse in the present perfect. If he hasn't yet misused the office, it isn't because he is unwilling. It just hasn't been necessary yet. Finding a way to get himself elected may provide the scenario—and there is no better way to remain in that particular office than to start a splendid little war. We shall see.

Still, we have to consider the subjunctive question "What *would* you do?" In the British series, Elizabeth also doesn't seem like her husband's ruthless moral equivalent until the very end, when we realize that perhaps she has been *subjunctively* worse all along. Our human moral character isn't determined solely by what we *are* doing and have *done*, or even by these combined with what we actually *will do* in the future. The best judgment of character also takes into account what you *would* do to have what you want or what you need, or to get something for another. There are plenty of sociopaths getting by in the world because they are able to get what they want and need without tipping anyone off to their real moral depravity. I am pretty sure we all deal with such people almost daily. This subjunctive standard thus needs to be included in an informed judgment. So we know Frank is capable of murder, but is Claire? And what else is each capable of?

## An Indirect Route

It isn't easy to figure out what people *might* do, given the right circumstances. We can't even be sure about ourselves. Am I capable of killing someone, say, in self-defense, or to defend someone else? Or what about in revenge, if someone had harmed a person I love and feel responsible for protecting? I just don't know. And I'm glad not to know. So the question carries a problem. How do we think about what we are glad not knowing? One way is to ask a more general question, a question about context—*relevant* context. Most people would probably kill, or anything short of killing, if they believed they had no choice. But where there is a choice, different communities and different political systems see matters differently. Vladimir Ilyich Lenin freely advocated the execution of his political enemies, authorized it, and believed it justified. Yet, he is not usually listed among the genocidal monsters of the twentieth century. Routinely, the French and Spanish took turns lining up their political enemies against walls and shooting them in great numbers. None of the colonial powers (including the United States) flinched at bringing on the deaths of millions and tens of millions of innocent people in the course of colonizing undeveloped countries and then using the colonized populous as surrogates and pawns in the Cold War.

This generalized situation provokes a broader question, then. Aristotle says that our moral development is limited by our political community. One can rise above the values of one's community, but not wholly. So in a democratic republic, such as the United States, our moral judgments may really depend on whether our political system facilitates moral development. This may seem like a question that is rather distant from whether Claire is worse than Frank, but I will try to convince you otherwise. There is a lot of truth to the old saw that we have gotten the leaders we deserved. Do we deserve Frank (assuming that at this point, we still haven't elected him to the office he holds)?

We commonly praise people who, in the course of carrying out the duties of a political office, have been responsible for the deaths (and, indeed, the murder) of thousands and thousands of human beings. One assumes that George Washington, for example, perhaps (indeed probably) actually killed people when he was rising in the British colonial army. Any US President has to be willing to use the military and the intelligence community to protect the country. We have had presidents who killed people long before Frank Underwood, although one assumes we have not had many actual murderers. Still, our system demands people capable of, frankly, murder. Although he doesn't admit much, even Dick Cheney might be willing to admit this.

It is clear that at least some inspiration for Frank's character is taken from Cheney's ruthless style (House Minority Whip, 1989, before becoming dangerously close to the Presidency for eight harrowing years). One shudders to imagine what Cheney might be capable of, in addition to what he has actually done that he is presently not incarcerated for (and for which he will apparently go unpunished). There are obvious analogies, of course, between Frank and Cheney. Our writers have probably stolen some Cheney moves, especially as the public imagines Cheney's designs on becoming President (by any means necessary), recognizing, as he surely did, that he could never be *elected*. And indeed, Cheney has a Claire-like spouse, as well, in terms of the nonprofit path to influence. But one might equally point out that Bill and Hillary Clinton bear a resemblance to Frank and Claire. I don't have to spell it out, I'm sure.

I have no doubt that the Cheneys and Clintons served as touchstones for these characters. There are numerous other political couples one might name, and not just Americans. Take a look at Justinian I and Theodora, or Antony and Cleopatra, or Odysseus and Penelope, among the other poisonous couples of history. You'll find patterns in each pair that have been used by these writers. I think the Clinton–Cheney blending is flesh on the bones, but it isn't the key or the meaning of the characters or their union. The important clues lie in the democratic context of the American republic, just as the British series investigates something quite fundamental to the disease of British parliamentary democracy. These contexts produce different kinds of ambition, and the moral character of the agents of such a government is adapted to that system as surely as are the classic couples of history. What people have done, are doing, and might be willing to do flow from the system of rewards and consequences of acting one way or another within a larger system.

## Learning from Our Betters

Can individual people really expect to be morally better than the political system that provides their laws, their ideals, and their heroes and villains? Can we rise above our governmental forms to become, somehow, better? We find it hard to look at ourselves with unclouded eyes, and we wince at the criticisms hurled our way from the people and the press of other nations. But we also don't want to endure fundamental *self*-assessment. If we were able, a good portion of the most recent Bush administration would be in prison, as Richard Nixon himself would have been, also, and who knows who else. Reinhold Niebuhr (1892–1971) famously said,

> [S]elf-criticism is a kind of inner disunity, which the feeble mind of a nation finds difficulty in distinguishing from dangerous forms of inner conflict. So nations crucify their moral rebels with their criminals upon the same Golgotha, not being able to distinguish between the moral idealism which surpasses, and the anti-social conduct which falls below that moral mediocrity, on the level of which every society unifies its life.[1]

Here in America, our moral mediocrity casts a wide net and tacitly condones much. Americans don't like the idea of anyone being morally *better* than anyone else—we admit it only grudgingly, on special days set aside for, well, whomever we can't find a way to destroy with sleazy tales of slumming it or the simple fictions we prefer to enduring inner criticism from someone actually morally superior to ourselves.

The full list of our moral betters turns out to be, at present, just Martin Luther King, Jr., and even in his case I think many people take a quiet satisfaction in recalling his personal failings while paying the required lip service his achievements. Nobody apart from MLK has a real holiday, and many legislatures resisted and swerved to get rid of his. My favorite example was the 16 years during which Virginia declared the holiday "Lee-Jackson-King Day" (yes, *that* Lee, and suffice to say it isn't *Jesse* Jackson).

Our moral superiors get an extra two minutes in the news cycle on the anniversary of some notable event—especially assassinations, which we morbidly love to revisit, and then we whisper about FDR's and JFK's affairs or TR's recklessness and egomaniacal personality, or RFK's petulance, or what have you. We even managed to roll the significant virtues of Washington and Lincoln into a single day that no one would remember at all if there weren't sales at the retail stores to remind us, or if February wasn't so god-awful boring.

The British are less squeamish about what makes a person *better* than just any old bloke at the pub, but they have a thousand shades of "better," better in this way but *not* that way, so that no one gets to ride the high horse too long (except perhaps Lord Nelson, and one doubts whether he'd have any such notice if he hadn't the decency to die in battle). The Brits thus have a thousand ways to tear a person down, but they seem at home with the idea that some people are better than others. This discussion belongs in *Downton Abbey and Philosophy*. But it is another reason to think that the American series might really have to take a different turn from the British miniseries. One reason Elizabeth has Francis assassinated is to save his own good name—and Americans would rather go down in flame and shame than sacrifice anything so dear as life for the sake of a paltry bit of posthumous praise.

So Americans wear their discomfort openly when it comes to any talk of "betters," moral or otherwise, but they are pretty much at home with the idea that some people may be genuinely *worse* than others. That might be one reason we have so many grades of prisons and so very many people in them. We don't know who's good, but we bloody well know who needs locking up, and we don't stop short of scrubbing the floor with enemy combatants (booo, hsssss, enemy combatants). And unlike every other civilized nation, we don't mind "putting down" a few dozen fellow citizens every year in Texas and Oklahoma and Florida and other barbarous borderlands where nobody much notices what happens to poor people, especially if they are also minorities. In the more civilized places, we just have the police shoot or choke the suspicious-looking ones, if they try to sell untaxed cigarettes or steal cigars or shop at Walmart or play in the park, or walk down the street and scare people with their hoodies and dark skin. Yes, that is the American way: People like that are bad and must die, evidently, but at least we didn't say we were *better* than them, like those British assholes, thank God.

No, the egalitarian conceit of the citizens of the United States rejects superiority only *upward* from wherever we are, our peculiar moral mediocrity, and never down, into risking a modicum of sympathy for those who "need controlling." The huddled masses yearning to breathe free look okay from within the mass, but from behind the picket fence of South Carolina, well, they seem more like a problem to be "handled," by Stamper or some other loyal American(s). I remember reading the results of Hogan's Survey of Ethical Attitudes when given to prison inmates. Inmates say the same things that people on the *outside* say, always rating themselves just a little lower than they would prefer to be, morally, but not really *bad*. But then you ask them, "Who *is* bad?" it's always anyone who *would do* something I just *wouldn't do*. So armed robbers think rapists are bad, and rapists think murderers are bad, and murderers think child molesters are bad, and child molesters, well, they don't live very long on the inside. And this, for better or worse, is the moral mediocrity Niebuhr was talking about, that cannot distinguish criminals from great moral teachers. In such a political system, is it any wonder that Frank and Claire are as they are? The wonder is that Dick and Lynne and Bill and Hillary aren't worse.

## Democracy behind the Eight Ball

Plato and Aristotle were pretty smart, and both of them held democracy in contempt. They believed that it appealed to what is lowest in human nature rather than to what is best. Neither of them would have expected a mob motivated by what is lowest and most common among us to be a guide to good decision making. I don't think they could have imagined the British House of Commons or the US House of Representatives, but if they had, horror would surely have been their feeling, both initially and upon reflection.

Indeed, Plato and Aristotle also agreed that no one could prevent democracies from falling into tyrannies. They had plenty of opportunity to watch that happen in Athens, several times. And it was, after all, a democracy that put Socrates to death. It wasn't just snooty disdain for "the common," or the morally mediocre, that motivated their acerbic prose about democracies. It was watching people with no scruples do whatever they believed necessary to wrest power from a changeable mob, a crowd of Athenians that was easily frightened and probably unfit to govern itself even when calm. The crowd will do anything, justify anything, kill anything, and steal anything. Groups will behave in ways that they would not tolerate from individuals and will celebrate those who lead them in such behavior. The crowd is so unstable that democracy inevitably becomes tyranny. For all their disagreements, Plato and Aristotle could not see how a crowd could possibly get good leaders. There really is a thick relationship between the character of individuals and the groups they belong to. Is it possible, just possible, that Frank and Claire are *us*, in the sense of US(A)?

It is impossible to deny that democracies, and indeed republics generally, do eventually become tyrannies. If that has not yet happened in Britain or the United States—and that isn't altogether clear—then you could count a couple of very smart Greeks among the most surprised witnesses of history. If an ape looks in the mirror, no saint will be looking back—and I say this with apologies to apes, who deserve better than to be compared to the main characters in *House of Cards*. On the other hand, these democracies *can* say that they have lasted longer than anyone thought they could. Yes, there have been civil wars, and yes, we have come close to losing the American republic a few times. On the other hand, the American republic has proven surprisingly resilient.

## We the People

We might not all agree on which times in US history we came closest to losing the whole shebang. Everyone will list our Civil War first, but thereafter it's a discussion. A great number of people would probably list the various crises of the Cold War, especially the Cuban Missile Crisis, as being high on the list. Others, such as Mark Twain and William James, would say that our decision to enter the colonial gambit with the European powers cost us our national soul. If there is one thing we could not afford to do, as a nation, it was exploit other nations and peoples for our national advantage. But I would place high on that list, for you to consider, the panic of the early 1950s that goes by the name of McCarthyism.

The American republic was perhaps saved in the moment when Joseph N. Welch, head counsel for the US Army, in the endless

hearings initiated by Senator Joseph McCarthy and his rabid anticom-
munists, finally found the words necessary to help the public see that
McCarthy was a paranoid bully who was an enemy of freedom. The
moment went like this. Welch said:

> Until this moment, Senator, I think I have never really gauged your cru-
> elty or your recklessness. Fred Fisher is a young man who went to the
> Harvard Law School and came into my firm and is starting what looks
> to be a brilliant career with us. Little did I dream you could be so reck-
> less and so cruel as to do an injury to that lad. It is true he is still with
> Hale and Dorr. It is true that he will continue to be with Hale and
> Dorr. It is, I regret to say, equally true that I fear he shall always bear
> a scar needlessly inflicted by you. If it were in my power to forgive
> you for your reckless cruelty I would do so. I like to think I am a gen-
> tle man, but your forgiveness will have to come from someone other
> than me.

When McCarthy tried to renew his attack, Welch interrupted him:

> Senator, may we not drop this? We know he belonged to the Lawyers
> Guild. Let us not assassinate this lad further, Senator. You've done
> enough. Have you no sense of decency, sir? At long last, have you left
> no sense of decency?

McCarthy tried to ask Welch another question about Fisher, and
Welch cut him off:

> Mr. McCarthy, I will not discuss this further with you. You have sat
> within six feet of me and could have asked me about Fred Fisher. You
> have seen fit to bring it out. And if there is a God in Heaven it will do
> neither you nor your cause any good. I will not discuss it further. I will
> not ask Mr. Cohn any more questions. You, Mr. Chairman, may, if you
> will, call the next witness.

This is taken from the Wikipedia article on Welch, but the exchange
can be viewed on YouTube as well (https://www.youtube.com/watch?
v=K1eA5bUzVjA). This was the moment when a television audience became self-aware as citizens of what they had been allowing.
Some condemned McCarthy, while most only quietly withdrew their

support and he slinked away in shame. I do not mean to claim that Joe Welch saved the nation, precisely; I mean to say that a democratic republic that can long endure requires Joe Welches. Someone has to find the words (or images) that enable the ape to look in the mirror and *see* an ape. The bad news is that in our polity, we will usually do much damage before anyone finds the words. We the people move slowly when it comes to recognizing our mistakes and glacially when it comes to rectifying them. But up until now, there has always been a Welch moment when it was needed, even if it doesn't come in time to save those who are tortured, killed, ruined, and otherwise "crucified" as a result of our moral mediocrity. Maybe it was good fortune, but maybe not, when Joe Welch found the words. The same society that made Joe McCarthy made Joe Welch. The good guys are out there. It is hard, so far, to find them on *House of Cards*, but that was true in the British version too. Keep your eye on that Secretary of State.

## A Guess at a Riddle

The British trilogy of miniseries that is responsible for blazing the television trail has some interesting features that we lack on this side of the Pond (like a King and a robust, if deeply oppressive, sense of decency). One thing both governments have in common, however, is the problem of the Lower House. If any Tom, Dick, or Francis can be elected to the lower house, then the cleverest boy (or girl) in that unruly free-for-all may well lay hands upon supreme power, but that is exceedingly rare in the United States. The British bear the burden of an ineffective and nearly useless Upper House. The Prime Minister is easier to pull down, but exercises more power than anyone in the Lower House in the United States could hope to gain. But ...

In only *one* case has it ever happened that a person moved from the Lower House to the Presidency entirely by appointments. It was Gerald R. Ford, whose path the writers of *House of Cards* followed in making Frank Underwood into a President. Everyone knows that Ford did not seek the Presidency under his own steam and that he was unelectable (as he discovered in 1976). Some see him as a lapdog of the corrupt Republican Party, but the truth is surely more complicated.

He was an able worker in the fields of the Lower House and nothing like Frank Underwood. The challenge faced by the *House of Cards* writers was to find a way to make someone like him President, and the path has to be very twisted, involving as much luck as calculation. No one man could do it, believably, by intrigue in the treacherous Lower House. In short, they needed Claire.

It is not yet revealed whether the course taken by the British series will be followed by the American writers. Much of what transpired over there has been repeated here, with the creative turns you'd expect. But there was never an open conflict between Elizabeth and her Francis such as we have seen in Season 3 of the Netflix version. We have only now, after three seasons arrived where the first four installments (of the total 12) got us in the earlier series. Our antihero there, Urquhart, actually enjoys a long and distinguished career as Prime Minister, although we don't see most of his career depicted in the series. He ends up serving one day longer than Margaret Thatcher herself. He does some good things, but his past finally catches him. I do not think this is what will happen in our series in the United States.

By degrees we have come to our answer about Frank and Claire, but we have done so by a side entrance. I suggest that the greater logic at work is this: Frank *is* the House of Representatives, as a symbol, and Claire *is* the Senate, as a symbol, morally speaking. I do not mean only the recent Houses and Senates, I mean the whole history of the House and Senate. Frank's character and his moral limits are the same as those of the House. He is much more likely to go bad, and he is mercurial, changing with every circumstance and adapting to it. Claire is far more considered, elevated, from a privileged background, deliberate. Frank goes slumming. Claire sleeps with an artist who flatters her. Frank pisses on his father's grave. Claire doesn't speak about her background. They have done different things in the past and are doing things that will bring different consequences in the present, and in the future subjunctive they are capable of different things, as suits their peculiar powers.

The crucial moments in the first two seasons occurred when they jogged together (that's Conference Committee) and shared a cigarette (that's backroom stuff). Yet, they always had one thing in common, this Upper and Lower House in the *House of Cards*: *They wanted executive power*. And such has always been the character of the legislative branch. Our writers posed us the hypothetical question as to what would happen if ever the House and Senate were in bed together and succeeded in getting executive power. It is very unlikely, but it is possible. The system has been designed carefully always to pit the three branches against one another, and to prevent the creeping tendency of each branch to usurp the authority of the others. Still ...

In Season 3, the writers began to struggle with the answer to that question—and I confess, I think they really were struggling with what they had created. They had both Frank and Claire, separately, have a flirtation with the prospect of governing honestly and even nobly. But they are too far down the road of perdition to pull themselves up to that place. The lure of holding power is too tempting, and the stress of governing is beginning to erode their alliance. When it gets right down to it, the character of the House is different from that of the Senate because they value different things, even if power (and acquiring it) had seemed like an end in itself. Having power means using it, and people with elevated tastes use it differently from, well, people who like barbecued ribs. It can't work—in the sense that a split is inevitable. But these two houses, the House of Frank and the House of Claire, know too much about each other, and they have different powers. This is going to get worse.

When we see what Frank is willing to do and use our imaginations to translate it into the rough and tumble of our Lower House, and when we see what Claire is willing to do and imaginatively transmute it into the actions of our Senate, we see the true American House of Cards. The inverted flag waves a warning here. The truth of the matter is that what is lower in us can rule what is higher in us only with the cooperation of the higher part. This is what Plato and Aristotle both said. Francis may not realize it, but he is completely powerless without Claire's cooperation. She can destroy him in an instant, but why would she?

And here we arrive at the true heart of the matter: What *does* Claire want? If we follow the analogy I have suggested, while the lower house wants to run the country, the upper house wants to run the *world*. Claire might be more ambitious than Frank, and, indeed, the Senate wants that power to control foreign policy—has always wanted that power. Think of how Senator Lodge sank our participation in the League of Nations after the first war to end all wars. If it were possible to make one person responsible for the Second World War, that person would be Henry Cabot Lodge. So our Senate isn't incorruptible, but it is difficult to twist. And yet, Joe McCarthy was a Senator. A bad Senator, like McCarthy or Lodge, is far, far more dangerous than a bad Congressional Representative. Yet, by way of abuse and the dissimulations that pile on it over the years, a high-born calling can become a perverse pursuit. I can answer the question as to how Francis and Claire got to where they are: They wanted the same things, or, more precisely, they wanted exactly compatible things (including, apparently, Meechum, their bodyguard). But they are not the same, and they can and have come apart.

It may seem crude, but the shocker of the second season, the ménage à trois with their bodyguard, is the clue. *If you trace* in your mind what happened after the camera cut away, showing first that Claire kisses Meechum, and then the two men kiss, as the writers *want you to do*, you will see that they are foreshadowing the inevitable. So how does this sex go? Is Claire the object, between two men? No. Is Frank submissive to either or both of the others? No. You *know* this. Then just how *does* it go? The answer: Frank and Claire take turns doing whatever they want to Meechum, sometimes cooperating. And who, then, is Meechum? He is the military, isn't he? Utterly loyal, utterly deadly. They can seduce him, but they have underestimated him.

I think that what will happen to Frank and Claire will happen to both of them, and I think Meechum will do it, ultimately. The toxic pairing of Lower and Upper morality with executive power leads to one and only one thing: the misuse and subsequent underestimation of the military. The warning in the series, symbolically, is that we cannot use our military for our pleasure and expect to have our republic survive. That is what we have been doing since we went to a volunteer military. This is where the danger lies for the Americans, and the writers of *House of Cards* know it well. If the American republic is to fall into a tyranny, it will be the military that takes over. Perhaps we are not as afraid of this as we should be.

So who is worse, Claire or Frank? The answer is that they are far worse together than either is alone. It is not the individuals but the union that has no decency, as Joe Welch might put it. But with their union very much in doubt, it may be well to remember that Claire might be more ambitious than Frank. Why, after all, does she want the UN assignment, and why does she want to be the high-stakes player at the table when matters concern the whole world? And is Frank not stifling her ambitions? He had best be careful. Hasn't he seen how the British series ended?

# Note

1. Reinhold Niebuhr, *Moral Man and Immoral Society* (Louisville, KY: Westminster John Knox Press, 2013), 89.

# President Frank Underwood's White House Staff (Contributors)

**Leslie A. Aarons** is an Associate Professor of Philosophy at City University of New York (CUNY) LaGuardia Community College. She teaches and publishes in environmental ethics, public philosophy, feminist philosophy, and continental philosophy. She is dedicated to manifesting her *Überwensch*, aspiring continually to greatness, and living a life of creative adventure.

**Randall Auxier** has been griping about politics for decades. In exchange for a paycheck, he complains unimportantly to a semicaptive audience of Southern Illinois University Carbondale students, and he listens to the students whine about even less important things, which seems impossible until you actually hear it done. Unsatisfied with this pretty decent arrangement, Auxier began some years ago bitching about things on the radio and in newspapers, magazines, and popular culture books and on a blog. This leaves him almost no time for anything else, so he is considering running for office.

**Chris Byron** is a doctoral student and teaching assistant in philosophy at the University of Georgia. He specializes in Marxism and political philosophy. He has published several book reviews and essays on human nature, along with ethical justifications for transitioning to a socialist society. He will continue to agree with Frank Underwood that "democracy is overrated" until it is extended to the workplace.

*House of Cards and Philosophy: Underwood's Republic*,
First Edition. Edited by J. Edward Hackett.
© 2016 John Wiley & Sons, Ltd. Published 2016 by John Wiley & Sons, Ltd.

You might think that **Kody W. Cooper** is a Postdoctoral Research Associate at Princeton University. You might think that he wears wool socks and Birkenstocks in the winter. And that he has a fear of umbrellas (those pointy tips could put your eye out!). And that, *pace* Freddy, he prefers Kansas City BBQ to Southern-style. Yes, you might think that. I couldn't possibly comment.

**Shane D. Courtland** received a PhD in Philosophy from Tulane University (in August 2008) and is currently employed as an assistant professor at the University of Minnesota, Duluth (UMD). In addition to teaching at UMD, Courtland is the director of the Center for Ethics and Public Policy. His publications have appeared in *Pacific Philosophical Quarterly*, *Journal of Environmental Philosophy*, *Journal of Applied Philosophy*, *Southwest Philosophy Review*, *Hobbes Studies*, *Reason Papers*, *Utilitas*, *Stanford Encyclopedia of Philosophy*, Routledge's *American Philosophy: An Encyclopedia*, and Wiley-Blackwell's *The Ultimate South Park and Philosophy*.

**Ian Diorio** is a full-time pastor and adjunct professor of theology at Hope International University. He holds a doctorate in leadership and has done graduate work in theology and philosophy. Ian sometimes wishes that Frank Underwood could help him with church politics.

**Austin Dressen** is an obsessive binge watcher of the Netflix original series when he is not listening to psychedelic music or writing. He lives in Minnesota, where he works as a consultant and teaches kids how to ski on Saturdays. An aspiring philosopher, Austin has written numerous essays and articles. Most recently, he coauthored "Praise & Blame in Philosophy of Religion" (*Toronto Journal of Theology*, 2014) with Charles Taliaferro. While he would not vote for Frank Underwood, he welcomes all of the entertaining questions and lessons that Frank inspires.

**Don Fallis** is a Professor of Information Resources and an Adjunct Professor of Philosophy at the University of Arizona. He has written several articles on lying and deception, including "What Is Lying?" in the *Journal of Philosophy*. But, despite his expertise in this area, Fallis is not at all a schemer.... Only someone as Machiavellian as

FU would ever accuse him of spreading misinformation, intentionally or not.

**John Scott Gray** is a Professor of Philosophy and Humanities at Ferris State University in Big Rapids, Michigan. His research interests include a wide range of applied philosophy, including the philosophy of sex and love, political and social philosophy, and ethics. He has coauthored a textbook on Popular Culture titled *Introduction to Popular Culture: Theories, Applications and Global Perspectives*. When not taking bribes from students for higher grades, he lives in Canadian Lakes, Michigan, with his wife Jo and son Oscar, and enjoys reading, collecting sports cards, and playing hockey.

**J. Edward Hackett**, PhD, is a Senior Lecturer at the University of Akron, and an Adjunct Professor of Philosophy at Kent State University and John Carroll University. He is author of *Being and Value in Scheler: A Phenomenological Defense of Participatory Realism* (Lexington, forthcoming), and is a coeditor of an upcoming anthology, *Phenomenology for the 21st Century*, with J. Aaron Simmons (Palgrave Macmillan). He is a specialist in phenomenology and ethical theory, and works at the intersections of phenomenology, pragmatism, and analytic ethics. And, as you can tell from this short bio, he takes himself way too seriously.

**Myron Moses Jackson** is Visiting Assistant Professor of Philosophy at Grand Valley State University. Earning a PhD from Southern Illinois University Carbondale in 2013, his dissertation argues for an ironic exceptionalism of American freedom symbolized through personalistic cultures predicated on novel hybrids and pluralistic rituals. His current research employs the process philosophy of Alfred North Whitehead to inquire into the capacity of virtual integration and entertainment, both metaphysically and aesthetically, to cultivate peace, truth, beauty, art, and adventure among civilized societies. In the meantime, he's trying to find some ribs and chill with the *politrix* behind him like Freddie.

**Katherine K. Johnson** is Assistant Professor of Philosophy and Director of the Ethics and Social Justice Center at Bellarmine University. Kate specializes in ethics and is in charge of teaching bioethics in the Doctor of Physical Therapy, Master of Science in Nursing, and Master of Health Science programs. A native of New England, she now resides in Louisville, Kentucky, with her husband John (whom she sometimes calls "Freddy"). While eating racks of ribs, she teaches her students the most fundamental moral imperative: "There is but one rule: hunt or be hunted."

**László Kajtár** is constantly worried about political spin doctors who weave stories as instruments of political power, and so he is a doctoral student of philosophy, working on storytelling. He conducts his research at Central European University, Budapest, Hungary, about issues at the intersection of aesthetics and the philosophy of mind. He has taught about the philosophy of fiction and about contemporary issues in aesthetics. His book reviews have appeared and will appear in the most significant journals of philosophical aesthetics, and he has published in multiple volumes about philosophy and pop culture.

**Angelica Kaufmann** is a Philosopher of Mind interested in the insights that Psychology and Anthropology can provide to contemporary theories on the evolution of the mind. Angelica was educated in Milan, Italy, and Edinburgh, Scotland. She is about to complete her PhD at Antwerp University. Angelica lives in London.

**James Ketchen** is an Assistant Professor in the Department of Law and Justice at Laurentian University, where he teaches courses in legal philosophy. He got into this gig because he has an abiding fascination with watching guys like Frank "get away with it" and asking, of no one in particular, "How'd he do that?"

**Brian Kogelmann** is a doctoral student in the Philosophy Department at the University of Arizona. He is a CGK fellow at the Center for the Philosophy of Freedom, a Bernard Marcus fellow at the Institute for Humane Studies, and an Adam Smith fellow at the Mercatus Center. He writes about political philosophy and the philosophy of economics, and he does not live in an ideal society.

**Greg Littmann** is Associate Professor of Philosophy at Southern Illinois University Carbondale. He has published on the philosophy of logic, evolutionary epistemology, and the philosophy of professional philosophy (no, really). He has also written numerous chapters for books relating philosophy to popular culture, including volumes on

*Boardwalk Empire*, *Breaking Bad*, *Game of Thrones*, *Sons of Anarchy*, and *The Walking Dead*. He would never sell out his principles by writing in support of someone else's political agenda in return for money, but it would be nice to be asked.

**Matt Meyer** is an Assistant Professor of Philosophy at the University of Wisconsin–Eau Claire, as well as a covert political operative for Chief of Staff Doug Stamper. He splits his time between DC; Eau Claire, Wisconsin; and Saint Paul, Minnesota, where he lives with his wife, Jill. (Don't tell her about the covert political maneuverings, please.) He enjoys doing PR work for Friedrich Nietzsche, as well as other existentialists and phenomenologists. When he is not pulling strings behind the scenes, he enjoys reading, biking, running, and, oh yeah, watching great TV like *House of Cards*.

**Steven Michels** is an Associate Professor of Political Science at Sacred Heart University in Fairfield, Connecticut. He is the author of *The Case against Democracy* and of essays on *The Daily Show* and Bruce Springsteen. He maintains that being a tenured professor is in many ways the opposite of being a politician, but he will still take your donations. As to the charge that there was illegal collusion between him and Brendan Murphy, Nick Kapoor, and C. J. Fleck on drafts of his chapter, on the advice of counsel he asserts his Fifth Amendment right against self-incrimination.

**Sarah J. Palm** studied Cinema and Photography at Southern Illinois University. She also has a degree in Criminology and Criminal Justice, which helps her to understand the criminal psychology of characters like Frank Underwood. She is currently a freelance video editor and a pop culture blogger at popculty.tumblr.com. This is her first time contributing to the Philosophy and Pop Culture series, but, barring an unfortunate train mishap, she hopes it will not be her last.

**Tomer J. Perry** is a PhD Candidate in the Political Science Department at Stanford University and a Research Fellow at the Edmund J. Safra Center for Ethics at Harvard University. Tomer is writing his dissertation on democratic theory and how it can help us address questions of global justice. When not engaged with political philosophy, Tomer plays (and writes about) board games, the up-and-coming art form (and leisure activity) of the digital age. He always knocks his ring on a table before he leaves a room, because he believes that success (in life, as well as in board games) is a mixture of luck and preparation. Besides, it hardens his knuckles and sounds cool.

**Stephanie Rivera Berruz** received her PhD in Philosophy at SUNY Buffalo in 2014. Her main interests lie in social and political philosophy with an emphasis on philosophy of race and feminist philosophy, as well as Latin American philosophy. She approaches these topics at their intersections as she is committed to the importance of diverse approaches to philosophical praxis. Her dedication to these topics stems from an investment in exploring her own identity as a Latina in philosophy. Her research has explored racial and gendered embodiment, the relationship between language and identity, the concept of boomerang perception in Latina feminist scholarship, and the metaphilosophical question of Latin American philosophy.

**Brendan Shea** is a tenure-track faculty member at Rochester Community and Technical College in Rochester, Minnesota, where spends his time writing and teaching about logical and scientific reasoning, ethics, the philosophy of religion, and the history of philosophy, among other things. Along with his more "academic" work, he has written nine chapters for books on popular culture and philosophy, with subjects ranging from *Twilight* to *Alice in Wonderland* to Leonard Cohen. When watching *House of Cards* for the first time, he thought it might be kind of fun to have Frank Underwood as a student in one of his philosophy classes. On a second watching, however, he realized this would be absolutely terrifying.

**Roberto Sirvent** is Associate Professor of Political and Social Ethics at Hope International University. His research explores the intersection of law, theology, and political theory. Roberto spent his last year of law school working for a US senator. He says his experience was nothing like *House of Cards* or *The West Wing*. But it was pretty close to *The Office*.

**Jason Southworth** teaches philosophy in south Florida. He has written chapters for other pop culture and philosophy volumes, such as *Batman*, *David Lynch*, and *Green Lantern*. He thinks these cute text bios are about as necessary as Frank Underwood talking to the camera.

**Kenneth W. Stikkers** is a Professor of Philosophy at Southern Illinois University Carbondale, where he has taught since 1997. He also has an appointment as Professor in the Department of Economics and Sociology at Autonomous University of Sinaloa, Mexico. His areas of research are wide, but recently he has been concerned with issues raised in the relationship between philosophy of economics and ethics.

**Charles Taliaferro,** Chair of the Department of Philosophy, St. Olaf College, is the senior coeditor of a six-volume *History of Evil* with over 130 contributors worldwide (Routledge, forthcoming 2015). His colleagues worry that his work on this project and on the *House of Cards* is leading him into a life of vice as he has confessed to bribing an official in Austria (offering payment to be called on to raise a question at a philosophy conference) and blackmailing a fellow professor (paradoxically, Charles used threats to get the professor to join a workshop in ethics).

**Ruth Tallman** is an Assistant Professor of Philosophy at Barry University, Miami Shores, Florida. She has written chapters for other pop culture and philosophy volumes, such as *Superman*, *Sherlock Holmes*, and *Walking Dead*.

**Nathan Wood** is a doctoral student and teaching assistant in philosophy at the University of Georgia. He specializes in environmental ethics, ethical theory (particularly virtue ethics), political philosophy, and epistemology. If knowledge is power, then with his academic career in philosophy he likes to believe that, alongside Frank Underwood, he has also chosen power over money.

**Michael Yeo** is an Associate Professor in the Department of Philosophy at Laurentian University. His main area of specialization is ethics. He worked for six years as an ethicist at the Canadian Medical Association. His interest in politics traces back to his days of working as an intern in the Ontario Legislature under a program administered by the Canadian Political Science Association. Recent publications include "The Rights of Science and the Rights of Politics" and "Fault Lines at the Intersection of Science and Policy: Interpretive Responses to the Trial of Scientists in L'Aquila."

# Index

*House of Cards and Philosophy: Underwood's Republic,*
First Edition. Edited by J. Edward Hackett.
© 2016 John Wiley & Sons, Ltd. Published 2016 by John Wiley & Sons, Ltd.